JAMES I. PACKER

DOING THEOLOGY

for the

PEOPLE

OF GOD

Studies in Honour of

J. I. PACKER

EDITED BY DONALD LEWIS
& ALISTER McGRATH

 APOLLOS

APOLLOS (an imprint of Inter-Varsity Press)
38 De Montfort Street, Leicester LE1 7GP, England

©1996 by Regent College

Published in the United Kingdom with permission from InterVarsity Press, Downers Grove, Illinois 60515, U.S.A.

Computer typeset by Paul Chapman.

First published in 1996.

British Library Cataloguing in Publication Data

A catalogue record for this book is available from the British Library.

ISBN 0-85111-450-4

Printed in the United States of America ∞

Contents

Part II: Biblical and Exegetical

Part III: Historical and Interdisciplinary

Acknowledgments

The editors wish to thank the staff at InterVarsity Press for their enthusiasm for, and gracious help with, this *Festschrift*—particularly Andy Le Peau and Jim Hoover, and especially Ruth Goring, who was always patient and helpful and without whose careful copy editing this volume would have never have made it to press. We also thank Paul Chapman, a Regent College student whose professional background in typesetting, layout and many other areas of the publishing business was invaluable in putting this book together; David Stewart, Assistant Librarian of the Regent-Carey Library, for his tracking down so many obscure references; Ken Pearson and Alex MacLeod, both Regent College students who assisted in various and sundry tasks related to the work; Freeman Barton of the Library of Gordon-Conwell Seminary in South Hamilton, Massachusetts, for his assistance in obtaining bibliographical details of some of Dr. Packer's publications; Linda Frydrychova, faculty secretary at Regent College, who spent many hours at the fax machine on behalf of the editors; and finally, Dal Schindell, Director of Publications at Regent College.

Donald M. Lewis
Alister E. McGrath

Preface

To James I. Packer on His Seventieth Birthday

Donald M. Lewis and Alister E. McGrath

THE ARTICLES INCLUDED IN THIS BOOK HAVE BEEN written as a present for J. I. Packer on the occasion of his seventieth birthday and his retirement from full-time teaching responsibilities at Regent College, Vancouver. This work is only a small tribute from a few friends—but these articles represent a much larger group of colleagues, friends and former students who wish to honor him.

As editors we have invited a handful of Dr. Packer's friends to contribute to this work, and in doing so we have challenged them to be visionary: specifically, to set out an agenda for evangelical theology over the next several decades. It will be for the readers of this volume to determine whether or not what we had hoped for has been achieved. Of course, the fact that among J. I. Packer's friends are some of the best-known and most respected scholars in the evangelical world has been a great advantage to us: finding willing and gifted contributors has not been as difficult as selecting from among them.

In approaching our task we realized that we could easily have had a much larger volume, or in fact several volumes! For the most part we have asked contributors who have known J. I. Packer for a number of years and who have worked with him closely in varied contexts. Several whom we approached were obliged, with reluctance, to decline because of pressing time commitments (especially in view of the short time-frame which we presented to the authors!) but wished their congratulations to be expressed to Dr. Packer. They included some well-known friends: the Most Reverend Dr. George Carey, Archbishop of Canterbury; the Reverend Professor Anthony Thiselton, Professor of Theology at Nottingham University; Charles Colson of Prison Fellowship, Washington, D.C.; the Reverend Dr. R. T. France, former principal of Wycliffe Hall, Oxford; Dr. R. C. Sproul of Ligonier Ministries, Lake Mary, Florida; and the Reverend Dick Lucas, Rector of St. Helen's, Bishopsgate, in London, England.

Dr. Packer often quips to his students that his lecturing and writing style matches his surname: "Packer my name; packer by nature." And indeed, he has been a packer by any standard, having compressed into one life more than most of us could live out in several.

James Innell Packer was born on the 22nd of July, 1926, in the city of Gloucester, in the west of England. His father was a railway clerk, his mother a teacher. The nominally Anglican family was not particularly religious, and it was not until he was in his first term as an undergraduate reading Classics at Oxford that he was seriously challenged with a call to Christian discipleship. Through the influence of the Oxford Inter-Collegiate Christian Union (OICCU) he came to faith and became a Christian disciple; an avid jazz musician, he sacrificed his role in a jazz band in order to attend the OICCU's Saturday evening Bible exposition, a long tradition of Oxford undergraduate life for evangelical students.

In this context, however, the new convert encountered a form of "holiness" teaching then popular among some British evangelicals, and this evangelical spirituality almost destroyed his fragile faith. The OICCU, however, was given a library by a former member, and the young Packer was put in charge of it. Amongst the books he discovered a twenty-three–volume set of the works of John Owen (1616–1683), the greatest of the English Puritan theologians. Delving into Owen, he read his work *Sin and Temptation*. The effect was twofold: first, it led him to the rich vein of Puritan theology and spirituality which he has mined ever since; second, it introduced him to the classic English Reformed tradition, which proved to be far more intellectually credible and spiritually nourishing than he anything he had known previously. Owen became his mentor to such an extent that a friend aptly described him as an "Owenian." It was Owen's *Death of Death in the Death of Christ* which led him to a "particular" view of Christ's atonement; Owen's *Pneumatologia* shaped his view of the relationship of regeneration to conversion; and Owen's *True Nature of a Gospel Church, Discourse on Spiritual Gifts* and *The Nature of Apostasy* which in Dr. Packer's words, "have done more over the years than any other books to shape my thoughts on what local church life should be."[1]

Upon graduation at the age of twenty-two, J. I. Packer taught classical languages at an Anglican seminary near London. Here he sensed the confirmation of a call to ordained ministry within the Church of England, and thus he returned to Wycliffe Hall in Oxford to complete a B.A. in theology, which he received in 1950, the same year in which he was ordained. In 1952 he met a Welsh nursing student, Kit Mullet, who was working in a London hospital. They married in 1954 and eventually adopted three children—Naomi, Ruth and Martin.

While wooing his bride-to-be, he completed a doctorate in theology at Oxford under the supervision of the eminent Puritan scholar Geoffrey Nuttall. His interest in the Puritans had first been sparked while an undergraduate but was nourished especially by his contacts with Martyn Lloyd-Jones, the Congregationalist pastor of Westminster Chapel in London. His thesis focused on the theology of Richard Baxter, but while greatly appreciating many aspects of Baxter's theology, Packer explicitly rejected Baxter's acceptance of an unlimited atonement and the moralistic tone of "Baxterianism" as it developed in the subsequent century.

When James and Kit Packer first met and married, their expectation was that his ministry would be parish-based, but after serving a two-year curacy in Birmingham, he was offered a teaching position at an Anglican seminary, Tyndale Hall in Bristol, where he served until 1961. A well-known conference speaker, he established contacts with a number of American evangelical seminaries, especially after the publication of his first book, *"Fundamentalism" and the Word of God* (1958), in which he effectively countered criticisms of evangelical positions and practice and exonerated British evangelicalism from charges of American "fundamentalism." His reputation as a scholar and apologist was further enhanced by his *Evangelism and the Sovereignty of God* (1961), in which he demonstrated the compatibility of Calvinist doctrine with a serious commitment to evangelism.

In 1961 the Packers moved to Oxford, where Dr. Packer was considerably freer to write and travel in his capacity as librarian (1961–1963) and then warden (1963–1970) of Latimer House, an evangelical library and study center. During his time at Latimer House he became embroiled in two major controversies. The first involved him in a common cause with Anglo-Catholics who opposed the proposed union of the Church of England with the English Methodists; this was not out of an opposition to Christian unity, as was demonstrated by his contribution to *Growing into Union: Proposals for Forming a United Church in England* (1970). The second dispute was more personal and painful, as it was provoked by his friend and mentor Martyn Lloyd-Jones, whom he regarded as "the greatest man" he had ever known. In 1966 Lloyd-Jones publicly urged Anglican evangelicals like John Stott and Packer to leave what he considered to be a doctrinally compromised Church of England and to join the evangelicals in the "Free Church" tradition. Instead of abandoning his denomination, Dr. Packer took a leading role in seeking its renewal through the National Evangelical Anglican Congress (convened at Keele in 1967), which is now regarded by many as a crucial turning point leading in the resurgence of Anglican evangelicalism in the Church of England. In 1970 the Packers moved to Bristol, England, where Dr. Packer became the principal of Tyndale Hall, which in 1972 united with two other seminaries to become Trinity College, of which Dr. Packer was made associate principal.

The publication of *Knowing God* in 1973 changed the direction of Dr. Packer's life. Known to this point as an apologist and academic theologian, he became a household name throughout the global world of evangelicalism. His fame as a practical, devotional writer vastly increased his reputation at a popular level.

Another momentous change in direction occurred in 1979, when Dr. Packer responded to the appeals of a friend from his days as an undergraduate at Oxford, Dr. James Houston. The latter had emigrated to Canada in 1970 to begin a new venture in theological education, seeking to establish—in concert with a group of Christians in Vancouver—a theological college whose primary aim was the educating of laypeople in Christian theology. For Dr. Packer, now in his late forties, this was an opportunity to be involved in an exciting and somewhat risky new venture while distancing himself from some of the painful memories of his English experience.

The North American location allowed him to be more closely involved in the International Council on Biblical Inerrancy and to travel more easily among North American evangelicals, few of whom appreciated or understood his British and Anglican identity. All the while Dr. Packer was writing. His *Beyond the Battle for the Bible* (1980) sought to move the inerrancy discussion beyond defensive polemics to a positive and constructive agenda. Since 1984 he has produced a number of major works (which are listed in the appendix to this book). The major themes of his writings have included the doctrine of Scripture, the doctrine of God, the work of the Holy Spirit and the contribution of the English Puritans of the sixteenth and seventeenth centuries.[2]

In all of his writing and speaking Dr. Packer has sought to serve the church, the whole people of God. Like so many great theologians, he has been drawn into controversy out of pastoral concerns, intensely aware of the fact that bad theology damages people. He has sought, however, in all of the controversies in which he has been involved, to be a peacemaker and a true Christian ecumenist. It is a pleasure to honor so great a writer and thinker, and to further the work which he has so capably carried out in his distinguished career.

Notes:

[1] J. I. Packer, introduction to John Owen, *Sin and Temptation: The Challenge to Personal Godliness,* ed. J. M. Houston, Classics of Faith and Devotion series (Portland, Ore.: Multnomah Press, 1983), p. xxv.

[2] For a fuller treatment of Dr. Packer's life, the reader is directed to C. Catherwood, *Five Evangelical Leaders* (Wheaton, Ill.: Harold Shaw, 1985), pp. 169–204, and Alister McGrath's forthcoming biography of Dr. Packer. For a theological assessment of his contribution, see Roger Nicole, "J. I. Packer," in *Handbook of Evangelical Theologians,* ed. Walter Elwell (Grand Rapids, Mich.: Baker, 1994), pp. 379–87.

Part I: Systematic

1

Theology: A Multidimensional Discipline

John R. W. Stott

Having enjoyed Jim Packer's friendship for about forty-five years, ever since he was finishing at Oxford and I was the young Rector of All Souls Church in London, I am grateful for the chance to add my tribute to this evangelical theologian *par excellence,* even if my contribution to his *Festschrift* is akin to a shrimp paying homage to a whale! I thank God specially for Jim's extraordinary combination of gifts. He somehow manages, at one and the same time, to be faithful and innovative, godly and human, open and critical, profound and popular.

❖ ❖ ❖

At first hearing the very concept of "theology" sounds grotesque. How can man (male and female) study God? How can God allow himself to become the object of human scrutiny and evaluation? In his relation to us is he not subject rather than object? So how can creatures investigate their Creator, the clay the potter, the finite the Infinite, and sinners the Holy One? The very idea is as brash as the alleged (though apocryphal?) letter of a schoolgirl to the Church of England Enquiry Office. "Dear Sir," she wrote: "We are doing God this term. Please send full particulars!"

Yet "theology," whatever its etymology may seem to suggest, does not necessarily have any inappropriately arrogant overtones. For God in Christ has deliberately presented himself to us, in our space-time existence, and has invited us to apprehend him by our three higher senses, by sight, hearing and touch (1 Jn 1:1ff.). So the arresting title of Dr. Packer's best-selling book, *Knowing God,* is not an anomaly, but fully consistent with the expectations which Scripture raises in us.

My thesis is that authentic Christian theology, although in our day unceremoniously dislodged from its former throne as "Queen of the Sciences," nevertheless remains a rich, multidimensional discipline, which demands a cluster of complementary responsibilities. I have chosen six of them.

1. Christian Theology Is Biblical Theology
(Theology and Revelation)

I am not now thinking of the so-called Biblical Theology Movement, which was launched with the publication of Karl Barth's *Römerbrief* in 1919 which decisively rejected old-fashioned liberal optimism and which later involved a number of well-known European specialists in Old and New Testament. Now, however, at least in the opinion of the liberal establishment, this movement has been discredited. For the fashion today is to emphasize the diversity of Scripture at the expense of its unity and to declare that there is no such thing as "biblical theology," only a number of mutually incompatible "biblical theologies."

It is essential, to be sure, that we acknowledge and safeguard the distinctive individuality of each biblical author. But the pendulum has swung too far. A. M. Hunter was right to insist that "there is . . . a deep unity in the New Testament, which dominates and transcends all the diversities."[1] Professor Charlie Moule suggests where this unity lies. While recognizing "the very wide range of diversity" in the New Testament, he writes: "The rainbow spectrum thus presented is undeniably thrown by one luminary alone. Common to every writing of the New Testament, without even the exception of the Epistle of James, is devotion to Jesus Christ."[2] This combination of unity and diversity is exactly what we would expect, granted our belief in the double authorship of Scripture, the one mind and mouth of God speaking through the many minds and mouths of the human authors.

Our first and fundamental conviction about Christian theology, then, is that it is a response to divine revelation. For we would know nothing about God if he had not taken the initiative to make himself known. Without revelation theology would inevitably degenerate into idolatry, since there would be no criterion by which to distinguish between true and false images of God. But the biblical revelation protects us from idolatry. True, it also imposes limits on our belief, yet in this limitation lies liberty. For the truth sets us free from bondage to fad and fashion, folly and falsehood.

The divine revelation, to which Christian theology is a response, is not mediated only through Christ and the biblical witness to Christ, but also through the created order. Following Calvin's teaching on the similarities and dissimilarities between general and special revelation, it was Sir Francis Bacon, the seventeenth-century scientific pioneer, who spoke about God's two "books"—the book of his word and the book of his works. And in our day it is refreshing to read *Christian Belief in a Postmodern World* by Professor Diogenes Allen of Princeton Theological Seminary, in which Parts I and II are entitled "The Book of Nature" and "The Book of Scripture."[3] But the theologian who has been most creative in his elaboration of the harmony between what he calls "theological science" and "natural science" is Professor Thomas Torrance of Edinburgh.[4]

Although this is an oversimplification, and the analogy is not exact, it is helpful to affirm that what theology is to Scripture, science is to nature. For both theology and science are human constructs, attempts to understand, synthesize and apply the data of revelation. The well-known statement of Johann Kepler, the seventeenth-century astronomer, about "thinking God's thoughts after him" is equally applicable to Bible study (theology) and nature study (science).

Moreover, both theology and science have bounds set for them by the limited character of the data of revelation. Indeed it is a necessary aspect of theology's proper humility that it restricts itself to what God has revealed in Christ and in Scripture, and does not trespass beyond it. If truth may be divided into "the secret things" and "the things revealed"[5] (Deut 29:29), then we must distinguish between the agnosticism appropriate to the former and the dogmatism appropriate to the latter. Speculation may have a place in theology, but only when it plainly advertises itself as such. Whether the scientist is faced with any comparable limitations, I am not qualified to say, although the replacement of Newton's "mechanistic" model of the universe by models variously described as "dynamic," "elastic" and even "uncertain," and associated with the modern physics of Einstein and Max Planck, is at least suggestive.

At all events, we may say that our theological investigations will never lead to a final *Eureka!* in this life, or even in the next. For Paul

likened his partial knowledge to the immature musings of a child and
the distorted reflections of a mirror (1 Cor 13:11f.). And although he
looked beyond childhood to maturity, and beyond reflections to a
"face to face" encounter with God, he also indicated that even this
would not be the end. For, contrary to popular hymnology, love is
not the only grace which "abides." The truth is rather that "these
three remain, faith, hope and love" (1 Cor 13:13). And if hope
abides, it must have an object, some future reality to which it looks
forward with expectation. What can this be but an ever richer and
fuller apprehension of him whom our soul loves and desires? Since
God is infinite in his being, we shall never come to the end of him.
Theological exploration will continue forever.

Meanwhile, the vision from the burning bush overwhelms us, and
the voice bids us keep our distance and remove our shoes, since the
ground on which we are standing is holy.

2. Christian Theology Is Historical Theology
(Theology and Tradition)

Christians are (or should be) strongly committed to history. For the
living God of the biblical revelation is the God of history, the God of
Abraham, Isaac, Jacob and Joseph, the God of Moses and Joshua, the
judges, kings and prophets, the God and Father of the Jesus of history, the God of the apostles and of the postapostolic church. It is in
the arena of history that God's eternal purpose is being unfolded. So
Christians should never deserve the epigram attributed to the Spanish American poet and philosopher George Santayana, that "those
who ignore history are condemned to repeat it."

Certainly modern attacks on the received Christian faith, and
modern deviations from it, are never the "new Christianity," "new
reformation," "new theology" or "new morality" which they boast of
being. Nor are their perpetrators the innovators they like to think
they are. For truly "there is nothing new under the sun." What claim
to be new versions of Christianity prove to be old ones, dredged up
from the past, deceptively reclothed and re-presented. One way in
which to heed Jesus' warning to "watch out for false prophets" (Mt
7:15) is to develop our historical sense. Otherwise contemporary
defenders of the faith may credit their opponents with a bogus origi-
nality, when in fact they are only reinventing the wheel. Christian
people would feel more stable and secure against heresy if they realized that it had been formulated and refuted before.

We should not think of historical theology as being only the history of heresy, however; it is also and positively the history of Christian doctrine. And this in turn has two meanings. It is sometimes used to refer to progressive or cumulative revelation within Scripture itself, as for example in the doctrine of the Trinity which could be affirmed in the New Testament only because the unity of God had been secured in the Old. More frequently, however, the history of doctrine alludes to the changing formulation of biblical truth down the generations of church history.

Because of the medieval Catholic conviction regarding the immutability of the church and of its doctrine (*semper eadem*), it was not until the nineteenth century that historical theology came to be recognized as a legitimate Christian discipline, as theologians wrestled with the tension between change and changelessness, between a doctrine's unchanging essence and its ever-changing cultural formulations. The classic example of this struggle is to be found in John Henry Newman's *Essay on the Development of Christian Doctrine* (1845), in which he elaborated what he saw to be the signs of genuine development, such as continuity of principle and logical sequence.

Newman's essay appeared shortly before the publication of Darwin's *Origin of Species* (1859). So it was inevitable that some Christian thinkers should press the concept of evolution into service as a model for doctrinal change. In this century, however, theologians have tended to prefer "development" to "evolution" as the more appropriate analogy. This is certainly so, for example, in regard to New Testament Christology, as Professor C. F. D. Moule has argued. For if evolution "means the genesis of successive new species by mutation of natural selection," development by contrast "will mean something more like the growth, from immaturity to maturity, of a single specimen from within itself." So the different New Testament presentations of Jesus were "not successive additions of something new"; they were rather "the drawing out and articulating of what is there," indeed "what was there from the beginning."[6]

Another and different way of thinking about the history of doctrine was proposed by James Orr in his justly famous book *The Progress of Dogma*.[7] By "dogma" he was referring to "those formulations of Christian doctrine which have obtained ecclesiastical sanction and are embodied in the creeds" (p. 13), and by "progress" he meant that the development of dogma followed "a recognisable law." This relates to the "singular *parallel* there is between the historical course of dogma, on the one hand, and the scientific order of the text-books on systematic theology on the other." That is, "the law of these two developments—the logical and the historical—is the same" (p. 22). The chronological order in which the Holy Spirit of truth enabled the church to get its mind clear on different doctrines was the logical order, so that each formulation built on the previous one and became in its turn the foundation of the next.

All this continuous theologizing, on the basis of the biblical revelation, comes under the heading of "tradition." For tradition is precisely the church's interpretation of Scripture from one generation to the next, as (it hopes and prays) it is enlightened by the Holy Spirit. But the interpretation does not possess the authority which belongs to the text being interpreted. We must follow Jesus both in his distinction between Scripture as the Word of God and tradition as the teaching of men, and in his insistence that all the traditions of the elders (which today will include those of the evangelical elders) must be subordinated to the supreme, reforming authority of Scripture (Mark 7:1ff.). This principle means that we always have the duty and the right to appeal back from tradition to the Scripture which it claims to be interpreting.

Not all tradition is misguided, however. And we evangelical people need a better doctrine of tradition, and a greater respect for it. To reject all tradition because it is not Scripture is to show disrespect for the Holy Spirit. Some Christians talk and behave as if they suppose the Holy Spirit came into operation, and even into being, when they arrived on the scene!

3. Christian Theology Is Systematic Theology
(Theology and Reason)

Although Anglican leaders in this century have tended to argue that authority is a "threefold cord" consisting of Scripture, Tradition and Reason, and to claim Richard Hooker as the originator of this notion, the historic formularies of Anglicanism plainly attribute supreme authority to Scripture.

This does not deny the importance of tradition and reason, but assigns to them their proper and humbler place. It is not the office of tradition and reason to stand in judgment over Scripture; it is the office of tradition and reason to sit in modesty under it. The role of tradition and reason is to elucidate, synthesize and apply Scripture. Indeed, if it is in historical theology that the importance of tradition is seen, it is in systematic theology that reason comes into its own.

The legitimacy of systematic theology has been assumed from the beginning, as theologians have endeavored to collect the teaching of Scripture on different themes, to trace their development, to relate them to each other, and to weave them into a coherent whole. It is clear in the New Testament itself that the apostles recognized the existence of a body of doctrine which they variously called "the truth," "the faith," "the tradition," "the teaching" or "the deposit," and which had to be guarded and passed on. This came to be condensed in the creeds and confessions of the church, and to be elaborated with growing sophistication in the later patristic, medieval Catholic, Orthodox, Reformed, Lutheran, Independent, Puritan and modern systematic theologies.

At the same time it is right to heed those who warn us of the two main dangers to which systematic theologians are exposed. First, God did not see fit to reveal himself in a neat and orderly fashion, but rather through the profusion of nature and the cultural riches of the Bible's sixty-six books. In consequence, we are taking something of a liberty when we attempt to reduce to order what appears disordered, or to impose a structure on what is unstructured.

The second danger is that systematic theologians may become so enamored of their construct that, if God were to cause fresh truth and light "to break forth out of his holy Word" (as John Robinson put it to the Mayflower Pilgrims in 1620), they are tempted to trim the truth to fit the system instead of adapting the system to absorb the truth.

Let Charles Simeon be our spokesman in expressing this danger. In his preface to the *Horae Homileticae* he wrote:

> The author is no friend to systematizers in theology. He has endeavoured to derive from the Scriptures alone *his* views of religion, and to them it is his wish to adhere with scrupulous fidelity; never wresting any portion of the Word of God to favour a particular opinion, but giving to every part of it that sense, which it seems to him to have been designed by its Great Author to convey. He is aware that he is likely, on this account, to be considered by the zealous advocates of human systems as occasionally inconsistent; but if he should be discovered to be no more inconsistent than the Scriptures themselves, he will have reason to be satisfied. He has no doubt but that there is a system in the Holy Scriptures (for truth cannot be inconsistent with itself); . . . but he is disposed to think that the Scriptural system, be it what it may, is of a broader and more comprehensive character than some very exact and dogmatical theologians

are inclined to allow.[8]

Yet the vocation of the systematic theologian remains. This is partly because God has made us rational and inquisitive beings, with a mind resolved to make sense of our beliefs and experiences, and partly because God's revelation through nature and Scripture, although presented unsystematically, soon yields to its persistent students logical consistencies which they had not at first observed. This is not the imposition of a structure, however, but the discovery of a hitherto hidden and beautiful coherence.

At the same time, wise theologians always preserve in their system a measure of openness and flexibility. Dr. Packer himself sets us an example in his fine essay from thirty-five years ago, entitled *Evangelism and the Sovereignty of God*. He rejects "the passion for systematic consistency, a reluctance to recognize the existence of mystery and to let God be wiser than men, and a consequent subjecting of Scripture to the supposed demands of human logic." For example, people cannot see how human responsibility and divine sovereignty can be reconciled.

> They are not content to let the two truths live side by side, as they do in the Scriptures. . . . The desire to over-simplify the Bible by cutting out the mysteries is natural to our perverse minds. . . . Our minds dislike antinomies. We like to tie up everything into neat intellectual parcels, with all appearance of mystery dispelled and no loose ends hanging out. . . . How to avoid both extremes? By making it our business to believe both these doctrines with all our might, and to keep both constantly before us for the guidance and government of our lives. . . . C. H. Spurgeon was once asked if he could reconcile these two truths to each other. "I wouldn't try," he replied; "I never reconcile friends."[9]

4. Christian Theology Is Moral Theology
(Theology and Ethics)

A notable feature of God's self-revelation is that a strong moral imperative is built into it. God has not disclosed to us his purpose and will, in order that we may merely "know" and "believe" his truth, but rather that we may "obey" it. He has never taken much interest in intellectual dilettantes who dabble in theology as an interesting pastime but have no intention of allowing it to affect their lives. God will not take us seriously if we do not take him seriously and "tremble" in humility at his word (Is 66:2). There are two main applications of this principle, relating first to all humankind and secondly to the redeemed people of God.

God's quarrel with the human race, as unfolded in Romans 1–3, is that, although they have known something of God and of goodness (whether through creation or Scripture, through the moral law written on stone or in the heart), they have not lived up to their knowledge. Instead, they "suppress the truth by their wickedness." This is the essence of their ungodliness, against which God reveals his wrath (Rom 1:18). Determined to do their own thing and go their own way, they therefore reject any truth which thwarts or even threatens their self-centeredness. Hence they are culpable, indeed inexcusable.

The second example of this principle is to be seen in God's own people. The reason they have come to know God's truth is that they have resolved to obey his will. For, as Jesus said, "if anyone chooses to do God's will, he will find out [literally, 'know'] whether my teaching comes from God or whether I speak on my own [authority]" (Jn 7:17). Thus knowing depends on willing, intellectual conviction on moral choice.

And as we began, so we must continue. God's continuous summons to us is that we will so listen to his word as to believe and obey it. For if we claim to enjoy fellowship with the God of light, even while we are walking in the darkness of sin, "we lie and do not live by the truth," literally, "we do not the truth" (1 Jn 1:6). That is, our life contradicts our claim. By contrast, God's purpose is that we "walk in the truth" (2 Jn 4; 3 Jn 3f.), conforming our lives to its moral standards. Throughout John's letters truth is not just to be "known" and "believed," but to be "done."

The tragedy of false teachers is that, instead of "holding on to the faith and a good conscience," they have rejected the voice of conscience and so "have shipwrecked their faith" (1 Tim 1:19). As Calvin wrote, when commenting on this verse, "a bad conscience is the mother of all heresies."

The true teacher, however, determines never to separate duty from doctrine, behavior from belief. Paul's instruction to Titus was plain: "You must teach what is in accord with sound doctrine" (Tit 2:1). In other words, he must teach on the one hand "the sound doctrine," a recognizable body of apostolic truth, and on the other, "the things which fit it," namely the standards of ethical conduct which are appropriate to the gospel. Theology and ethics belong indissolubly to each other. We must never teach either an ethic without theological foundations, or a theology without ethical consequences.

John Mackay, formerly President of Princeton Theological Seminary, insists much on this in his perceptive little book *A Preface to Christian Theology*. He takes "the balcony" and "the road" as symbols respectively of detachment and involvement. "The balconized spectator," he writes, who has made no "irretrievable commitment" to Christian duty, ". . . becomes the proud patron of both God and man." Such people sit on the fence and never take sides. The road, on the other hand, is "the symbol of a first-hand experience of reality," which "issues in decision and action." "Knowledge of things divine," he continues, "can be obtained only by those people in whom personal concern has been born and an absolute commitment produced." Without such concern and commitment no true knowledge of God is possible.

So we must repudiate every theology which lacks ethical seriousness. We must ourselves "descend from the balcony to the road." And we must remember the statements, which John Mackay also quotes, from "the Form of Government of the Presbyterian Church in the USA," that "truth is in order to goodness," and that "the great touchstone of truth is its tendency to promote holiness."[10]

5. Christian Theology Is Contextualized Theology
(Theology and Mission)

Some theologians are justly criticized for living in an ivory tower. For in an ivory tower one is yet further distanced from the world than on a balcony. A balcony is a place of detachment, but from it one can at least watch what is going on, even if one is not personally involved. An ivory tower, however, is a place of refuge, in which one is so far removed from harsh reality as to be ignorant of it and even unconcerned about it. On a balcony one is an observer, but in an ivory tower an escapist.

True, some claim still to be able to theologize in isolation from the world, and even to do so with greater objectivity and therefore with greater clarity. But this concept runs counter to the very essence of God's chosen method of communication. For no part of his revelation was given in a vacuum; every part was given in a context. So must it be with our theologizing. Communication without contextualization is an impossibility.

Perhaps it is here that the enduring legacy of all liberation theologies is to be found and appreciated. We evangelical Christians have been legitimately critical of them, especially of their hermeneutics (interpreting salvation in socioeconomic, ethnic, political or sexual terms, and the exodus as a paradigm of modern revolutionary movements) and of their seemingly naïve espousal of Marxist social analysis and violent revolution. "Dangerous innocence" one reviewer has called it. Yet we can have no quarrel with the longing to liberate human beings from everything which dehumanizes them and is therefore profoundly offensive to the God who created them in his image. Indeed, we should be ashamed that we were not the first to develop a truly biblical theology of liberation, and that instead we have been guilty of dragging our feet.

In particular, we should have been more open to liberation theology's emphasis on "praxis," and on the need to "do theology" (as in the title of this *Festschrift*) in the marketplace rather than in the monastery, and in "base (i.e., grassroots) communities" rather than in theological seminaries. Henri Nouwen, who visited Peru in 1981–1982, was profoundly impressed by Gustavo Gutiérrez and his pioneer liberation thinking. From it he learned (as he wrote in his journal) "one of the oldest of truths: that *theologia* is not primarily a way of thinking, but a way of living. Liberation theologians do not think themselves into a new way of living, but live themselves into a new way of thinking."[11] This may overstate the antithesis, but the point is forcefully made.

The principal danger to which contextualizers are exposed is the tendency to make a fetish of modernity (or postmodernity), and even to accommodate the biblical revelation to its claimant demands. To do this is always a grave mistake. Speaking on apologetics to a conference of Christian leaders in Wales in the 1940s, C. S. Lewis said:

> Our main temptation in the modern world will be that of yielding to the winds of (strange) doctrine, not that of ignoring them. We are not at all likely to be hidebound; we are very likely indeed to be slaves of fashion.[12]

C. S. Lewis himself resisted this temptation and greatly admired the famous leaders of church history who did the same and stood firm. One such was *Athanasius contra Mundum*. Lewis contributed the introduction to a new edition of *St. Athanasius on the Incarnation* (Mowbray, 1953). In it he wrote: "It is his glory that he did *not* move with the times; it is his reward that *he* now remains, when those times, as all times do, have moved away."

In other words, it is not necessary to move with the times in order to address the times. On the contrary, we are not called to endorse but to challenge the presuppositions, values, ideals, standards and lifestyle of our non-Christian contemporaries, while at the same time restating the gospel in a way which resonates with them and which offers them a viable and attractive alternative. Theology is of little use if it cannot be communicated as gospel. Authentic Christian theology has an ultimately missiological purpose. James Denney once said: "I haven't the faintest interest in theology which does not help us to evangelize."[13] Again, "the doctrine of the death of Christ and its significance was not Paul's *theology;* it was his gospel."[14]

More recently, but along the same line, Dr. Alister McGrath has voiced a trenchant criticism of academic theology:

> Mission and theology are so closely interrelated that they cannot be permitted to become divorced in the manner in which western academic theologians have become accustomed. After all, in Jesus Christ God himself came down to earth, down to the level of us mortals, and it ought not to be beyond the capacities of theologians to do the same. Theology must come down to earth, to serve the church and its mission to the world—and if it will not come down to earth, it must be *brought* down to earth by so marginalising academic theology within the life of the church that it ceases to have any relevance to that church, in order that a theology orientated towards the pastoral and missiological needs of the church may develop in its wake.[15]

This determination to communicate the gospel to our contemporaries will of course affect the concepts we develop and the vocabulary we use. "You must translate every bit of your theology into the vernacular. I have come to the conviction that if you cannot translate your thoughts into uneducated language, then your thoughts were confused." So wrote the most effective Christian communicator of the middle of the twentieth century, C. S. Lewis.[16]

But if we are really concerned for the reevangelization of western society, it will not be enough to proclaim the gospel in modern idiom. We also have a demanding apologetic task. In his address at the opening of the 101st session of Princeton Theological Seminary in 1912, Gresham Machen said:

> We may preach with all the fervour of a reformer, and yet succeed only in winning a straggler here and there, if we permit the whole collective thought of the nation and of the world to be controlled by ideas which, by the resistless force of logic, prevent Christianity from being regarded as anything more than a harmless delusion.[17]

The early church fathers grasped the necessity of a Christian apologetic which addressed the Greco-Roman world of their day. And in our day courageous Christian voices are beginning to be heard. Richard John Neuhaus has called for the reclothing of "the naked public square" with Christian "meanings" and values, and Os Guinness, arguing that the United States is experiencing the fourth major crisis of its history, namely "the crisis of cultural authority," sees no solution but the developing of a new "public philosophy" to replace the old.[18] Meanwhile in the United Kingdom, Bishop Lesslie Newbigin has popularized the emphasis of the sociologists of knowledge on the social conditioning of belief. "Every society depends for its coherence upon a set of what Peter Berger calls 'plausibility structures,' patterns of belief and practice accepted within a given society, which determine which beliefs are plausible to its members and which are not."[19]

All this is part and parcel of our responsibility to contextualize Christian theology. It is possible only for those who practice "double listening," tuning in both to the voice of God as he speaks through his ancient word, and to the varied voices of the modern world in all its alienation and pain, in order to relate the one to the other.

6. Christian Theology Is Doxological Theology (Theology and Worship)

If mission is to proclaim God's holy name among the nations, worship is to glory in his name as proclaimed (Ps 105:1, 3). Thus mission and worship belong together. It would be impossible to know God and not to worship him. Moreover, the name of God stands for the fullness of his being, particularly as he has revealed it in creation and redemption. Both are called his "mighty acts." In fact, several Psalms could be called "Hallelujah sandwiches," in that they begin and end with a summons to worship ("Hallelujah!"), while the doctrinal meat in the middle is an exposition either of God's grace in redemption (as in Ps 103) or of his skill in creation (as in Ps 104). This double theme runs all through Scripture. The prophets delighted to identify the God of the Covenant with the God of Creation. For example, "[Yahweh] is the everlasting God, the Creator of the ends of the earth" (Is 40:28; cf. Jer 32:17ff.). And the same truth will inform and inspire the eternal worship of heaven. For John hears the heavenly hosts as they declare the worthiness of God to be worshiped, both because he "created all things" and because through the slain Lamb he has "purchased" or redeemed his people (Rev 4:11; 5:9f., 12f.). At times the church may well have overemphasized redemption at the expense of creation, but Matthew Fox's call to develop a "creation spirituality" at the expense of redemption is an unbiblical overreaction.

I have so far written nothing about "spiritual theology." Indeed, I confess that the recent evangelical adoption of the word and concept of "spirituality" troubles me for three reasons. First, it is a traditionally Roman Catholic term, which means that inevitably it carries with it some Catholic baggage. Then we spread confusion by using the same language for different notions. Second, the term *spirituality* threatens to perpetuate the disastrous dichotomy between the sacred and the secular, the spiritual and the material. Third, the evangelical borrowing of *spirituality* is unfortunate because it establishes an unbiblical term, while at the same time overlooking a better and biblical one, namely *discipleship*. For *discipleship* (like *spirituality*) is an umbrella word, which includes a whole range of Christian responsibilities like public and private worship, disciplined meditation and prayer, moral standards, Christlikeness of character and conduct, work, witness and mission.

Certainly the preeminent aspect of discipleship is the worship of God, signifying not just liturgical services but the living of our whole lives "to the praise of his glory" (Eph 1:6, 12, 14). For worship is not an activity which can be detached from others; it is the essential quality which characterizes them all. We are to present our bodies to God as our "spiritual act of worship" (Rom 12:1), because all our deeds are done through our bodies (our eyes and ears, mouth and lips, hands and feet) and so become constituent elements of our worship of God. Sunday worship services are valuable to God only if they are a distillation into an hour or two of the dedication of our whole life to him.

It is not only that true theology issues in worship, however, or that our knowledge of God issues in our adoration of God. It is also that our very theologizing itself should be done in a spirit of humble praise. I found it disturbing, therefore, to read Angela Tilby's description of the joint annual conference of the Society of Biblical Literature and the American Academy of Religion in December 1993. More than seven thousand religious scholars converged on Washington, D.C. There were lectures, seminars, discussions and entertainment, but there was little "religion." "This was not a place to discuss what *relationship* one might have with the Lord Jesus. Worship services were held quietly, but not advertised. On the whole," she concluded, "today's religious academics are not noticeably pious."[20]

Totally different was the attitude of the apostle Paul. One of the most striking features of his letters is the natural way in which his expositions and exhortations turn into both prayer for his readers and praise to God. At least a dozen times in the letters traditionally attributed to his authorship, he breaks off suddenly with "thanks be to God" or "to him be glory."[21] It should be natural to us also that thought slides into praise. There is something inauthentic about any theology which does not become doxology. I can myself testify to the godliness of Jim Packer's own writing, in that, while reading his *Knowing God*, I felt compelled to stop reading and start worshiping the God I was reading about.

Helmut Thielicke, in his small but suggestive book entitled *A Little Exercise for Young Theologians,* urges us to think about God in the second person ("you"), and not slip into the third person ("he").

> This transition . . . from a personal relationship with God to a merely technical reference, . . . is the first step towards the worst and most widespread ministers' disease. . . . A theological thought can breathe only in the atmosphere of dialogue with God. . . . Consider that the first time someone spoke of God in the third person, and therefore no longer *with* God but *about* God, was that very moment when the question resounded "Did God really say . . . ?"[22]

More eloquent still is a passage from the pen of Professor T. F. Torrance, in which he expresses something of his own doxological theology. Having stated his conviction that "knowledge of God is the basic act of the human mind," he continues:

> Theology is not just a second-order activity of reflection, but a first-order activity of inquiry pursued in a deepening empirical as well as a theoretical relation to the living God. It is a form of intense intellectual communion with God, in which our minds are taken captive by his love and we come to know God more and more through himself. Even though we are found using third-personal language, theological inquiry of this kind is carried out face to face with God, so that it may properly be regarded as a form of rational worship in which awe and wonder and joy give vent to themselves in prayer and praise.[23]

❖ ❖ ❖

I began by suggesting that theology is a multidimensional discipline, and I have tried to show how it relates to revelation, tradition, reason, ethics, mission and worship. One might sum it up by saying that Christian theology is a serious quest for the true knowledge of God, undertaken in response to his self-revelation, illumined by

Christian tradition, manifesting a rational inner coherence, issuing in ethical conduct, resonating with the contemporary world and concerned for the greater glory of God.

Such a theology is not developed quickly or by purely human endeavor. It requires the humility of Christian patience and of dependence within the Christian community on the Holy Spirit of truth. I could not conclude more appropriately than by using a Trinitarian prayer attributed to Calvin:

> Heavenly Father, in your Son Jesus Christ are hidden all the treasures of wisdom and knowledge. Enlighten our minds by your Holy Spirit, and grant us that reverence and humility without which no-one can understand your truth, through the same Jesus Christ, your Son, our Lord.

Notes:

[1] A. M. Hunter, *The Unity of the New Testament* (London: S.C.M. Press, 1943), p. 109.

[2] C. F. D. Moule, *The Birth of the New Testament* (London, 1962; 3rd ed. revised A. & C. Black, 1981), p. 17.

[3] Diogenes Allen, *Christian Belief in a Postmodern World*, "the full wealth of conviction" (Louisville, Ky.: Westminster/John Knox Press, 1989).

[4] E.g. Thomas F. Torrance, *Transformation and Convergence in the Frame of Knowledge*, "explorations in the interrelations of scientific and theological enterprise" (Grand Rapids, Mich.: Eerdmans, 1984).

[5] All scriptural quotations in this article are taken from the New International Version of the Bible, copyright the New York International Bible Society.

[6] C. F. D. Moule, *The Origin of Christology* (Cambridge: Cambridge University Press, 1977), pp. 1–4.

[7] The lectures were delivered in 1897; the book was published by Hodder & Stoughton in 1901.

[8] Charles Simeon, *Horae Homileticae* 8th ed. (London, 1848), p. xxiii.

[9] J. I. Packer, *Evangelism and the Sovereignty of God* (London: Inter-Varsity Press, 1961), pp. 16, 19, 25, 35.

[10] John A. Mackay, *A Preface to Christian Theology* (New York: Macmillan, 1941), pp. 28, 34, 44, 49, 106.

[11] Henri Nouwen, *Gracias! A Latin American Journal* (Maryknoll, N.Y.: 1983; Orbis, 1993), p. 159.

[12] C. S. Lewis, "Christian Apologetics," *God in the Dock: Essays on Theology and Ethics* (Grand Rapids, Mich.: Eerdmans, 1970), p. 92.

[13] From R. V. G. Tasker's preface to the 1951 Tyndale edition of James Denney's *The Death of Christ* (London, 1902), p. 8.

[14] Ibid., p. 66.

[15] Alister McGrath, *The Enigma of the Cross* (London: Hodder & Stoughton, 1987), p. 174.

[16] "Christian Apologetics," p. 98.

[17] J. Gresham Machen, *The Christian Faith in the Modern World* (London: Hodder & Stough-

ton: 1936; Grand Rapids, Mich.: Eerdmans, 1947), p. 63.

[18] Richard John Neuhaus, *The Naked Public Square* (Grand Rapids, Mich.: Eerdmans, 1984); Os Guinness, *The American Hour* (New York: Macmillan/Free Press, 1993).

[19] Lesslie Newbigin, *The Gospel in a Pluralist Society* (London: S.P.C.K., 1989), pp. 8 and 53.

[20] Reported in the *Church Times* on 17 December 1993.

[21] Rom 6:17, 11:33ff., 16:25ff.; 1 Cor 15:57; 2 Cor 2:14, 8:16, 9:15; Gal 1:5; Eph 3:20f.; Phil 4:20; 1 Tim 1:17, 6:15ff.

[22] Helmut Thielicke, *A Little Exercise for Young Theologians* (Grand Rapids, Mich.: Eerdmans, 1962), pp. 33–35.

[23] Thomas F. Torrance, *Reality and Scientific Theology* (Edinburgh: Scottish Academic Press, 1985), pp. xi–xii.

2

Systematic Theology as a Practical Discipline

Kenneth S. Kantzer

SYSTEMATIC THEOLOGY IS AN EMINENTLY PRAC-
tical discipline or science. It is a "discipline" in the sense that it is a
field of study, and a "science" in that it implies a public and open
method and that it yields knowledge.[1] This discipline goes by many
names. Until modern times the Christian church most frequently la-
beled it "sacred doctrine" or Christian "doctrine" or "teaching." Calvin called it "instruction." In this article I am using the term in this
traditional sense.[2] Entirely apart from the rather loose ways in which
the term "systematic theology" is used in today's vocabulary, it is
worthwhile noting that among contemporary Roman Catholic and
Protestant theologians there is now no agreement as to the precise
meaning of the term.[3]

David Hollaz, an eighteenth-century Lutheran theologian, offered
a definition of theology which is both faithful to the magisterial Reformers, Luther and Calvin, and useful for evangelical Protestants.
He wrote: "Theology must be defined: [It is an] Eminently practical
system, teaching from the revealed Word of God all things which
sinful man, who is to be saved, needs to know and do, in order to
attain true faith in Christ and holiness of life."[4]

Systematic theology, therefore, is practical because it seeks to help
sinners alienated from God to come to know God, find acceptance
with him, learn how they can please the One they love supremely
and find usefulness in his kingdom. It seeks to answer the question:
What must I think and say and do about God, human beings and the

created universe in their interrelationships?

The practical nature of systematic theology is rooted in two things: first, the fundamental human need to know God better because he is the supreme Being sovereign over his universe; and second, because it seeks to enable humans to become rightly related to him and thus find their appropriate role in God's universe.

The Theological Disciplines and Their Tasks

Systematic theology is not the only practical discipline. It is related to several other disciplines generally listed under the rubric of theology.

First, exegetical theology *seeks to determine what is the best text of Scripture and what it means.* That is, what did the original author mean in the final form of the literary document as it came from the hand of the author or editor?

Exegesis, of course, means many different things in the world of contemporary biblical scholarship. I am using the term in the traditional sense of the attempt to understand the meaning intended by the biblical author as expressed in the text as it stands written. The first task of biblical exegesis is to determine the final form of the literary piece we are seeking to interpret—in short, textual criticism. This is not to denigrate the rights of historical criticism, source criticism, redaction criticism, form criticism or other allied ways of examining a text and its background. In practice, these studies can be ways of helping us to interpret better the text we have.[5]

I am also interested in the historical background of biblical statements and how these ideas came to find their way into the final text, but exegesis seeks the author/editor's meaning in the literary text we have in its final form as a literary piece. At worst, these studies can be means by which we reject the meaning of the text in its final form in favor of a quite different idea—an idea we conjecture to lie behind the meaning set forth in the final form of the literary piece.

In a significantly different sense, many theologians distinguish between the meaning of what the text says (the task of exegesis, as I perceive it) and what the text means (which is often quite different from what it says). In this case the modern interpreter is turning away from the meaning of the text to his own idea which the reading of the text suggests to him and which he deems profitable. Krister Stendahl, the former dean of Harvard Divinity School, notes that what the text means is often far more important to the modern exegete than what the text says.[6] However, this replaces any "authority" of the biblical text with the ability of the biblical text to stimulate ideas in the mind of the reader. Such ideas may be quite different ideas from those of the biblical text.[7]

Second, biblical theology *seeks to answer the question: What is the teaching of the various parts of the Bible as viewed in their historical perspective in the unfolding of special revelation?* In short, biblical theology is not necessarily truer to the Bible, but it has a different approach.

Some students of the New Testament argue that we cannot speak of a biblical theology but only of divergent biblical theologies in the plural. Perhaps the most articulate defender, at least in English, of the view that sees only contradictory theologies in the Bible is J. D. G. Dunn.[8] He argues that we have very different theologies embedded in the New Testament.[9]

On the surface, at least, this is unquestionably true. The theology of Leviticus is not identical with the theology of Paul. The Christian church, however, has solidly maintained that there is an ultimate unity throughout the Bible. Only on this basis could it possibly be a revelation from a God of truth and, naturally also, only thus could it be a practical guide for our life and thought.[10]

Third, historical theology *seeks to answer the question: What has the church understood as the truth about God and our life in relationship to him and his created universe, and how has this truth been applied down through the history of the church?* The role of the church's teaching from the past is like that of an elder brother in the faith. It not only helps us interpret biblical passages but also shows how the Scriptures were applied practically in the historical and cultural situations of the past. By observing the changing situations to which Scripture has been applied across the centuries, we are aided in our own practical applications of Scripture to our day.[11]

Fourth, systematic theology *seeks to bring together the teaching of the whole of the Bible and apply it to all of life.* The sense in which theology is systematic is important. I understand theology to be systematic in the sense that it is orderly. One may have a reason for putting together its various parts, but that reason need not be that each part logically requires every other part. To conceive of systematic theology in this latter sense (what is often referred to as a "logical" system) would destroy the freedom of God and require a completely determined God and a completely determined universe—both of which seem to me flatly to contradict the nature of God and the universe as revealed in Scripture. In quite a different sense of the word "logical," any valid systematic theology would be logical. It would not ultimately be incoherent and contradictory.[12]

And fifth, the discipline commonly referred to exclusively as practical
theology *really relates to how to communicate and persuade people of the
truth and the need to act upon it.*

The Practical Nature of Systematic Theology
In this article we are concerned with systematic theology as a practical discipline. But when it is done rightly it becomes more and more
evident that it is closely related to each of the other disciplines. None
of them can be carried on rightly in isolation from the others. And all
are truly practical. All contribute directly to what we need to know in
order to live satisfactory human lives. Hollaz's definition of systematic theology, clearly representing both the Reformation and the
common evangelical understanding and practice of the term, displays
immediately its essential biblical matrix.

For an evangelical this does not necessarily mean that we find no
religious truth except in the Bible. Many evangelicals accept the validity of natural revelation. Humanly discovered truth, however, does
not come with the force of a command of God; and systematic theology must always be based on Scripture, though many insist that
scriptural truth can be supported by truth from other sources, and
this evidence is at times valuable both as a tool for evangelism and as
a confirmation of biblical truth for the unbeliever.[13]

"Torah" is the term most frequently used by the Bible to refer to
itself. Its essential meaning is instruction and, in this case, divine instruction. The phrase "Word of God" in both the Old and New Testaments is used to refer to the divine instruction coming from God
found in Scripture.[14]

Without committing himself to the final authority of Holy Scripture, Paul Tillich makes the distinction between the autonomous man
who is self-instructed and the theonomous man who is God-
instructed.[15] In evangelical terms to be instructed by God means to
be biblically instructed. Hence the evangelical places himself or herself practically under the Bible's teaching. If you convince him or her
that the Bible teaches something, that settles the issue. This is the
Reformation principle of *sola Scriptura*. Only Scripture comes with
divine authority, and only Scripture (i.e., only God) can bind the
human conscience.[16]

The task to which systematic theology sets itself, or what it seeks
to provide for human beings, therefore, shows clearly its practical
nature. Systematic theology seeks to systemize and present as a unified whole the truth concerning God and his relationships to hu-

mankind and the universe as this is authoritatively revealed in the Holy Scriptures and, in turn, to relate this truth to human thought and life.

Note that this truth is not simply a body of ideas; it is far more than this. It is truth that comes to us with divine authority. It is truth derived from a divine revelation. If the omniscient, all-loving God has seen fit to give us a revelation of what is truly the good life, and how it can be attained, then it is sheer folly for finite, sinful human beings to ignore that truth.

Furthermore, *systematic theology has the task of making this divine truth available in practical ways to needy humans.* The biblical revelation came to us bit by bit, spread over many centuries, and was initially revealed to people living in diverse cultures. With the help of biblical exegetes and church historians, systematic theologians divide up this raw material according to topic. They seek every facet of truth contributed by the whole Bible pertaining to each topic. They relate each of these pieces of truth to other aspects of revealed truth. They must also seek to understand the contemporary world and its culture so that they can appropriately apply revealed truth to situations involving practical, personal obedience.

All of this, of course, is based on the tremendous assumptions that Scripture actually does give truth about God and man, that that truth comes to us in Scripture with divine authority, and that the truth of Scripture is unified—not a flat uniformity, but on the other hand not a chaos, not a jumble of contradictory ideas, but truth that comes with adequate authority, meaningfulness, clarity and consistency so that it can be followed in the living out of our lives.

Naturally, for all its practical importance, systematic theology never replaces the Bible. It would be folly to think that once the believer has benefited from the serious study of systematic theology or Bible doctrine, he or she no longer has need of the Bible. The Bible and systematic theology serve different purposes. The Bible is God's instruction spelled out in real life. It comes to us in the way we can best use it as we face life's problems. Theology or Christian teaching (and theology need not be written to be of value) represents our putting it all together in a single focus to enable us to know what we must think or do about the practical problems we face.

The study of systematic theology is especially helpful for immature Christians who are not familiar with the broad scope of the instructions contained in the Bible. For example, when they read 1 Corinthians 14, they need to be reminded of 1 Corinthians 11. If we would be obedient to God, we need a comprehensive view of divine instruction when we face a decision. Yet we grasp the Bible most powerfully in the setting of the biblical text.[17]

I urge my students, therefore, not to preach a theological system from the pulpit or in a Sunday school class. They need a theology, and they should encourage every believer to have a theology; but they should preach and teach the Bible, because that is the way we are best able to absorb biblical instruction and use it to solve the tensions of life.

The heart of biblical preaching, therefore, ought to be the exposition of Scripture, not systematic theology. But the best of such preaching must always be theologically informed, and to be truly profitable exposition of Scripture, it must inform theologically those who are being instructed. It must set the content of a particular passage of Scripture within the context of the comprehensive biblical teaching on the subject. That is, it must be set in the context of the related branch of systematic theology, even though the central message and emphasis are determined by the biblical text.[18]

The task of systematic theology is sometimes confused or even set forth in quite different terms so as to pervert slightly, or in some cases severely, the practical nature of the study. For example, systematic theology does not seek an exposition of the creeds of the church. Evangelicals accept the truth, though not the final authority, of the Apostles' Creed, the decrees of the first seven councils of the ancient church, and most of the major Protestant creeds. Evangelicals tend to take these creedal statements seriously as respected human authorities, but insist that they are fallible. We make no ultimate commitment to them. We may, for example, reject certain items in individual creeds of particular churches; and we may reject the condemnatory clauses that lie at the beginning of the ancient creeds. The creed is not the focus of our attention, but is a guide to lead us better to understand and apply the Bible.

In similar fashion, systematic theology is not a defense of an inherited body of doctrine. Sometimes, it is true, evangelicals give the impression that that is precisely what they are doing. Indeed, they have such an inherited body of doctrine; and they may very well be extraordinarily grateful for it. Yet in doing systematic theology evangelicals are aiming in another direction. That does not mean that they will overthrow their heritage, and it certainly does not mean that they despise it or reject it. In the end, they may, in fact, find their doctrinal heritage confirmed rather than overthrown. But it is not the aim of the evangelical theologian to seek merely to defend an inherited body of systematic doctrine; and in their best moments, they do not form their systematic theology on this basis.

Similarly, the task of systematic theology is not to provide a defense of what is believed to be the most coherent interpretation of the natural data—the most reasonable system of truth. Biblical Christianity is reasonable, and it is coherent, though it may not always appear so to the warped thinking of fallen creatures. Yet the best defense of its truth is usually a clear exposition and understanding of it. A truly biblical systematic theology provides us with a doctrine that makes sense to a rightly functioning human mind. Yet we do not try to form a theology by pulling into it whatever we find to be coherent. This would be rationalism of the worst sort. We put into our theology what the Bible teaches or authorizes us to put into it. And when we have completed our task rightly, we find (a) this biblically constructed theology is coherent as instruction from a coherent God of truth and (b) this coherence becomes in turn a confirming evidence of its truth and its divine revelation.

This presents a special danger for every Christian functioning as a student of theology, and even more so it is a danger for teachers of systematic theology. They are prone to fit into their theology what seems most reasonable to them rather than exactly what Scripture teaches and no more. And since they believe what the Bible really teaches is coherent, they find an almost irresistible temptation to twist what it says so that it appears to them to be coherent. The task of systematic theology is not to shape a doctrine that will prove easy to believe or that will make it easier to convert or to convince or to make better Christians or to achieve any other good and pious motive we may have in mind.

Most well-meaning Christians who are eager to win others to Christ and wish to be useful (and practical) in Christ's kingdom are often severely tempted at this point. They take the trouble to study biblical Christianity so they can be better Christians as well as help others to be better Christians, and the temptation is great to reshape the Bible to say what seems to be helpful and practical. Yet the aim of studying theology is not to discover what we believe will foster the Christian life as we are able to determine this by human reason. This might destroy our soul. Rather the task of theology is to secure what God has revealed to us from his Word. Of course, we must teach and preach the instruction given in the Word of God as best we can so as to win others. We must seek to avoid raising false obstacles to acceptance of the gospel. If the truth is an offense to the unbeliever, we want to be sure it is an offense of the cross and not one that we have created.

The task of systematic theology is not to analyze religious or even Christian experience. Friedrich Schleiermacher, the so-called father of liberalism, argued that theology is built on an inductive analysis of religious experience.[19] It is true that religious experience may lead to truth and to genuine faith. Christian experience also may confirm the biblical truths and the genuineness of faith. Valid experiences may enable us to interpret truth more accurately. Biblical truth acted upon will lead to a rich Christian experience. But just as I do not construct my theology out of what seems to me to be reasonable, so I do not construct my theology out of the truths derived from an analysis of religious or Christian experience.

On occasions Karl Barth might seem to imply this sort of experiential view of how to do theology. For example, he says that we base our theology on the living Word of Christ as found within Scripture.[20] But in other passages he qualifies this carefully so as to make clear that it is the Christ who is set forth according to the teaching of Scripture that really determines our theology. Christ is not a principle or sieve through which we put the Scripture to find what in Scripture is significant for our theology.[21]

For the evangelical, rather, Christ is a principle of hermeneutics or interpretation, whose person and work and benefits (Christ understood in a broad sense as a sort of shorthand for all these items) are revealed in the whole of Scripture. There is, for example, a right way of searching the Scripture as testifying to Christ—not just discovering the predictive passages but as a revelation of the gospel, God's redemptive work, promised in the Old Testament and fulfilled in the New. It tells us of all the benefits God in his grace has in store for repentant sinners who put their trust in him.

The practical necessity and importance of the study of systematic theology is further evidenced by the very nature of our minds. Everyone has a view or attitude toward life. It may or may not be self-consciously formed as a philosophy of life. Few have a coherent and well-articulated philosophy of life. Some have only a jumble of ideas collected from inheritance and experiences along the way, without any attempt to bring them into consistent formulation. Everyone thinks in the sense that a flow of ideas passes through the mind. We all make decisions as to what we choose to do and when we will do it. This flow of ideas and this set of decisions may be good or bad. So

Hordern writes:

> There is no escaping theological questions. We simply do not have the alternatives of theology or no theology. Our alternatives are either to have a well thought out theology, a theology which has passed the tests of critical thought, or to have a hodgepodge theology of unexamined concepts, prejudices and feelings. One of the weaknesses of Protestantism today is that so few Protestants know what they believe or why.[22]

The Bible itself in many passages stresses the importance of knowing the truth. It is the duty and privilege of every believer to know the biblical message. Discussions of systematic theology as a formal discipline or science often convey the impression that systematic theology is an esoteric subject available and useful only to learned scholars. But that is far from the view of the Bible. Writing to his understudy, Timothy, the apostle Paul charges him to preach the Word for in Jesus Christ, our Lord and Savior, you yourself found salvation. Scripture tells us what we need to know about the Savior. And it also provides instruction from God that is profitable for the forming of doctrine, for reproof, for correction of what is wrong and for instruction in what is right so that the man or woman of goodwill becomes perfect, doing only what is good and eventually becoming all that a holy God wishes his child to be. The very wayfaring man, though a fool, is to profit from it. This is the thrust of the message of the apostle Paul to his understudy.[23]

The Bible, moreover, sets forth for us all the moral and spiritual resources we need and shows us how we can apply them to achieve our God-given goals for life. It instructs us as to how to think about God, what God has done for us, what we need to do and how that truth is to be applied to our lives. It exhorts and encourages us to put these truths into action. Only thus can we learn to know God intimately, how to please him, and how to live useful lives in our relationships to ourselves, to others, to creation and to our God.

This, of course, implies a valid hermeneutic, however elementary it may be, so that we really understand the instruction that God has given to us in the Holy Scripture. John Calvin's great fear, as he warns us specifically in his introduction to the *Institutes,* is that believers will follow what he says in his *Institutes* rather than use the *Institutes* to guide them into the study of Scripture. He did not wish his systematic theology to be our final guide. That would constitute him as our Lord and dethrone God. Rather his highest hope was that his teaching in the *Institutes* would lead believers to a better under-

standing and application of the Scripture. It would be helpful if all
professional theologians would share Calvin's concern.[24]

Holy Scripture tells us truth, truth that comes to us with God's
own authority and truth that we desperately need for our ultimate
good. And it is possible for us to understand it with the guidance of
the Holy Spirit. We must depend upon him to teach us its truth and
guide us in applying this truth so as to enable fallen sinners to live
worthwhile Christian lives.[25]

The study of Christian doctrine or the science of biblical dogmatics is simply the work of getting all the Bible says on every topic laid
out in full so it is meaningful and then applying it to our thought
and life.[26] In one sense, therefore, every single believer must be a
theologian or student of divine instruction.[27] Every believer is given
special grace to perform this task of understanding and applying the
Scripture.[28]

Yet the Bible speaks of a divine calling to teach the Scripture. God
calls

> some to be apostles, some to be prophets, some to be evangel-
> ists, and some to be pastors and teachers, to prepare God's
> people for works of service, so that the body of Christ may be
> built up until we all reach unity in the faith and in the knowl-
> edge of the Son of God and become mature, attaining to the
> whole measure of the fullness of Christ.[29]

The apostle Paul places an extraordinarily high value on the gift of
teaching. He enjoins young Timothy to entrust this crucially important gift to others who will exercise it faithfully.[30] Later he adds:
"Watch your life and doctrine closely. Persevere in them, because if
you do, you will save both yourself and your hearers."[31]

For the fulfillment of this task, some are better equipped by
God—given talents and a special call of the Holy Spirit—than are
others. As the apostle makes plain:

> Since an overseer is entrusted with God's work, he must be
> blameless—not overbearing, not quick-tempered, not given to
> drunkenness, not violent, not pursuing dishonest gain. Rather
> he must be hospitable, one who loves what is good, who is self-
> controlled, upright, holy and disciplined. He must hold firmly
> to the trustworthy message as it has been taught, so that he can
> encourage others by sound doctrine and refute those who op-
> pose it.[32]

Because of the crucial importance of biblical teaching to the study
of systematic theology, this discipline becomes an immense aid to

further Bible study. There is, of course, a so-called deep Bible study which counts verses beginning with three-letter words, or determines where Jesus moves next so as to get biblical geography straight. Unfortunately, when it is done, the student may feel that he or she has arrived at valuable and deep Bible study. While some of this may certainly have value, on the contrary the best and deepest Bible study seeks to know all that the Bible reveals about God himself and our relationship to him. In fact, we need to learn *all* that God has revealed to us on any subject.

For example, suppose we are faced with a problem regarding the advisability of securing a divorce, either to guide our own actions or to help others as they face that issue. The Bible tells us (1) God hates divorce and doesn't wish anyone whatsoever to be divorced. (2) Divorce is permissible. (3) Remarriage is not necessarily contradictory to what God has revealed. (4) Divorce is permitted on the ground of adultery. (5) A woman who has been deserted by her husband is freed from obligation to her husband.

Now what shall we do if we seek to be obedient to our Lord? I know passages in the Bible which say each of these things. In my case it may seem to be merely an academic question, which would be a pure waste of time to pursue. But to many true Christians this is decidedly *not* an academic question. It is a nagging problem calling for immediate and desperate decision. In such a case, if I want my life to be guided by God or to help others find God's will for themselves, I *must* engage in serious study of the Bible.

In similar fashion the study of theology is important for the purity of the church. Some think this study splits up the church by engendering dogmatic strife. This, too, sometimes happens as when we search the Scripture to set the other fellow straight. But that need not be the case.

Again we are not seeking a theology to unify the church, but the truth which instructs and unifies it in obedience to God. The Bible clearly teaches that lines must be drawn between truth and falsehood, between obedience and disobedience. Only doctrine permits this. If error leads a church astray and is harmful, we should, if we love the church, seek to keep it from error. The apostle Jude warns us: "Beloved, when I gave all diligence to write unto you of the common salvation, it was needful for me to write unto you, and exhort you that ye should earnestly contend for the faith which was once delivered unto the saints."[33]

James Stalker writes, "Excessive aversion to controversy may be an indication that a Church has no keen sense of possessing truth which is of any great worth, and that it has lost appreciation for the infinite difference in value between truth and error."[34]

No pastor can perform his duties rightly without a serious grasp of biblical instruction and the determination to impart that teaching to his congregation in its fullness. Luther warned us against the danger of partial knowledge and partial obedience:

> Christ is the chief Shepherd, and under Him He has many shepherds. What are these shepherds to do? They are to lead Christ's flock to pasture. . . . To give pasture is nothing else than to preach the Gospel, by which souls are made fat and fruitful, and that the sheep are nourished with the Gospel and God's Word. For a pastor must not only lead to pasture by teaching the sheep how to be true Christians: but, in addition to this, he must also repel the wolves, lest they attack the sheep and lead them astray with false doctrine and error. For the devil does not rest. Now today one finds many people who can let the Gospel be preached, provided that one does not cry out against the wolves and preach against the prelates. But even if I preach in the right way and tend and teach the sheep, this protecting and guarding does not suffice to keep the wolves from coming and leading the sheep astray. For what is built if I lay stones and watch someone else knock them down? The wolf can surely let the sheep have good pasturage. The fatter they are, the more he likes them. But he cannot bear the hostile barking of the dogs. Therefore to him who takes this to heart it is important to tend the sheep in the right way, as God has commanded.[35]

So systematic theology is important for both the propagation and the defense of the gospel. We are to witness to the whole truth of God. And it is the preaching and teaching of the whole body of scriptural truth that allow it to be heard in all its glory, beauty and winsomeness. In fact, the best means to propagate the gospel is often a clear explanation of Christian truth.

A century ago James Orr reminded us that opposition in his day was against not just an individual Christian doctrine here and there, but was directed against the whole Christian world and life view. Therefore, we need to present and defend Christianity in its wholeness.[36]

If that was true in Orr's day, it is certainly far more true in contemporary Christendom at the end of the twentieth and the beginning of the twenty-first century. Again, it should be noted that we do not construct a theology which we believe can be most easily defended, but rather theology drawn from Scripture. It is the clear presentation of the whole truth that represents our best apologetic.

Finally, the study of systematic theology should enable us to preserve a proper balance. Granted that we are to preach and teach the whole counsel of God, what specific degree of emphasis is to be accorded each particular doctrine? We must determine this on the basis of the teaching of Scripture. It is the whole truth of God coming with his authority that we need to know and communicate. A piece of truth isolated from the whole truth is usually a dangerous guide. Every heresy, for example, encamps on isolated verses which it takes as the whole and out of which it draws rational conclusions which go beyond or, worse yet, often go against the clear teaching of the other passages of Scripture. Time and time again history tells us the story of those who have led the church astray by adding their own rationalistic insights or experience-based conclusions to the teaching of Scripture and who then sought to foist this teaching upon the church.

Systematic Theology as a High-Risk Enterprise

So far I have been speaking of the practical value of the discipline of systematic theology. Yet it must be admitted that there are very significant dangers in constructing a systematic theology. The more clearly we see these, the better we can avoid them. Emil Brunner lists four such objections, which he then seeks to refute.[37]

First, it is said, the study of systematic theology destroys the simplicity of faith. So far from providing practical and useful service for our lives, it has exactly the opposite effect. By subtle distinctions and assertions, it leads at best to fruitless speculations and at worst to hurtful controversies instead of a loving appreciation of, and fellowship with, the person of Christ. It takes our affection off Christ and sets us to the task of systematic study. This dulls not only our love for God but also our concern for the good of others. If I wish to grow to Christian maturity and become more and more like Jesus Christ, I must avoid systematic theology like a pestilence.

Of course, the study of systematic theology can do and, in fact, has actually done this at times. Every good creation can be perverted. But it need not do this. The ultimate aim of all our study is, quite literally, a love for, appreciation of and fellowship with the person of Jesus Christ, our redeeming God. We study that we may know him. The truth we seek is truth about a person. Does studying a love letter drive you from the person you love? Moreover, I do not want to be ignorant of the world in which I live and to which I must apply the divine instruction of Scripture.

And we must ask, what is fruitless and hurtful controversy? Certainly the tracing out of truth that God has revealed to us for our good is not a fruitless study. It is only going beyond what is revealed that may well be fruitless.

Similarly, what is hurtful controversy? We can hate the wrong things, or we can use doctrine to foster our selfish and private gain or those of our own organization. But the truth that God has given should turn us away from most controversy and from all wrongful controversy. Some controversy, as we noted, is necessary to maintain the truth. Yet truth may bring controversy which, in fact, may hurt. But if it is a hurt that God knows is necessary and really good for us, we must not avoid such controversy, but face it as truth God in his love for us has given to us for our good.

The second danger mentioned by Brunner is that the Christian needs to act rather than to waste time on reflection. But is all reflection wasted? Of course not! We are commanded to meditate on the law of God day and night.[38] The real question is, when is meditation wasteful, and when is it not wasteful but worthwhile? It is never wasteful to seek to know God and to let our minds dwell on the worthwhile, the good and the true.

But someone may protest, can't we expend too much time and energy in worshiping God and not enough in doing good? For example, isn't that precisely what the mystical hermit does when he secludes himself from all human society and the work of the world in order to know God better? No, we shall not spend too much time in worshiping God if we also are faithful to obey God in what he has commanded. In the act of obeying God in what we already know to be his will for us, we shall be prevented from spending too much time in the seeking of more truth, or in worship and contemplation of God. The mystic recluse, in fact, is disobedient if he is not concerned about the world.

Still, the divinely ordained life is a mixture of worship and work with no exact proportion prescribed for all. We know on biblical authority that the life pleasing to God must include a generous mixture of both. We can justly condemn a life devoted exclusively to one or the other.

John Wesley, for example, went beyond the clear application of Scripture when he expressed doubts about the spirituality of anyone who spent less than three hours each day in personal prayer. Since God has not revealed any precise amount of time anyone must devote to prayer and worship, we dare not condemn others for spending more or less time in prayer and worship than we are convinced is good for us. God knows what is best suited to each person, and what that amount is remains his or her personal business, so long as there is no complete absence of prayer and worship or of the study of God's Word.

Essentially the same principle holds for the proportion of our life we devote to evangelism and care for the physical needs of those in want. God knows each of his children perfectly, and he knows what he wills for each of them. We do not. We must only take care that our life habits are not more determined by our social environment than by the Word of God. In general, it has often been observed that Eastern Christians must guard against overworship; Western Christians must guard against overwork. All of us must submit our lives to the Holy Spirit of God in accordance with the instruction of Scripture, which we must know and apply faithfully and honestly.

In the third place Brunner notes that the study of systematic theology by its attempt to lay down rules and dogmas binding on all believers everywhere and under all circumstances destroys the freedom of the Christian child of God. A creed binds us and narrows our vision. The code of ethics spelled out restricts our activity and inhibits our freedom to act.

This is like saying, "Don't confuse me with the facts, I've already made up my mind." In one sense, the truth restricts our freedom to err. In reality, however, the truth makes us free. A good creed provides us with the truth we need to know so that we may arrive at more truth and not wander helplessly in error and ignorance. A good understanding of the biblical instruction for the conduct of life ("code" is a pejorative word) keeps us off dangerous paths that might destroy us or hinder our freedom to act to our best advantage.

Emil Brunner lists a fourth danger in the study of systematic theology. Such intellectual capacity as is available should be used to further the intellectual defense of the truth of the gospel in order to win the outsider rather than to create stumbling blocks to faith.

As with the previous objections to the study of systematic theology, this has included within it a piece of truth. Every church faces this sort of problem. We cannot concentrate all our energies on perfecting saints. We must evangelize sinners. And apparently God sees an absolute need for both. Moreover, only by knowing the truth can we discover what we ought to defend. The urgent instruction of

Holy Scripture will drive us to evangelism. Only an excessive kind of "polishing" of the saints will ever lead us to a lessening of the evangelistic imperative.

Finally, *additional dangers* not suggested by Brunner are frequently faced by the church. Because the moral temptation to evade the truth is so great at this point, *we may choose to construct a system of theology without the guidance of the Holy Spirit.* Such study is foredoomed to failure, because it is only the Spirit of God who is able to open our hearts and minds to see the truth of Scripture and to apply it honestly and seriously to our lives.

Again, *we may seek to answer every foolish question we conceive of or some foolish person asks and thus run into the danger of overcompleteness.* We need to consider what is the right amount of completeness. The Bible gives us all we need to know for the guidance of our spiritual and moral life. When the Bible is silent, we should be silent. Where the Bible speaks, there we must speak. God does not see fit to gratify our human curiosity on every point, but in the Scripture he has given us all the truth that we need to know for pleasing him, living obedient lives and rightly serving our fellow human beings.

We may also get off on tangents of doctrine and thus develop an unbalanced system of theology to the exclusion of the grand central themes of the Word of God. The faithful study of theology drawn from Scripture and available for us as we depend on the Holy Spirit is our best guarantee to a balanced view of the truth and in turn to a truly godly life.

We may also become enamored of our own systematic theology. This is a special danger for those who believe that the Christian faith is coherent and, above all, is a particular danger for teachers of philosophy and systematic theology. We can avoid this only by reminding ourselves constantly that it is not our theology we have created; but to the degree that it is true and good, it is the instruction that God has given us. And it is only in complete dependence upon the Holy Spirit and by his guidance that we are able to discover the truth and relate it properly to our lives and to the lives of others.

And once again, *we need to be warned against adopting a system of theology on the wrong grounds.* We can easily fall into the role of a Christian rationalist. This is—may I repeat because it is so frequently forgotten—a special danger of the teacher of systematic theology and especially of the theologian who believes (as I do) that the right use of reason appropriately illuminated by the Holy Spirit supports Christian faith. We must exercise great care to avoid putting into our theology what seems to us to fit most neatly into the beautiful whole we have concocted. Rather, we must limit our theology to what is demanded by the loving instruction of our God as set forth in Holy Scripture.

Scripture also warns us not to seek to please our audience. If a form of Christian rationalism is the special danger of systematic theologians, the desire for audience approval is a special danger for evangelists and ministers who speak to the world's "itching ears." We are men and women under orders. We do not create our own gospel. We are responsible for ascertaining and communicating the truth that God has revealed to us. And we determine that not by judging what people are eager to receive, but rather by what God in his infinite wisdom has chosen to reveal through his written Word.

Two additional and quite unavoidable dangers are found in constructing systematic theology. Even the most godly theologian or student of doctrine working humbly under the guidance of the Holy Spirit will experience them. Yet there are ways by which we may seek to lessen the evil effects of these dangers.

First is the danger of limiting our usefulness because of prejudices against the truth. This is the counterpart of constructing a systematic theology on the wrong grounds—the grounds of what is palatable or acceptable to those one is trying to win. By virtue of our faithfulness to the truth of the Scripture and our very unwillingness to bend it to what is attractive to unbelievers, we may on occasion hold to a doctrine which arouses antagonism. Evangelical opposition to free abortions provides an excellent example of this. Unfortunately, this opposition to abortions turns off many of our contemporaries. This does not mean that we are simply to omit this aspect of biblical teaching in our presentation of the truth of God. Rather we need to take great care as to how we present it. The issue does not reflect, as many moderns perceive it, a biblical or evangelical rejection of human freedom, especially of the freedom of women. Rather we are very strongly pro-life *and* pro-freedom *and* pro-choice within the guidelines laid down by our heavenly Father, who knows and has revealed to us in the Scripture what is best for us. Human freedom of choice has its limit: one person's freedom always stops where the next person's freedom begins. Therefore, we are not free to murder, and we are not free to abort an unborn child.

A second unavoidable danger sometimes limits the usefulness of Christians whose life is guided by Scripture. Instead of unbelievers turning away from our message because they object to Christian and biblical standards they deem too narrow for them, our own standards set by the straight and narrow path of Scripture may on occasion cause us to wall ourselves off from those we wish to reach. My unwillingness to rear my family in a thoroughly liberal church where the gospel is repudiated will serve as an example of this. I believe the Scripture requires that I rear my children in the nurture and admonition of the Lord. This demands that, if possible, they should have the benefit of a believing church that will nourish their faith. Unfortunately this means that I am not free to enter wholeheartedly with my family into an unbelieving church fellowship. Consequently I am unable to bring to such a church the witness to the gospel that would otherwise be possible.

Conclusion

Evangelical systematic theology is from start to finish a thoroughly practical discipline. It is, it is true, a fallible human endeavor. Yet it is based on an all-wise and all-loving God. It seeks to bring the wisdom of God to bear upon all the practical issues of life. When it has been strong, it has produced men and women with souls of iron. Great theologies have provided great character, great witness, great sacrifices, great servants of God, and because they are first great servants of God, also great servants of their fellow humans. In short, great theologies have produced great churches.

But great churches have also produced great theologies. Which produces which is not the point, for it is obvious that each contributes to and builds into the other. They are clearly related, and each serves and supports the other.

In his writings Paul Tillich poses a fundamental problem for us. He asks, Can Christianity today be relevant and still remain Christian? He answers, Yes, but to remain relevant Christianity must undergo a radical revision; and what he proposes is a far cry from traditional or biblical Christianity.[39]

As an evangelical, my answer is: Certainly it is relevant; and it is relevant because it is biblical. It will remain relevant and practical so long as it remains biblical. It is our duty (not only as teachers of doctrine and systematic theology but as Christians)—it is our duty to know the truth based upon the revelation of God in Holy Scripture and to bear witness to that truth and to show why it is relevant, why it is practical, why it is important and why, indeed, it is essential for the living of the good life in God's world.

Notes:

[1] For an excellent discussion of theology as a science, see Karl Barth, *The Doctrine of the Word of God*, 1/1, trans. and ed. G. W. Bromiley and T. F. Torrance (Edinburgh: T. & T. Clark, 1975), pp. 3–11.

[2] John Calvin, *Institutes of the Christian Religion*, ed. John T. McNeill, trans. Ford Lewis Battles, 2 vols. (Philadelphia: Westminster Press, 1975), 1:xxxiv. See Emil Brunner, *The Christian Doctrine of God*, trans. Olive Wyon (London: Lutterworth Press, 1949), pp. 89 and 90. See also the extraordinarily valuable study by Wolfhart Pannenberg, *Theology and the Philosophy of Science*, trans. Francis McDonagh (Philadelphia: Westminster Press, 1976). The section "Part Two: Theology as Science," pp. 228ff., is particularly helpful.

[3] See Schubert Ogden, "What Is Theology?" *The Journal of Religion* 52 (1972): 22–24. Roman Catholics, even at the most basic level, cannot agree as to what they mean to do when they "do theology." See John J. Connelly, "The Task of Theology," *The Catholic Theological Society of America: Proceedings of the 29th Annual Conference* (Chicago: Catholic Theological Society of America, 1974), pp. 1–58. Protestants are still less agreed. See, for example, Maurice Wiles, *What Is Theology?* (Oxford: Oxford University Press, 1976), pp. 42ff.; and John M. Frame, *The Doctrine of the Knowledge of God* (Phillipsburg, N.J.: Presbyterian and Reformed, 1987), pp. 76 and 77.

[4] Cited by Heinrich Schmid, *The Doctrinal Theology of the Evangelical Lutheran Church*, 3rd ed. revised, trans. Charles A. Hay and Henry E. Jacobs (Minneapolis, Minn.: Augsburg, 1875), p. 15.

[5] See especially E. D. Hirsch, *Validity in Interpretation* (New Haven, Conn.: Yale University Press, 1967). See also Tremper Longman III, *Literary Approaches to Biblical Interpretation* (Grand Rapids, Mich.: Zondervan, 1987); and Anthony C. Thiselton, *The Two Horizons: New Testament Hermeneutics and Philosophical Description* (Grand Rapids, Mich.: Eerdmans, 1980).

[6] See his *Interpreter's Dictionary of the Bible*, George Arthur Buttrick et al., eds. (Nashville, Tenn.: Abington Press, 1962), 4:418–32.

[7] For a valuable analysis of the quite varied understanding of what it means to "exegete" or to "use" Scripture, see David Kelsey, *The Uses of Scripture in Recent Theology* (Philadelphia: Fortress Press, 1975).

[8] J. D. G. Dunn, *Unity and Diversity in the New Testament* (London: S.C.M. Press, 1977).

[9] Sometimes Dunn seems to suggest that these theologies are contradictory; but he is tolerant, and it is quite okay with him if, indeed, others pick one of the poorer choices. More frequently, he argues that they contradict each other, but really all of them are basically and equally satisfactory. For a careful analysis of this position, see Donald A. Carson, "Unity and Diversity in the New Testament: The Possibility of Systematic Theology," in D. A. Carson and John D. Woodbridge, eds., *Scripture and Truth* (Grand Rapids, Mich.: Zondervan, 1983), pp. 65–95. Note especially his treatment of J. D. A. Dunn on pages 72–77.

[10] For a defense of the inner unity of the various segments of biblical theology, see Walther Eichrodt, *Theology of the Old Testament*, trans. J. A. Baker (Philadelphia: Westminster Press, 1951). Eichrodt organizes Old Testament theology around the "covenant," but other arrangements are surely possible. See also Jacob Jocz, *The Covenant: A Theology of Human Destiny* (Grand Rapids, Mich., Eerdmans, 1968); Herman N. Ridderbos, *Paul and Jesus: Origin and General Character of Paul's Preaching of Christ*, trans. David H. Freeman (Philadelphia: Presbyterian and Reformed, 1958); Walter C. Kaiser, *Toward an Old Testament Theology* (Grand Rapids, Mich.: Zondervan, 1978); F. F. Bruce, *Paul and Jesus* (Grand Rapids, Mich.: Baker, 1974); and George E. Ladd, *A Theology of the New Testament* (Grand Rapids, Mich.: Eerdmans, 1974).

[11] See Karl Barth, *Church Dogmatics*, 1/2, *The Doctrine of the Word of God*, trans. G. W. Bromiley and T. F. Torrance (Edinburgh: T. & T. Clark, 1956), pp. 603–60.

[12] This paragraph and a number of other introductory notes in this article as well as a few sentences from the text first appeared in and are here taken from my article in the volume edited

by John D. Woodbridge and Thomas E. McComiskey, *Doing Theology in Today's World* (Grand Rapids, Mich.: Zondervan, 1992), pp. 465–93. The material is used by permission of Zondervan Publishing House. General items discussing the nature of theology are more fully covered in that article.

[13] For a fine presentation of the legitimate role of natural revelation from an evangelical viewpoint, see Bruce S. Demarest, *General Revelation: Historical Views and Contemporary Issues* (Grand Rapids, Mich.: Zondervan, 1982).

[14] In the New Testament the primary reference of the phrase "Word of God" is to Christ, the gospel and the message about Christ. It can also refer to the written Scripture. See, for example, Mark 7:13, where the teaching of Moses in the Scripture is designated the Word of God because it is a message coming from God. Students of Scripture distinguish between the living Word of God, Christ, and the written Word of God, Holy Scripture. For the divergent ways the phrase was used in ancient religious literature and in the Bible, see *Theological Dictionary of the New Testament,* ed. Gerhard Kittel, trans. and ed. Geoffrey W. Bromiley, 10 vols. (Grand Rapids, Mich.: Eerdmans, 1967), 4:69ff. For a somewhat different view of the phrase, see *Dictionary of New Testament Theology,* ed. Colin Brown, 3 vols. (Grand Rapids, Mich.: Zondervan, 1978), 3:1078–146.

[15] Paul Tillich, *Systematic Theology,* 3 vols. (Chicago: University of Chicago Press, 1963), 1:83–85 et passim.

[16] This was the thrust of Martin Luther in his famous treatise *The Freedom of the Christian Man* (published under the title *Christian Liberty*), ed. Harold J. Grimm (Philadelphia: Fortress Press, 1957).

[17] Biblical preaching, however, cannot ignore the complex ways parts of the Bible are related to each other. We dare not preach as though the bits and pieces of the Bible need only to be juxtaposed so that no piece is omitted from our theology or our preached message. For example, parts of Scripture must be understood in the historical context of covenantal relationships set forth in the Bible (Heb 8:13). The "befores" and "afters" of Scripture greatly affect all attempts to understand Christian ethics, Christian worship and even Christian beliefs.

[18] The alternatives to such a relationship between preaching and systematic theology are unthinkable: (1) the pastors alone—who receive a formal theological education—will be exposed to systematic theology and thus become the initiated, the elite of the elect, or (2) the ordinary lay Christians in the pew must develop their own systematic theology with no help or modelling when such help would prove enormously stabilizing in their own lives. The strength of the church depends upon such preaching as is informed by and informing systematic theology.

[19] Friedrich E. D. Schleiermacher, *On Religion: Speeches to Its Cultured Despisers,* trans. John Oman, introduction by Rudolph Otto (New York: Harper, 1958), pp. 119ff. Later Schleiermacher modified his views somewhat, but not decisively. See his *Christian Faith,* 2nd German ed., ed. and trans. H. R. Mackintosh and J. S. Stewart (Edinburgh: T. & T. Clark, 1928), pp. 142ff.

[20] Barth, *Doctrine of the Word of God,* 1/1, pp. 111ff. Here Barth argues that Scripture points to Christ, but its trustworthiness as a pointer is in doubt. For example, Scripture errs in its theological teaching. See 1/2, p. 509 and many other passages.

[21] Karl Barth, *Evangelical Theology: An Introduction,* trans. Grover Foley (New York: Holt, Rinehart and Winston, 1963), p. 30ff. Here Barth argues that both theologians and Christian witnesses must place themselves under the authority of Holy Scripture and be guided by it. They dare not pick and choose from what it says, rejecting it here and approving it there, like some teacher grading a student's exam.

[22] William Hordern, *A Layman's Guide to Protestant Theology,* rev. ed. (New York: Macmillan, 1955), p. xvii.

[23] 2 Timothy 4:1-2; 3:14-17.

[24] Calvin, *Institutes* (introduction to the *Institutes* of 1559), 1:4.

[25] 1 Corinthians 2, especially verses 14ff.

[26] Psalm 19:7-13 (RSV) puts it beautifully: "The law of the LORD is perfect, reviving the soul; the testimony of the LORD is sure, making wise the simple; the precepts of the LORD are right, rejoicing the heart; the commandment of the LORD is pure, enlightening the eyes; the fear of the LORD is clean, enduring for ever; the ordinances of the LORD are true, and righteous altogether. More to be desired are they than gold, even much fine gold; sweeter also than honey and drippings from the honeycomb. Moreover by them is thy servant warned; in keeping them there is great reward."

[27] As our Lord declared: "It is written in the prophets 'and they shall be taught by God.' Every one who has heard and learned from the Father comes to me" (Jn 6:45 RSV).

[28] 1 John 2:20, 26, 27. The apostle even states that we have no need for any teacher other than the Holy Spirit. This is not to say that other teachers are useless; but the only really necessary teacher is the Holy Spirit.

[29] Ephesians 4:11-13 NIV. See also Galatians 1–2; 1 Corinthians 2; John 17:17; Romans 6–8; and elsewhere.

[30] 2 Timothy 2:2.

[31] 1 Timothy 4:16 NIV.

[32] Titus 1:7-9 NIV; see also 1 Timothy 3:1-7. In these passages Paul includes many quite personal qualifications.

[33] Jude 3 KJV.

[34] James Stalker, *Imago Christi: The Example of Jesus Christ* (London: Hodder & Stoughton, 1899), p. 287.

[35] From Luther's sermons on 1 Peter. *Luther's Works: The Catholic Epistles,* ed. Jaroslav Pelikan and Walter Hansen (St. Louis, Mo.: Concordia, 1967), 30:134–35. From *Luther's Works* Volume 30—*Luther's Works: The Catholic Epistles,* copyright 1967 Concordia Publishing House. Used by permission.

[36] James Orr, *The Christian View of God and the World as Centring in the Incarnation: Being the Kerr Lectures for 1890–1891* (Grand Rapids, Mich.: Eerdmans, 1948), pp. 8ff. See also his note on pages 370–72.

[37] Emil Brunner, *The Christian Doctrine of God,* trans. Olive Wyon, 2 vols. (London: Lutterworth, 1949), 1:6–8.

[38] Psalm 1.

[39] Paul Tillich, *The Shaking of the Foundations* (London: S.C.M. Press, 1949).

3

Toward a Theology of the Biblical Text

Roger T. Beckwith

THERE ARE FEW INDEED TO WHOM THE CONTEM-
porary church owes more for fostering faith in the divine authority of
Scripture than James Packer. Beginning with his *"Fundamentalism"
and the Word of God* (1958), in which a short but penetrating section
on the biblical text is included, through *God Has Spoken* (1965, revised edition 1979), and on to nearly all his writings in one part or
another, the authority of God's written Word is a recurring theme
and a constant concern.

The biblical text, like the biblical canon, is a material aspect of the
subject of the Bible, which writers usually handle in isolation; but its
relevance and importance are unquestionable, for just as it is true that
without a canon there could be no Bible, it is equally true that without a text there could be no Bible. If, then, the Bible is a topic of
theology, so is its canon and text. They are normally approached
historically, but they need to be approached theologically as well.

The historical inquiry about the canon and that about the text are
significantly different in their aim. The former inquiry works forwards, to trace the developing conviction of God's people about the
books which are to be reckoned as Scripture. The latter inquiry
works backwards, to trace the earliest form of the text from which
subsequent forms evolved. Both inquiries are working from diversity
toward unity, but the former inquiry is working forwards to a period
when the evidence is getting increasingly abundant and clear, while
the latter inquiry is working backwards to a period when the evi-

dence is getting increasingly scanty and obscure, and inference rather than testimony has to be one's guide. Textual criticism, as it is called, is a balance of probabilities, and there is much room for difference of opinion as to where the balance lies.

As Originally Given

Turning to the theological aspect of the biblical text, one of the assertions most frequently made by conservative evangelicals today is "the divine inspiration and infallibility of Holy Scripture, *as originally given*" (University and Colleges Christian Fellowship [UK] Basis of Faith). One can perfectly well defend what is explicit in this assertion from the statements that the Bible makes about the operation of the Holy Spirit upon those who wrote the Scriptures in the first place. In 2 Peter 1:21, for example, we read that "no prophecy [of Scripture (compare verse 20)] ever came by the will of man: but men spoke from God, being moved by the Holy Ghost."[1] What they wrote was not simply their word but the word of God. However, the implication of the phrase "as originally given" goes beyond this basic affirmation, for it implies that what was true of the Scriptures when they were first written is not necessarily true of them as we have them today. And herein lies a problem. For the New Testament is not making this assertion about the inspiration of the prophets for any abstract reason, but in order that we may know how to treat their writings today. Thus, in verse 19 it says of their writings, "to which you do well that you take heed, as to a lamp shining in a dark place," and in verse 20, "no prophecy of scripture is of private interpretation."

Theological statements of this qualified kind were not normally made before the closing years of the nineteenth century. They were a consequence of the revolution in the textual criticism of the New Testament brought about by the edition of B. F. Westcott and F. J. A. Hort (1881). Westcott and Hort claimed that the traditional Greek text of the New Testament, which is found in the great mass of the manuscripts, and on which the "Textus Receptus" of the Renaissance and the vernacular translations stemming from it were based, was not the original form of the text but a revision dating from about the fourth century, constructed out of earlier Western, Alexandrian and Neutral traditions of the text. They called this revision "Syrian" and placed their reliance instead on the fourth-century manuscripts *Codex Vaticanus* and *Codex Sinaiticus,* which they reckoned "neutral," though not perfect. To get still further back toward the original text, one had to compare readings and test them by various rules. One could then claim to have got as near to the original text as is now possible. Westcott and Hort's theory was accepted by the great Princeton theologian B. B. Warfield, who expounded it in a book of his own (*An Introduction to the Textual Criticism of the New Testament,* 1887), and from that point onward the infallibility claimed for the Scriptures began to be attached to a form of the text not now entirely accessible.

Westcott and Hort's theory is no longer defended in the form in which they propounded it. The traditional text is not today called Syrian but Byzantine, and a number of Byzantine readings which they rejected have been found in the early papyri. The text they called neutral is now regarded as an Alexandrian revision. Most modern textual critics favor an eclectic text, but the original text continues to be regarded as to some degree inaccessible, even in circles where the traditional text has found new champions.[2]

A second difficulty about the phrase "as originally given" is of rather a different kind. This difficulty concerns not the form of text to which it refers but the meaning of the phrase itself. If we could get back to the earliest form of the text, as it left the hand of the original author, would that be the form of the text to which divine authority properly and entirely attaches? Many biblical books seem to have been added to afterwards, either by the original author or by someone else, but not necessarily without divine sanction. What is the original text of St. John's Gospel? Does it include chapter 21 or not? Is St. Mark's Gospel complete at chapter 16, verse 8, or is its ending lost, or is the longer ending the original ending? In the Old Testament, is the book of Deuteronomy (in which Moses often appears as the writer) complete without the account of Moses' death? What is the original text of a composite book like Proverbs, in which there are fresh headings at Proverbs 10:1; 24:23; 25:1; 30:1; and 31:1? Are the speeches of Elihu (Job 32–37) part of the original text of the book of Job? Certainly, it is forbidden to add to God's words or to diminish from them (Deut 4:2; 12:32; Prov 30:6; Rev 22:18f.), but does that necessarily mean that all editorial work on a sacred text is in the nature of the case uninspired and prohibited?

This question is now posed more sharply as a result of the discovery of the Dead Sea Scrolls, which have vitally affected every field of biblical study, including the study of the text. Up to the time of their discovery, it was possible to maintain (even if with some difficulty) that the Masoretic text of the Hebrew Bible was the only genuine Jewish form of the Old Testament text—the Samaritan Pentateuch was a sectarian variant, and the Septuagint owed its peculiarities to its translators. The library at Qumran has made it impossible to maintain this any longer. Hebrew manuscripts of the Old Testament in all three traditions were found there, evidently read and used by the same Jewish religious community. Certainly, the Masoretic form of text predominates, but the Samaritan is also found there, and so are Septuagint-type texts in Hebrew and not in Greek. Side by side with the Masoretic form of the text of Jeremiah, for example, is the Hebrew original of the much shorter and differently arranged Septuagint text. Clearly, three traditions of the Hebrew text then existed among the Jews, one of which they shared with the Samaritans, another of which had been employed by the Septuagint translators, and the third of which was becoming predominant and was later standardized.[3]

This new evidence is discussed with great thoroughness by Emanuel Tov in his book *Textual Criticism of the Hebrew Bible* (Minneapolis, Minn.: Fortress, 1992). Tov argues that many of the Old Testament books may have had a compositional stage rather than a single act of composition, at the end of which the text was considered complete and was accepted as authoritative and binding in that form. From this point the stage of copying and transmission began. However, he postulates a degree of overlap. While some reckoned a text complete and devoted themselves to copying and circulating it, others may have continued to develop it and may have judged it complete at a later date and in a different form. This would certainly account for the phenomenon of two or three forms of the Hebrew text, so widely varying from each other, for some of the books, and would almost necessitate this development of multiple forms occurring in different places. F. M. Cross Jr.'s theory of Alexandria as the home of the Septuagint-type text, Palestine as the home of the Samaritan-type and Babylonia as the home of the Masoretic-type is open to criticism as it stands, but may be pointing us in the right direction.

As the Dead Sea Scrolls are only fragmentary and simply *indicate* a plurality of forms of the biblical text, rather than completely documenting it, much still depends on inference. Moreover, the question is further complicated by various other facts. Those who look for tendencies in different forms of the text do not find the same tendencies throughout the different books of the Masoretic text or of the Septuagint. There are certain "nonaligned" manuscripts among those found at Qumran, which do not clearly belong to any of the three great families and yet in some cases contain many readings which seem authentic. Textual changes continued to occur, to some extent, even after the end of the compositional stage and throughout the transmissional stage, owing to errors of transcription, assimilation of parallel passages and similar causes. And the basic issue of a plurality of forms of text, not a single form, at the end of the compositional stage and the beginning of the transmissional stage, is the most intractable problem of all.

If Tov is right, then, it seems that the Old Testament text, "as originally given," was (at least in the case of some books) a developed text, produced by more than one hand and transmitted in more than one form. These forms are accessible to us, insofar as they are accessible, through the transmitted manuscript of the Masoretic Hebrew, the Samaritan Hebrew and the Septuagint Greek, together with such parts of the last named as we now possess in Hebrew and not just in Greek.

Turning our thoughts to the New Testament books, the manuscripts are more abundant and approach nearer in date to the time of composition, but here too there are occasional problems over what we mean by the original author, and many uncertainties in detail about the original form of the text.

God's Singular Care and Providence

Exclusive concentration on the text "as originally given," it can now be seen, inevitably drives one toward a degree of agnosticism. It is therefore helpful to reflect that before the time of Westcott and Hort, the emphasis of theologians was quite different and concentrated on the reliability of the transmitted text. As John Jewel, the Elizabethan reforming bishop, expressed it in his *Treatise of the Holy Scriptures,* 1570:

> There is no sentence, no clause, no word, no syllable, no letter, but it is written for thy instruction: there is not one jot but it is sealed and signed with the blood of the Lamb . . . no word, no syllable, no point or prick thereof, but it is written *and preserved* for thy sake. (*Works*, Parker Society, 4:1175, italics added)

Or, as the *Westminster Confession of Faith,* 1647, puts it,

> The Old Testament in Hebrew . . . and the New Testament in Greek . . . being immediately inspired by God, and *by his singular care and providence kept pure in all ages,* are therefore authentical; so as in all controversies of religion, the Church is finally to appeal unto them. (ch. 1, sect. 8, italics added)

This emphasis on the reliability of the transmitted text was sometimes even pushed to the excess of claiming inspiration for the Masoretic vowel points, as is done in the *Helvetic Consensus Formula,* 1675, but this was only an extreme example of a sober conviction. The church was not, of course, unaware in this period that there were certain differences between manuscripts, and from the beginning of the eighteenth century or earlier it began to collate these differences—Kennicott and others working on the Hebrew Bible, Hody and others on the Septuagint and Mill and others on the Greek New Testament. The differences were found to be numerous, but small, and of no real doctrinal significance.[4]

Belief in the providential preservation of the Scriptures has, in fact, been the common conviction (or at least assumption) of the people of God in every age. If this had not been so, it would have been impossible for people to use the Scriptures for the purpose for which they had been given. From the Intertestamental period onward, and even in the later books of the Old Testament, we find the contemporary text (or texts) of the Scriptures being referred to as giving authoritative guidance. The expression "as it is written," without further explanation of *where* it is written, but evidently meaning "as it is written in the well-known and authoritative Scriptures," first occurs in Ezra 3:4, Nehemiah 8:15 and 2 Chronicles 30:5, 18; but in the Dead Sea Scrolls, Philo, the New Testament and the Fathers this becomes one of the characteristic formulas used for introducing quotations from the Scriptures, designed to apply their authority to whatever question is at issue. The quotations are treated as having finality, and it is the contemporary text of the quotations which is treated in this way. Philo quotes from the Septuagint translation, as the New Testament often does and the Fathers regularly do, but when the Hebrew is quoted or reflected (as in the Dead Sea Scrolls and sometimes in the New Testament), there is nothing to suggest that anything other than contemporary manuscripts of the Hebrew is being used. Paraphrase, where paraphrase is employed, is evidently designed to draw out the most relevant implications of the passage quoted, and not to restore a more primitive form of the text. In all this, the practice of Jesus and his apostles in the New Testament is like that of their Jewish contemporaries.

What this implies is that God's "singular care and providence" was understood to extend not just to the traditional form (or forms) of the original text, but even to standard and accepted translations of the text, such as the Septuagint. The Septuagint is an interesting case in point, because, whereas it is an assumption that the men of Qumran used the various forms of the Hebrew text which they preserved as all being authoritative, we have more specific information about the Septuagint. On the one hand, it was treated as sacrosanct. The Letter of Aristeas contends that the Septuagint Pentateuch must never be altered (sections 310f, 317) and Philo speaks of its translators as being "just as if inspired" (*De Vita Mosis* 2.37). On the other hand, sustained attempts were made, from the first century B.C. onward, to revise the Septuagint in order to conform it more closely to the Hebrew. The *Kaige* school of revisers and retranslators (as it is called), which culminated in the work of Theodotion and Aquila, was already at work as early as this, and one of them is quoted in the New Testament (Acts 2:18).[5] The Hebrew was standard, as being the original, but the Septuagint was the revered translation. This attitude of venerating both the Hebrew and the Septuagint continued among the Fathers and is put into words by Augustine (*City of God* 18.42-44). He recognizes that there are differences but treats both texts as true, if rightly interpreted. Jerome, with his passion for the neglected *Hebraica veritas*, was less tolerant of diversity, but even Jerome found it necessary to make concessions to the existing practice of the church.

The Semitic-speaking Jews also were aware of textual differences. A *baraita* or ancient quotation in the Babylonian Talmud (*Megillah* 9a-9b) gives a curious list of the deviations from the Hebrew in the Septuagint Pentateuch, attributing them to divine prompting. A passage in one of the earliest midrashim (*Siphre on Deuteronomy* 356), repeated elsewhere in the rabbinical literature, states that there were three Hebrew Pentateuch scrolls in the temple, each taking its name from a small textual variant which it contained, and adds that the variants were emended, on the purely numerical basis of two scrolls against one. And there is further evidence of a similar kind.[6] The Jews were already moving toward standardizing a form of the Masoretic text, but the other forms of text which were known to exist were still treated with great respect.

Tentative Conclusions

It follows from all this that the quest for the original form of the biblical text, as the form originally inspired by God, is a proper quest, but it needs in future to be thought of as the original form *or forms*. The idea that there can be only one author and one form is probably a misconception.

It follows, secondly, that the habit of thinking of one form as infallible, and all other forms than one as necessarily corrupt, is improper. And this caution needs to be extended not just to different elements in the original text but also to traditional texts, which are the objects of the providential care of God, and may be more than one in number, but are the forms of text which the church has no choice but to use as its religious authority and has the example of Jesus and the apostles to justify it in doing so.

It follows, thirdly, that a standard and long-accepted translation like the Septuagint can also be treated as the Word of God without any impropriety. It is right to compare it with the Hebrew, but it is also right to use it with confidence in itself. Augustine's principle of accepting both, and relating them by exegesis, was not wrong.

And since, in matters of canon and text, we are left to argue by analogy from God's providential care of the Old Testament to his providential care of the New, it follows that here too the original form or forms of text should continue to be sought, but that the traditional form of text should also be used with confidence as the Word of God, and that standard and long-accepted translations like the Vulgate, the Peshitta, Luther's German Bible and the English Authorized (or King James) Version have a claim to similar treatment, alongside faithful modern translations, based on critical texts.[7]

Notes:

[1] All scriptural quotations in this article are from the Revised Version.

[2] A good statement of the case for the traditional text is made by a convert to that viewpoint, J. W. Wenham, in the third edition of his *Christ and the Bible* (Guildford, England: Eagle, 1993), pp. 177–95. The first edition (London: Tyndale Press, 1972, pp. 172–87) argues the case for an eclectic text.

[3] This is not, of course, to say that the Samaritans did not introduce sectarian variants into their text at a few points, or that the deviations of the Septuagint are not sometimes due to the translators, but simply that these explanations are no longer adequate in themselves.

[4] Many differences appear to be due to harmonizing additions, and some to variations designed to make unorthodox interpretations more difficult. On the latter, see B. D. Ehrman, *The Orthodox Corruption of Scripture* (London: Oxford University Press, 1993).

[5] On the *Kaige* school, which rendered the Hebrew *gam* (or *aph*) in this way, see Dominique Barthélemy, *Les devanciers d'Aquila* (Supplements to *Vetus Testamentum* 10, Leiden, Netherlands: Brill, 1963).

[6] See Abraham Epstein, "Biblische Textkritik bei den Rabbinen," in Adolf Büchler et al., *Recueil des travaux en mémoire du Jubilé de M. D. Chwolson* (Berlin: Calvary, 1899).

[7] The decree of the Council of Trent (session 4) that the Latin Vulgate should be "held as authentic" would therefore be defensible if the Council had not been promoting the Vulgate in rivalry to the original Hebrew and Greek.

4

Recovering Baptism for a New Age of Mission

David F. Wright

T HE 1995 GENERAL ASSEMBLY OF THE CHURCH OF
Scotland was asked by one of its education committees to authorize
the admission of unbaptized children to the Lord's Supper in certain
circumstances. Two or three years ago the Assembly had agreed that

> where a Kirk Session is satisfied that baptised children are being
> nurtured within the life and worship of the Church and love the
> Lord and respond in faith to the invitation "take, eat," it may
> admit such children to the Lord's Table, after pastorally oversee-
> ing the response of faith of such children to see when it is right
> for them to come to the Lord's Table.[1]

When this provision was under debate, questions were raised about
invidious division among the children of the congregation, some of
whom, in the Sunday school in particular, might not have been baptized. It was chiefly discrimination of this kind—some, baptized, being taken and others, unbaptized, being left—that the 1995 request
was intended to obviate. Why, it was argued, should children be excluded as second-class citizens on a technicality, merely because they
happened not to have been baptized?

The rejection of the suggestion afforded cold comfort. It was difficult to conceive how it could ever have surfaced in the Church of
Scotland, no less, which not only nurtures a sizable *amour-propre* as
far as theology is concerned (not without good cause, it should be
said) but sponsored barely a generation ago probably the most extended investigation of baptism that topic has ever received from a

church. The Special Commission on Baptism beavered away for a decade, 1953–1963, under Professor T. F. Torrance's convenership, reported at length in minute print to the General Assembly year after year, and published *The Biblical Doctrine of Baptism* (1958) and *The Doctrine of Baptism* (1966).[2] It was as fulsome in its theology of baptism as it was exhaustive in its research. Nevertheless, three decades later, a child's lack of baptism is regarded in some circles in the same church as incidental, unfortunate perhaps, but not to be allowed to debar the child from the Lord's Table.

Readers of this volume of essays in honor of one of the most powerful evangelical theologians of the twentieth century may be shaking their heads knowingly and muttering, "Well, what do you expect? The Kirk's not what it was, theologically." One does not need to be a James Packer to expose the nakedness of the proposal: if unbaptized children, why not unbaptized teenagers and adults?—to say nothing of a raft of other more substantial objections. But if we are of one mind in showing it the door, how healthy is the theology of Christian baptism among the evangelical churches today? It may not be only a few Church of Scotland bureaucrats who have relegated baptism to the status of a doctrinal Cinderella. But neglecting or illtreating baptism may have more serious consequences than losing one's theological respectability: it may damage the church's mission at a time in Western society when primary mission rises ever higher on all the churches' agenda. If theology finds its ultimate *raison d'être* in the vitality of the people of God, as James Packer has so splendidly exemplified, belittling or ignoring baptism must prejudice its missionary integrity. For baptism is above all the sacrament or ordinance of the church's missionary advance.

On a number of measures, baptism comes off a poor second to holy communion. Only very recently has it begun to attract major attention in ecumenical contexts. Not a few commentators have judged the section on baptism in the influential Faith and Order report *Baptism, Eucharist and Ministry* (Geneva, 1982) lacking in sophistication compared with the other two. The history of Christian baptism largely remains to be written, both for formative eras like the patristic age and the Reformation and from an overall perspective. Solid dogmatic treatises on baptism are scarcely two a penny in the publishers' catalogs. In terms of church order, the question who may administer baptism hardly rates a mention alongside who may preside at the Eucharist. What an irony that so much ink—or blood—should have been spilt over the latter, and so little concern evinced over who may rightly admit people to the church in baptism.

The Church as Baptismal Community

It has become a commonplace in recent ecumenical discussion to describe the church as a Eucharist community. It would be far truer to the New Testament to describe it as a baptismal community. To make this point is not merely to correct an ecumenical imbalance; it is to challenge evangelical indifference, for the New Testament's (and for that matter, the Reformation's) baptismal language is much more realist than modern evangelical piety has generally allowed. Without attempting a close exegetical study, it may nevertheless be worth reminding ourselves of a string of New Testament declarations.[3]

> Jesus came to them and said, "All authority in heaven and on earth has been given to me. Therefore go and make disciples of all nations, baptizing them in the name of the Father and of the Son and of the Holy Spirit." (Mt 28:18-19)
>
> "Brothers, what shall we do?" Peter replied, "Repent and be baptized, every one of you, in the name of Jesus Christ for the forgiveness of your sins. And you will receive the gift of the Holy Spirit." (Acts 2:37-38)
>
> We were all baptized by one Spirit into one body . . . and we were all given the one Spirit to drink. (1 Cor 12:13)
>
> You are all sons of God through faith in Christ Jesus, for all of you who were baptized into Christ have clothed yourselves with Christ. (Gal 3:26-27)
>
> There is one body and one Spirit—just as you were called to one hope when you were called—one Lord, one faith, one baptism; one God and Father of all, who is over all and through all and in all. (Eph 4:4-6)
>
> This water [around Noah's ark] symbolizes baptism that now saves you also—not the removal of dirt from the body but the pledge of a good conscience toward God. It saves you by the resurrection of Jesus Christ. (1 Pet 3:21)

Note the absence from Ephesians 4 of "one Eucharist"! I omit, as likely to be contentious, John 3:5, "Jesus answered, 'I tell you the truth, no one can enter the kingdom of God unless he is born of water and the Spirit,'" even though no biblical text was cited as often as this with reference to baptism in the early Fathers. Peter's summons in his Pentecost address may be taken as standing for the special interest in baptism shown throughout the Acts of the Apostles. The Ethiopian's question, "Look, here is water. Why shouldn't I be baptized?" (Acts 8:36) must reveal part of the burden of Philip's witness to him. What Paul heard from Ananias, "And now what are you waiting for? Get up, be baptized and wash your sins away, calling on his name" (Acts 22:16), helps to explain the boldness of Paul's baptismal teaching.

The centrality of baptism to the experience of the New Testament churches is evident also in the way it is cited to correct abuses of one kind or another. To the divided parties of Corinth it was enough to say "Is Christ divided? Was Paul crucified for you? Were you baptized into the name of Paul?" (1 Cor 1:13). How many pastors today would instinctively tackle the gross misunderstanding of "going on sinning so that grace might increase" as Paul did?

> We died to sin; how can we live in it any longer? Or don't you know that all of us who were baptized into Christ Jesus were baptized into his death? We were therefore buried with him through baptism into death in order that, just as Christ was raised from the dead through the glory of the Father, we too may live a new life. (Rom 6:2-4)

Colossians 2:12-13 shows how readily Paul invoked the burial imagery of baptism:

> . . . having been buried with him in baptism and raised with him through your faith in the power of God, who raised him from the dead. When you were dead in your sins and in the uncircumcision of your sinful nature, God made you alive with Christ.

How many among us would think of describing the Israelites of the exodus as "baptized into Moses in the cloud and in the sea" (1 Cor 10:2)? Or include "instruction about baptisms" (Heb 6:2—whatever the plural might denote) among the basics of the faith?

Low Baptismal Consciousness

The apostolic churches evince a baptismal consciousness rarely to be glimpsed in evangelical churches today. This is particularly the case in infant-baptizing communions. It would not be uncommon in the Church of Scotland, for example, for older teenagers or young adults coming forward for what until recently could be called admission to the Lord's Table to be unaware whether they had been baptized or not ("I must ask my parents"). But apart from such uncertainty, baptism occupies a fairly marginal niche in the teaching programs and hence the corporate mind of many an orthodox congregation. A different story might have to be told of believer-baptizers, but I would expect considerable variation, with conversion in many instances eclipsing baptism as the moment constitutive of Christian identity. On a nondenominational canvas, a problem typically encountered in mass evangelism—"she has become a Christian/been converted, and now she has to find a church to join"—is a quintessentially modern one, which would have been almost incomprehensible to the church of most earlier centuries. That is to say, the notion that one could "become a Christian" prior to and apart from being "baptized by the one Spirit into the one body" is one that the church of the Fathers and the Reformers would have found bizarre.

Why is it that the baptismal consciousness of so much church life in the West burns so low? Why is it that so few Christians who would otherwise identify cordially with the broad witness of the Reformation would think of defying devilish assaults on the soul as Luther did—with the words "I have been baptized"? The answers are no doubt to be sought in several different directions, not all of which need detain us here. They would include an understandable but exaggerated reaction against sacramentalist fundamentalism, which views participation in baptism as the be-all and end-all of church membership—a reaction still responsible for the ignoring or spiritualizing of biblical references to baptism in too much biblical exposition from evangelical pulpits. Coupled with this, one must cite the practice of indiscriminate baby baptism that still prevails in some European countries, especially where Lutheranism is the state church, and is still widely influential elsewhere, though more patchily than earlier in the twentieth century. Where baptism is so easily given and received, with so little effect, it cannot—so many biblical Christians would reason— amount to very much. Some would even claim that it is not better than nothing but actually worse than nothing! In broad terms this conviction inspires the work of the Movement for the Reform of Infant Baptism (MORIB),[4] whose newsletters reflect the analysis that indiscriminate infant baptism has created massive obstacles to the evangelization of England. On this reckoning it has, alas, been only too effective; its injection of a minimal dose of the virus of Christianity has successfully inoculated generations of English men and women against catching the real thing in later life. This diagnosis of the root causes of pervasive spiritual indifference may be losing its plausibility with the passing of the years, but its validity cannot be wholly discounted.

Baptism and De-Christianization
There may even be factors in the de-Christianizing religious situation

in the West which threaten to breathe new life into a turning-the-blind-eye generosity in baptismal administration. Interest in the institutional church seeps away at an alarming rate. As fewer and fewer people express any need for it, those who do are likely to be greeted with unquestioningly open arms. In this age of accountability, ministers will be increasingly tempted to notch up every chance of demonstrating that there is still a demand for what they have to offer, even if their services—in marrying and burying as well as baptizing—are increasingly demanded on sub-Christian or non-Christian terms. Where the consumer is king, it will surely prove harder for clergy to remain ministers of Christ's Word and sacraments in servicing the expectations of ever more minimally Christian folk-religion. Already Granny, rather than the child's parents, is the real promoter of many an infant baptism, and already pastors are grappling routinely with requests for baby baptism from cohabiting unmarried parents or from a single parent with the other one nowhere in sight.

The last paragraphs of course no more than draw attention to some of the implications for baptism of the messiness that complicates the life and ministry of Christ's church as the society within which it is set slides into an ex-Christian ethos. It is messy because it is a slide rather than an abrupt leap, and the carryover from the Christian past, in memory, instinct and conscience, lives on with varying degrees of vitality. It is messy no doubt for other reasons also, such as inconsistent or unprincipled church practice in earlier years which has now come home to roost. And we may be tempted to welcome the sharper lines of the harsh new environment of hostility, scorn and indifference toward Christianity simply because the messiness may diminish. This would be cold comfort, to be sure, but it holds out for baptism clear hopes of a recovery of its intrinsic connection with the Christian mission.

We should not imagine, however, that as the church increasingly finds itself, in Europe at least, in a primary mission field, this recovery of baptism will be straightforward. For inclusiveness is a prominent element in the religious psyche of the ex-Christian West, and baptism always marks boundaries. It is the rite whereby persons are included in the family of Christ, but only by drawing lines between church and nonchurch, between Christian and non-Christian. A baptismal ministry which seeks to be faithful to the New Testament's presentation of baptism cannot fail to run athwart the inclusivist spirit of the age. In a number of ways the pre-Constantinian experience of the church becomes more and more pertinent at the end of the second millennium. Not least is this the case for baptism.

Now the baptismal experience of the church of the early Fathers was very largely of believer's baptism, or perhaps better conversion baptism. Historical study is steadily consolidating the conclusion that infant baptism did not really come into its own, as the common practice, until after Augustine, perhaps in the sixth century. This is not to deny that some babies were baptized from at least the middle of the second century (grounds for confidence before this are lacking),[5] but rather to confirm historically what Karl Barth claimed, that infant baptism belongs to Christendom. Its flourishing took place in the context of that long phase of Western religious history marked by the coterminousness of the Christian and the civil communities. Christendom began in the era of the Christian Roman Empire after Constantine and has continued in Europe, and in less formalized ways in the regions of the world colonized from Europe, until the latter twentieth century. Even where establishment or national recognition of one particular church survives (in England and Scotland, for example), the reality rings increasingly hollow. For the first time for over a millennium and a half, Christians in Western, or at least European, society now live in a post-Christendom world. To that extent, pre-Constantinian Christianity must come into its own again.

Infant Baptism and New Testament Baptism

From several quarters infant baptism is likely to encounter growing criticism. In addition to factors already mentioned, such as the deeper historical uncertainty attending claims for the practice of normative pedobaptism from apostolic times and the disintegration of civil communities united by a shared Christian identity attested in universal baptism of babies, others lie nearer the biblical and theological knuckle. One reason for the muffling of the New Testament's clarion baptismal notes is the sheer embarrassment most evangelicals incur when attempting to make them ring true of baby baptism, or of young children baptized as babies. At this point I should perhaps make it plain that my purpose in this essay is not to reject the biblical and theological credentials of infant baptism, as I hope the following remarks will confirm. To attempt to do so in a volume dedicated to honoring Jim Packer would be discourtesy indeed. My concern is rather to persuade us to face up to the connections between the prevalence of pedobaptism, not least in Reformed Christianity, and the strange silence on baptism in the church. One cause of this silence, I would submit, is our gross discomfort in treating both forms of baptism—of infants and of believers (or in the very earliest distinction between them, in Hippolytus's *Apostolic Tradition* early in the third century, of those who cannot and those who can answer for themselves)—as "one baptism."

Of course we would testily repel any suggestion that we believed in two baptisms, and no doubt our baptismal orders of service employ some New Testament baptismal affirmations when babies are being baptized. But when we are free of such liturgical constraints, we display our true colors. The children of the church family do not grow up being taught that in baptism they died to sin and rose in Christ to newness of life. They do not learn of their identity as those who in baptism have put on Christ, or who were baptized by the Spirit into the body of Christ.[6] Moreover, because we have become accustomed to aiming off, as it were, in accommodating what the New Testament says about baptism to our infant baptism, even when we do baptize believing converts we lack the crispness of apostolic conviction that in baptism they pass from the bondage of Egypt to the freedom of the Promised Land—an Old Testament type that the New Testament encourages us to apply to baptism.

By now some readers will be indignantly protesting that I do their ministry and their church practice an injustice. The broad brush, however, is the only implement I can use in this wide-ranging portrayal of baptismal neglect. In the nature of the case, it can be only impressionistic as a generalization, but I could cite sufficient particular instances to make me believe that it will sound the ring of truth for many. The difficulty we experience in treating baby baptism as New Testament baptism, pure and simple, accounts, at least in part, for our uneasiness in the face of what a document like *Baptism, Eucharist and Ministry* says about baptism. A common evangelical response faults it for using verbs in the indicative mood rather than in the optative or in some other form expressing the ideal instead of the assumed reality. We would prefer such texts to convey the message that it ought to be true that all who have been baptized have been clothed with Christ, instead of assuming it to be true *simpliciter.* And we may wish to insert "or will be clothed with Christ," for the overconfident sacramentalism we detect in *Baptism, Eucharist and Ministry* unnerves us most of all when it purports to speak without qualification of pedobaptism.

Analyzing such ecumenical statements is, no doubt, a specialist skill in which few of us have been trained; my comments here barely scratch the surface. My point is this: we bridle at their language not always or solely for the reasons of high theological principle we verbalize, but because, in our almost single-minded preoccupation with babies as the recipients of baptism, we have become past masters at a kind of baptismal reductionism. We balk at the indicatives of *Baptism, Eucharist and Ministry* when it is the indicatives of the New Testament that truly bother us. We have got used to handling the latter, but we see no good cause to extend similar considerations to documents emanating from twentieth-century Geneva.

Note again the case that is being advanced here. As a result of thinking of baptism almost exclusively in terms of baby baptism—of making the latter not only the norm in practice but also the theological norm—we have subjected the New Testament's witness to baptism to a compliant reductionism. We have shrunk the apostolic testimony to what we can comfortably believe about pedobaptism.[7] Integral to these convictions is the awareness that infant baptism is only too often a failure. Far from being an initiation, a beginning, it rapidly turns out to be a dead end. One indubitable fact about Britain at the end of the twentieth century ought to have given the churches a sobering pause for thought long ago. I refer to the millions of infant-baptized persons who are now by any meaningful measure dechurched. The fault, to be sure, does not lie solely with the churches' baptismal policies, but they cannot escape a heavy weight of blame. It is difficult not to conclude that the baptismal practices of the mainstream churches of the Reformation in modern Britain in recent decades have been a colossal failure. Evangelicals in the main are as ready as any to recognize the failure. Endeavors such as MORIB are attempting to address it. But it is a thousand pities that too salient a feature of the evangelical response has been the downgrading of the significance of baptism. If so frequently the baptism of a baby leads not to his or her incorporation into the living community of faith but simply nowhere, what is so wonderful about baptism?

In practice, the center of gravity shifts to conversion, profession of faith, confirmation, admission to Communion. Confirmation, that fruitful seedbed of confusion, is treated as compensating for baby baptism's inadequacies, although what is being confirmed—the baptized person, the baptismal vows or promises, or baptism itself—and by whom—God the Holy Spirit, the minister or the candidate—has never met with a consensus. Although there are some grounds for viewing admission to Communion or confirmation as gathering up a feature or features of a primitive baptismal rite that got sundered from baptism itself, the modern observance is little more than a deposit of ecclesiastical tradition—by comparison, that is, with the dominical status of baptism. It is a matter of grief, therefore, when confirmation is viewed as "completing" baptism, or otherwise eclipses it in importance. The credibility of confirmation must be tested by the preeminence it gives to baptism. When adult believers are being baptized, there should be no need for confirmation or admission at all. When a group of candidates is presented for confirmation and one of them has not been baptized, any action should be avoided that appears to rate the baptism as a mere preliminary requirement— such as holding it in advance in the vestry or hall in the presence of the elders alone, or reducing it to the barest minimum in order to arrive as soon as possible at the real business of the service. Thus does human tradition make void the Word of God (cf. Mk 7:13).

The Reformers' Problems

It is again cold comfort to realize that the cluster of problems highlighted in this essay is largely the legacy of the sixteenth-century Reformers. Their appeal to the supremacy of Scripture—not so much Scripture alone as Scripture supreme over all other loci of authority—left them at first hesitant and latterly resourcefully versatile in vindicating the baptism of babies. It was, one may judge, by far the most significant constitutive feature of Protestant church life that they perpetuated without explicit scriptural warrant. The devising of a new rite of confirmation was probably their most lasting attempt to secure what they concluded was unattainable on the basis of infant baptism alone. A key figure in the development of evangelical confirmation was Martin Bucer, the Reformer of Strasbourg and later England. It emerged out of his struggles to establish in Strasbourg a viable program of Christian discipline to ensure the formation of an authentically Christian community. In the process he came

> to detach from baptism when given to infants much of its significance as the point of demarcation between the church and the world, and to reassign this to subsequent education and discipline and in due course to confirmation. . . .
>
> [He] ascribed specifically to paedobaptism a containing role, the marking of an outer ring, within which another and more decisive line would be drawn, coming into quasi-sacramental focus in confirmation.[8]

Several of the magisterial Reformers, while insisting on the strictest universality of infant baptism, experimented in other ways in their quest for a genuine fellowship of committed believers, an *ecclesiola* within the *ecclesia* of the broad people's church identified by pedo-baptism.[9] These endeavors to some degree acknowledge the attractiveness of the Anabaptists' vision of a covenanted community, but as stalwart champions of the ideal of late-medieval Christendom, the mainstream Reformers recoiled instinctively from the Radical Reformers' abandonment of one of Christendom's key foundations, universal infant baptism, in pursuit of that vision.

The obligation to have one's children baptized, on pain of legal sanctions, is a thing of the past, yet it has left a mark on expectations and aspirations that can still sometimes be discerned in the 1990s. The case for unrestricted administration of baby baptism is still occasionally made in all good faith. More common is the minister prejudiced in favor of acceding to every request for baptism, even in defiance of his denomination's stipulated conditions. Yet to recognize that our contemporary problems have their roots in the Reformation does not excuse our fecklessness in confronting them in the present. On the contrary, such a recognition should liberate us to grapple with them all the more vigorously, especially if we judge that in their unbudging allegiance to pedobaptism the Reformers were less critical of Christendom than they might have been. They were after all not only for the most part honorable men but also fallible human beings.

Shifting Convictions

So where do we go from here? By now some personal confession is overdue. I have hitherto defended, and still can and do defend, the biblical and theological credentials of baby baptism in time-honored Reformed fashion. Nevertheless, the conviction has been growing on me for some years that the practice of baby baptism in mainstream Protestantism (including Anglicanism) in Britain in recent decades has been fraught with immense harm to the church of Jesus Christ. The reasoning that undergirds this unwelcome conviction has been spelled out in the earlier sections of this essay, if not comprehensively, at least at sufficient length to enable readers to seize the gist of it. The conviction is unwelcome not only because I regard the standard Reformed justification of pedobaptism to be as sound as ever (see further below) but also because of the challenge it poses to my more general conviction that healthy theology and healthy practice go together. How can the biblical-theological basis for infant baptism be so secure if administering it faithfully creates so much agonizing for conscientious ministers of the gospel? And if squaring the circle in order to reconcile the high promise of baptism with its high failure rate leads to the minimizing of the significance of baptism that I have labored to demonstrate above? In my book, the toughest charge that pedobaptism has to answer is its responsibility, not alone but heavy enough, for disabling evangelical churchmen (but not the Reformers, it must be said) from believing and teaching the New Testament's witness to baptism at anywhere near its face value.

I am now inclined to regard infant baptism as consistent with Scripture but not required by it, much like episcopacy, or presbytery for that matter. What cannot be claimed for it on credible biblical grounds is that it is normative baptism, whether theologically or practically. That distinction must rest with believer's baptism or conversion baptism. Placing the theological rationale for baby baptism somewhat lower down the scale of *credenda* should enable us to tackle its discontents with greater freedom of movement. After all, it appears in none of the creeds of the universal church; I have argued elsewhere that the Nicene Creed's "one baptism for the remission of sins" cannot originally have encompassed the baptism of infants.[10]

Future Prospects

Once again, where do we go from here? We may expect infant baptism in part to wither on the vine, along with the dregs of Christendom. Already requests for it inspired by residual folk-Christianity are decreasing. In an age of growing sensitivity to children's rights, it is also likely that in more of the committed Christian families in our congregations parents will opt not to have their babies baptized— and if my argument is heeded, we will not strive officiously to persuade them otherwise. They will resort instead to the increasing availability of services of dedication or thanksgiving for the birth of a child. We may expect such services, even when not centrally provided by a particular denomination (as is the case still in the Church of Scotland),[11] to be more and more the resort of ministers concerned to avoid both abusing baptism and turning away empty-handed those seeking baptism for their children on unacceptable grounds. Services to mark the birth of a child come in various shapes and sizes.[12] It is critical that while they may function as alternatives to baptism, they must not become substitutes for it—infant baptism in all but water, as it were. They dare not leave the impression that a person, whether parent or child, has settled his or her account with the living God. To that extent, they should remain purposefully open-ended—open to the subsequent hearing of the gospel and the response of faith in baptism.

A growing number of churches now formally operate a dual-practice administration of baptism. In many cases this has come about from the union of churches of divergent baptismal order, as in the United Reformed Church in Great Britain. Other churches have simply given formal recognition of the acceptability of the parental choice not to have their offspring baptized as persons unable to answer for themselves. Yet other churches which have in no way qualified their expectation that children born to members will be baptized—again the Church of Scotland is an example—are nevertheless likely to feel the influence of this increasing flexibility in baptismal practice.

It enjoys the endorsement of no less than *Baptism, Eucharist and Ministry*, which must rank as the most widely studied document of the ecumenical movement. While it does not go so far as to recommend adoption of the dual-practice system, it points forcefully to the emerging consensus that sees much less difference than our forefathers did between infant baptism followed by nurture leading to personal profession of faith and infant dedication followed by nurture leading to baptismal profession of faith.

Evangelical Disagreement

This is an appropriate point at which to cite an important reason for evangelicals' devaluation of baptism which has so far been merely alluded to: namely, our deep-seated disagreement about it. A similar fate has befallen another bone of evangelical contention—ecclesiology; better to leave it buried than have it dug up and noisily scrapped over. Yet our failure to agree about the proper subjects of baptism represents a serious challenge to cherished evangelical convictions about the perspicuity of Scripture,[13] as well as leaving believers-baptists free to practice what pedobaptists regard as rebaptism.[14] Welcome evidence of some meeting of minds, not least in a recent article by George Beasley-Murray,[15] will strengthen the developing flexibility surveyed above. But flexibility must not be allowed to foster indifference to baptism.

The shift in my own thinking toward viewing the baptism of babies as something akin to an *adiaphoron* has been promoted by a deepening conviction of the centrality of baptism to the church's mission of the gospel. Baptism is, when all is said and done, one of the only two specific observances which the churches of the Reformation believe that Christ the Lord commanded his followers to perpetuate.

Saving Infant Baptism

This paper is not a call for the abandonment of infant baptism—although I have often thought that a moratorium on baptizing babies for, say, ten years would enable it to be resumed on a much sounder basis. But rather than indulging such daydreams, let me evince my *bona fides* by spelling out the terms that would alone to my mind justify the continuation of the practice.

1. A principled discipline of administration, so that only those parents who are regularly worshiping church members would expect to have their infants baptized. Easier said than done, I know; hence what follows next.

2. The adoption of a service or services to mark the birth of a child, to enable ministers to escape from the straitjacket of an all-or-nothing choice. I have no doubt at all that theologically and liturgically respectable orders are already on hand, and biblical precedents are not hard to seek.

3. The unambiguous owning of baby baptism as New Testament baptism—period. I see no defensible future for a pedobaptism which cannot bear the full weight of the New Testament's baptismal witness. If this creates problems for tidy theological systems, so be it; better to be faithful to Scripture than to the *magisterium* of any of our dogmatic theologies.

4. The nurture of baptized children as members of the church and the people of God. I view early admission to the Lord's Table as entirely consistent with such a stance. By one Spirit they have been baptized into the one body of Christ; their full belonging is not a matter of hope or prospect, but of present enjoyment.

5. The making of baptism an explicit and frequent reference-point in Christian education from the earliest stages. The baptized must grow up knowing that they are in Christ by baptism, that in baptism they died and rose again with Christ, and that through baptism they are his for ever. This fifth point is really an aspect of the previous one, but is to the best of my knowledge neglected enough to merit highlighting separately. It has many different facets, according to the different facets of New Testament baptism. For example, in terms of Galatians 3:27-28, baptized children should grow up knowing that baptism is the great leveler; in baptism individuals of all kinds are received on the common basis of grace alone.

6. A cluster of lesser practical requirements that would make baptism unambiguously a congregational occasion rather than a family one, and also heighten the dramatic vividness of the rite. If there has

to be a party, make it a church one; the baptism shall always take place in the home church at the time of a main Sunday service; the local minister shall baptize (even if the baby's aunt or granddad is a minister); imaginative efforts will be made to enhance the solemnity and awesomeness of the observance (why not immersion, like the Orthodox?); all billing and cooing over the baby will be banned (it was the late Alan Stibbs, with whom Jim Packer must have shared many a platform, who averred that baby worship had killed the gospel at the font).

7. The notes of the gospel to be sounded loud and clear, so that all present will be left in no doubt that baptism is a sacrament of the gospel. If infant baptism deserves to be saved from the ruins of Christendom, it will only be by returning it to baptism's New Testament configurations—ecclesial, kerygmatic, mystagogic, Christological. Then infant baptism will truly be an apostolic focus for the church's apostolic mission.

Notes:

[1] *The Church of Scotland General Assembly 1992* (Edinburgh: Church of Scotland, 1992), I, 553; II, 33.

[2] For details see the article "Baptism" by the present writer in Nigel M. de S. Cameron et al., eds., *Dictionary of Scottish Church History and Theology* (Edinburgh: T. & T. Clark, 1993), pp. 56–58.

[3] All scriptural quotations in this article are taken from the New International Version of the Bible, copyright the New York International Bible Society.

[4] Its president is Bishop Colin Buchanan. Details are available from Mrs. Carol Snipe, 18 Taylors Lane, Lindford, Bordon, Hants GU35 0SW, England.

[5] Cf. David F. Wright, "At What Ages Were People Baptised in the Early Centuries?" forthcoming in *Studia Patristica; idem.*, "The Origins of Infant Baptism—Child Believers' Baptism?" *Scottish Journal of Theology* 40 (1987): 1–23.

[6] Galatians 3:27 ("all of you who were baptized into Christ have been clothed with Christ") was an embarrassment to Augustine in controversy with the Donatists, as he tried to sustain his position that the baptism they received in schism was real, but wholly unbeneficial so long as they remained outside the Catholic Church. Armed with texts like Galatians 3:27, the Donatists impaled him on the horn of a dilemma: either deny that our baptism is real baptism or concede that, if real, it must bestow the Spirit, clothe with Christ, etc. For Augustine's response see David F. Wright, "Donatist Theologoumena in Augustine? Baptism, Reviviscence of Sins and Unworthy Ministers," in *Congresso Internazionale su S.Agostino . . . Atti* II (Rome: Institutum Patristicum "Augustinianum," 1987), pp. 213–24.

[7] The extent to which we have been unaware of the shift that has taken place is illustrated by appeals to the passivity of the child in baptism as theologically virtuous—and even sometimes (heaven forfend!) to the child's squalling as expressive of fallen nature's hostility to grace! The same reasoning would lead to the dosing of unwitting babies with the bread and wine of the Supper. While it is true that baptism is not self-administered, nor is the Supper. "Take and eat" is on par with "Be baptized" in respect of the recipient's initiative, as Karl Barth recognized.

[8] David F. Wright, "Infant Baptism and the Christian Community in Bucer," in Wright, ed., *Martin Bucer: Reforming Church and Community* (Cambridge: Cambridge University Press, 1994), pp. 95–106 at 101, 106. See also Amy Nelson Burnett, *The Yoke of Christ: Martin Bucer and Christian Discipline,* Sixteenth Century Essays and Studies 24 (Kirksville, Mo: Sixteenth Century Journal Publishers, 1994).

[9] David F. Wright, "Sixteenth-Century Reformed Perspectives on the Minority Church," in John H. Leith, ed., *Calvin Studies VII: Papers Presented at a Colloquium . . . January 28–29, 1994* (Davidson, N.C.: Davidson College Presbyterian Church, 1995), pp. 15–29.

[10] "The Meaning and Reference of 'One Baptism for the Remission of Sins' in the Niceno-Constantinopolitan Creed," *Studia Patristica* 19 (1989): 281–85.

[11] See Graeme Dunphy, *Celebrating Child-Birth in the Church: Baptism or Dedication?* Edinburgh: Handsel Press and Rutherford House, 1991).

[12] See the helpful discussion by Phillip Tovey, "'Can We Have the Baby Done?' Infant Initiation and Pre-baptismal Rites," *Anvil* 12 (1995): 137–44.

[13] Cf. my "Scripture and Evangelical Diversity with Special Reference to the Baptismal Divide," in Philip E. Satterthwaite and David F. Wright, eds., *A Pathway into the Holy Scripture* (Grand Rapids, Mich.: Eerdmans, 1994), pp. 257–75.

[14] See the present writer's "One Baptism or Two? Reflections on the History of Christian Baptism," *Vox Evangelica* 18 (1988): 7–23.

[15] "The Problem of Infant Baptism: An Exercise in Possibilities," in *Festschrift Günter Wagner* (Bern: Peter Lang, 1994), pp. 1–14.

5

Christology and the Quest of the Historical Jesus

Colin Brown

BACK IN THE 1950S, WHEN JIM PACKER WAS AT THE
beginning of his teaching career and I was a student at Tyndale Hall,
Bristol, I had him for church history, historical theology and philosophy of religion. Little did I know then the influence Jim Packer
would have on my life, my thought and the course of my life. My
goal in working for a degree in theology was to get a good ground-
ing for pastoral ministry. It never entered my head to think of an academic career. But events turned out differently. As Associate Rector
of my parish church, I am still active in parish ministry. But in 1961
I embarked on a new life. In the spring of that year Jim Packer left
to become Librarian of Latimer House, Oxford, and I found myself
as Jim's successor at Tyndale Hall, called to teach the very same
courses that he had taught me, and trying to fill the void created by
Jim's departure.

In honoring Jim Packer I offer some reflections on what I see as
the most critical issue in theology today—the question of the historical Jesus and the part that it plays in our knowledge of God. My discussion has three main sections:

1. Anselm and the Problem of Pictures Painted on Water or Air
2. The Abortive Quest of the Historical Jesus
3. The State of the Question Today

In the first section I note some consequences of trying to divorce Christology from the historical Jesus. In the second I look at consequences of trying to divorce the historical Jesus from Christology. In the third I offer some observations and recommendations.

1. Anselm and the Problem of Pictures Painted on Water or Air
1.1. *The Person and Work of Christ*

Among the many things that Jim Packer taught me was the value of Anselm's approach to the person and work of Christ in his *Cur Deus Homo (Why God Became Man)*. His work is a masterpiece of medieval contextualization. Contextualization has both strength and weakness. The strength lies in making ideas relevant to a particular cultural context. The weakness lies in precisely that fact: the more it speaks to a particular culture, the less it speaks to others. Despite misgivings that modern readers might have about Anselm's contextualization of the atonement in terms of feudal social thinking, his work remains a classic for what Jim Packer called its "God-ward reference"—how human beings may be reconciled to God and God to human beings.

But something else in Anselm's argument has stuck in my mind. It is a comment on the ancient recapitulation theory of atonement which paints a beautiful picture of the symmetry of grace. When death had entered the human race through disobedience, it was fitting that life should be restored through obedience. Since the sin which caused the fall came through a woman, it was fitting that the author of salvation should be born of a woman. Since the devil conquered Adam through a tree, it was fitting that he should be conquered by a man's suffering on a tree. But there is a difficulty. Beautiful as they are, such images will appear like pictures painted on water or air, unless they can be seen to be painted on something solid.[1] For Anselm that solidity was to be found in the rational coherence of the reason for the incarnation with other truths.

> Surely we argue conclusively enough that it was fitting for God to do the things we speak of, when we say that the human race, that very precious work of his, was altogether ruined; that it was not fitting for God's plan for man to be entirely wiped out; and that this same plan could not be put into effect unless the human race were delivered by its Creator himself.[2]

What was at stake was for faith to understand the divine logic.[3] This was achieved by proceeding from certain *givens*—that redemption could be accomplished only by God, that sin was an offense and a debt that could not be repaid, that death was the result of sin, that the redeemer must be perfect God and man in order to make satisfaction, that the Son owed the Father a life of perfect obedience, but not his death whose merit is rewarded by the gift of salvation.[4] By drawing inferences from these givens, Anselm believed that he had exhibited the inner necessity of why God became man *without actually examining the life and teaching of Jesus*.[5] In so doing Anselm grounded Christology in soteriology.

1.2. Problems

Knowledge is never merely a matter of taking a look and seeing. It requires penetration beneath the surface of things, and grasping why things are as they are in terms of what philosophers call "the web of belief."[6] This "web of belief" has to do with the nature of reality and our construal of it. In a sense, this was what Anselm was addressing. The linking of Christology with soteriology is part of a great tradition which reaches back to the early church and remains vital today. But to take Anselm's strategy just as it is invites the question whether Anselm himself has not painted his pictures on water or air. Three difficulties lie in the way of accepting it without modification.

First, there is the point that the argument works for those who share the various *given convictions* that we have noted. But this raises the question of whether these convictions really are the same as God's own reasons.[7] The argument looks like a counterpart to Anselm's flawed ontological argument. Whereas the latter sought to deduce reasons for believing in God's existence from the idea of God, *Cur Deus Homo* deduces the person of a Savior from a series of ideas.

The second difficulty lies in the fact that the argument's logic is not as compelling as it might appear. Anselm's strategy was to show that the Savior must possess certain qualities: he must be man (though not a sinner) in order to be our representative, and God in order to have the authority and power to overcome evil and death, and ensure that the saved will belong to God. But the argument is like a game which anyone can play and win: one loads the dice to roll the way one wants. To put it another way, one puts into the equation what one wants to get out. It is a game that can be played by both the orthodox and the heterodox. The way that Anselm played it led to a vindication of orthodoxy. But an Arian or semi-Arian could (and in fact did) argue that Christ could not be consubstantial with the Father in his divinity. For the Father is immutable and impassible (i.e., changeless and incapable of suffering), whereas Jesus suffered and died. One could say that Christ was *like God,* but not "the only true God" (Jn 17:3).[8] Alternatively, one would have to say with Tertullian that Jesus suffered as a man but not as God,[9] or one could take the same course as Moltmann and repudiate divine impassibility.[10]

The third difficulty with Anselmian strategy is perhaps the most formidable. It consists in the fact that the approach is (in the words of Wolfhart Pannenberg) entirely a Christology "from above."[11] It looks at the incarnation totally from the standpoint of divine inner logic without considering the historical figure of Jesus and the world in which he lived. The Jesus of history plays no part in his scheme. That he lived a life of perfect obedience and chose to die are *theological necessities* that are assumed to coincide with historical fact. Even with an approach less rigorous than Anselm's in its exclusion of the Gospels, we still have the problem of matching up what we read there and the presumed divine logic. How do the actions of Jesus in history and the events surrounding his death relate to the theological reasons deduced from dogmatic considerations? The strategy requires us to develop Christology on two tracks: the one "from above" gives theological explanation, while the other "from below" deals with earthly phenomena. But the task of Christology is not to impose on the Gospels a preconceived explanation that has been reached from other considerations, but to discover from the history contained in the Gospels why the Christian church acknowledges Jesus as the Christ who was truly God and truly man.[12] The Anselmian approach still has value. It poses the question: "What might a redeemer look like, if God were to intervene to help human beings trapped by sin and evil?" It offers a *possible* answer. But to see if any person has ever approximated that answer—or even to see if we were asking the right questions—we have to turn to history. Otherwise, we are left with pictures painted on water or air.

2. The Abortive Quest of the Historical Jesus
2.1. Schweitzer and the Original Quest
It was Albert Schweitzer (or to be more exact, his English publisher) who gave currency to the phrase "the quest of the historical Jesus."[13] The approach is diametrically opposite to Anselm's, for it insists on pushing aside theological considerations to discover "the facts" behind the Gospels. Schweitzer's book *The Quest of the Historical Jesus* (1906) established itself as a quasi-canonical account from its beginnings down to Schweitzer himself.

This is not the place to attempt to re-examine the views of

Reimarus, Schleiermacher, Strauss, Baur, Renan and countless others. It must suffice to say that Schweitzer set up his work like the Wimbledon tennis tournament as a knockout competition with seeded players. There were three main rounds, each deciding a key issue.[14] In the first round the issue was whether the study of the life of Jesus should be "*either* purely historical or purely supernatural." Here the victor was D. F. Strauss, who rejected the supernatural picture of Jesus in the Gospels as the product of myth-making. From here on Schweitzer would countenance only naturalistic interpretations. In the second round the key issue was whether to follow the Synoptic Gospels or John. The decision was won by the Tübingen School and Schweitzer's teacher, H. J. Holtzmann. Henceforth, John could not be taken seriously as history. In the final round the issue was between an eschatological Jesus and a noneschatological Jesus. Did the Jesus of history proclaim and die for the kingdom of God as a new world-order, or was he the Jesus of liberal theology who preached ethics and moral transformation?

The two final protagonists were William Wrede and Schweitzer himself. Wrede, whom Schweitzer regarded a thoroughgoing skeptic, was an old rival.[15] He maintained that Jesus never thought of himself as the Messiah, and that the so-called Messianic Secret (Jesus' charge to his disciples not to make his messiahship known) was the creation of the evangelist Mark. Schweitzer, on the other hand, saw eschatology as the key to understanding Jesus. Jesus really did believe himself to be the messianic Son of Man who would come on the clouds as judge. At first he told this secret only to Peter, James and John. Later Peter told it to the rest of the Twelve. Judas told it to the high priest, who used Jesus' confession of it as the ground for his execution (Mk 14:61-64; cf. Dan 7:13).

There is profound irony in Schweitzer's position. He believed that he had recovered the historical Jesus and made sense of the Gospel narratives. But it was at the price of seeing Jesus as a fanatic, driven by dreams that ended in disaster. For Schweitzer it was a good thing that "the true historical Jesus should overthrow the modern Jesus" of liberal theologians like Adolf Harnack.[16] But which was really better? Of Harnack it was said that "the Christ that Harnack sees, looking back through nineteen centuries of Catholic darkness, is only the reflection of a Liberal Protestant face, seen at the bottom of a deep well."[17] If Harnack's Jesus was the reflection of a liberal Protestant, Schweitzer's Jesus, "the authoritative ruler" who summons disciples in every generation, was the reflection of Nietzsche's Superman who unflinchingly marches against the stream in his pursuit of self-imposed goals.[18]

2.2. The Short-Lived New Quest

In the wake of Schweitzer and pre-1914 liberalism came the Dialectical Theology of Karl Barth with its stress on revelation, the Biblical Theology movement, and Bultmann with his form-critical and demythologizing programs, which in turn gave way to the so-called "new quest of the historical Jesus."[19] The term was coined in the 1950s to describe the movement among Bultmann's disciples who felt the need to have a historical Jesus as a basis for faith. In contrast with the source-critical methods of the original quest, the new quest sought to base its construction on the Bultmannian analysis of the early church's proclamation of Jesus' death and resurrection. But the demise of Bultmannian theology was soon followed by that of the new quest.

2.3. Kähler's Alternative

In the circumstances, it is not surprising that some have wondered whether the Gospels provided enough reliable material to recover the historical Jesus.[20] It is no less surprising that others have comforted themselves in Martin Kähler's denunciation of the quest and his insistence that the real Christ is the Christ of faith.

> The real Christ, that is, the Christ who has exercised an influence in history, with whom millions have communed in childlike faith, and with whom the great witnesses of faith have been in communion—while striving, apprehending, triumphing, and proclaiming—*this real Christ is the Christ who is preached.* The Christ who is preached, however, is precisely the Christ of faith. He is the Jesus whom the eyes of faith behold at every step he takes and through every syllable he utters—the Jesus whose image we impress upon our minds because we both would and do commune with him, our risen, living Lord. The person of our living Savior, the person of the Word incarnate, of God revealed, gazes upon us from the features of that image which has deeply impressed itself on the memory of his followers—and which was finally disclosed and perfected through the illumination of his Spirit.[21]

Kähler's statement has been applauded as a return to a balanced perspective. But it is not without problems. Kähler seems to be speaking on behalf of orthodoxy, insisting that one cannot set aside

Christian experience for positivistic research. But Kähler can be understood in other ways, as he was by his most famous pupil, Paul Tillich. For Tillich, Kähler's contribution lay in his insistence on "the necessity to make the certainty of faith independent of the unavoidable incertitudes of historical research."[22] Tillich himself achieved this by appropriating the Gospel stories for their *symbolic* value and transposing them in his philosophical theology as a means of relating to the ground of being.[23]

Kähler has been hailed as the theologian who rescued Jesus from the hands of the historian. But it is a Pyrrhic victory. For it is not as if anyone today has *direct* access to Jesus. The access that we have is always *mediated* in some way or other. It may be mediated by hymns, prayers and sermons. In that case, the Jesus to whom we have access is mediated by those who composed them, their choice of words, and what they evoke. Our access to Jesus may be mediated by our reading of the New Testament. In that case, it will be affected by *what we bring* to our reading—our knowledge of the language and world of the New Testament, our personal situations which cause us to relate to some passages more than others, our worldview and our ability to interpret. Contemporary hermeneutics and reader-response criticism are making us increasingly aware that reading involves interpretation, and that texts speak to us only as *interpreted texts*. In short, the choice is not between what the historians say and a direct knowledge of Jesus that we can get for ourselves. Rather, it is a question of whose *interpretation* we are to follow. If we look again at the passage from Kähler, it can also be read to mean that it is not the historical Jesus who has made an impact on history, but *the Christ that is proclaimed in preaching*. In that case, Christ has been taken out of the hands of the historian only to be placed in the hands of the preacher.

There is something troubling about "liberating" Jesus from the historian only to put him into the hands of the popular preacher and the image-making TV evangelist. I am reminded of the 1992 American presidential election, which pushed the art of image-making to new heights, and the man who pushed it furthest ended up the winner. The dubious logic of Kähler's statement is made apparent if we make a name substitution. "The real Bill Clinton [or George Bush, or Ross Perot], that is the Bill Clinton [et al.] who has exercised an influence in history, with whom millions have communed in childlike faith . . . *this real Bill Clinton [et al.] is the Bill Clinton who is preached.*" Sooner or later the public will ask probing questions—*historical questions* about whether the image that they have been led to believe really fits. The same is true in religion. We cannot avoid historical questions. But if properly asked and answered, they can be a great enrichment to faith.

3. The State of the Question Today
3.1. *The Classical Christology of the Creeds*
In the Apostles' Creed the church confesses its faith
>in Jesus Christ, [God's] only Son, our Lord.
>>He was conceived by the power of the Holy Spirit
>>>and born of the Virgin Mary.
>>He suffered under Pontius Pilate,
>>>was crucified, died, and was buried.
>>He descended to the dead.
>>On the third day he rose again.
>>He ascended into heaven,
>>>and is seated at the right hand of the Father.
>>He will come again to judge the living and the dead.[24]

The Nicene Creed goes further and defines the divinity of Christ in terms of his being "of one Being [*homoousios*] with the Father." The Chalcedonian definition of faith goes still further in defining not only the divinity of Christ as *homoousios* with that of the Father but also his humanity as *homoousios* with ours, like us in all things except sin. Behind these formulations lie prolonged and bitter controversies over how one should think about Jesus Christ. The finely tuned answers represent guidelines for thinking in terms of those controversies. The creeds anchor their definitions in history. But something is missing. Jürgen Moltmann puts his finger on the spot when he confesses that he has always missed the "presence of the earthly Jesus in the Christian creeds. Why is it reduced to a mere comma between 'born' and 'suffered'? Ought we not to add—at least in thought—

>Baptized by John the Baptist,
>filled with the Holy Spirit
>to proclaim God's kingdom to the poor,
>to heal the sick,
>to receive the rejected,
>to awaken Israel for the salvation of nations,
>and to have mercy on all human beings?"[25]

The creeds need to be fleshed out by the historical Jesus.

3.2. *The Third Quest of the Historical Jesus*
In the aftermath of the original quest and the short-lived "new quest"

we are now in the "third quest" of the historical Jesus. The pessimism of the Bultmann era concerning the possibility of any knowledge of Jesus is largely a thing of the past.[26] At the same time we must recognize a wide spectrum of views. At the radical end is the Jesus Seminar, Burton L. Mack and John Dominic Crossan.[27] Their approach might be described as a kind of archaeology which digs through layers of tradition in order to discover the earliest, multiply attested authentic accounts of the historical Jesus who lies buried beneath the rubble of tradition (which includes much of the New Testament itself). To that extent their work carries on the tradition of the old nineteenth-century quest. However, it differs in other respects.

For one thing, these scholars see Q (the presumed sayings source behind the teaching of Jesus in Matthew and Luke) as the earliest part of the canonical Gospels. Or rather, they see Q itself as a stratified text in which the earlier supposedly nonapocalyptic parts are to be separated from the later apocalyptic material. For another, they treat the Gospel of Thomas (a collection of sayings like Q which most scholars reckon to be late) as a primary source for material earlier than the canonical Gospels. The Jesus that emerges turns out to be a Jewish Cynic philosopher who, like other Cynics, lived without possessions or family, and shocked his hearers with his dark, troubling sayings. In Crossan's case, Jesus was also a magician whose unorthodox healing practices and common meals were a form of social subversion.

The case for a Cynic Jesus has been more carefully argued by F. Gerald Downing, but even he has not been able to adduce evidence for any Cynic passing through Galilee during the lifetime of Jesus.[28] Perusal of Downing's collection of Cynic sayings and alleged Gospel parallels shows how far the two were removed.[29] Crossan deftly overlooks the fact that Cynics were not magicians, and the magicians of the ancient world were not Cynics. The life-style of Jesus and his followers bears only superficial resemblance to that of the Cynics. Close examination shows Jesus, not as quasi-philosopher bent on promoting independent lifestyle, but as God's agent engaged in prophetic renewal of Israel.[30]

Crossan's reconstruction has prompted Frans Jozef van Beek to see it as a twentieth-century version of a Romantic preconception in the tradition of Strauss, Renan and Schweitzer. The face seen at the bottom of the well is not that of the nineteenth-century liberal Protestant, but that of "a capable, quite original, rather skeptical New Testament professor with the soul of a leprechaun."[31] The highly publicized activities of the Jesus Seminar and the promotional efforts of Mack's and Crossan's publishers bestow an importance on their work that is out of proportion to its merits and place in the scholarly community. In a recent survey of "A Century of Quests for a Culturally Compatible Jesus" Howard Clark Kee sees it as "the triumph of the peripheral."[32] For far more significant approaches to the historical Jesus we need to turn to the projected three-volume study of Jesus by John P. Meier,[33] Raymond E. Brown's account of *The Death of the Messiah*[34] and N. T. Wright's investigation of Christian origins.[35]

Perhaps the most distinctive feature of the "third quest" of the historical Jesus is the development of new approaches by way of forming general hypotheses to answer questions posed by our sources. These hypotheses seek to address questions often neglected in the past, and endeavor to understand Jesus in the context of the religious, social, economic world of Judaism. Attention is focused on questions like "Why did Jesus come into conflict with the Jewish authorities?" "Why was he handed over to the Romans and put to death in a manner normally reserved for political revolutionists?"

Within the confines of this essay it is impossible to outline, let alone analyze, the developments that are taking place.[36] It must suffice to note one or two. One major development is the attention given by both Jewish and Christian scholars to a feature almost totally neglected in the original and new quests—the Jewishness of Jesus.[37] Related to this is the study of geography and economic and political conditions of Jesus' world.[38]

In *Jesus and Judaism* E. P. Sanders takes as his starting point Jesus' action in the temple, which he sees as a key to Jesus' program of restoration eschatology.[39] Martin Hengel has made a study of Jesus in comparison with charismatic figures of Second Temple Judaism.[40] A. E. Harvey has approached the question of the historical Jesus by way of the social and religious constraints of his time.[41] Ben F. Meyer has developed an approach to history, drawing on the philosophy of Bernard Lonergan, which combines critical history with recognition of the divine and transcendent in the person and activity of Jesus.[42]

Yet another major development is the Spirit Christology of James D. G. Dunn, which draws attention to the role of the Spirit in understanding the identity of Jesus.[43] More recently Dunn has focused on what he calls "the partings of the ways" between Christianity and Judaism.[44] My own researches have pointed me in the same direction in focusing on the Spirit and Jesus, on the one hand, and the opposition to Jesus, on the other. In addressing issues raised by the "third quest," I have sought to explore two theses as a means of understanding the Gospel accounts of Jesus and those who opposed him.[45]

Thesis A argues that in giving prominence to the prophecy of John the Baptist (Mk 1:8; Mt 3:11; Lk 3:16; Jn 1:33) the evangelists want their readers to understand that this prophecy was fulfilled *initially in the earthly ministry of Jesus.*[46] Mark's version reads: "I have baptized you with water; but he will baptize you with the Holy Spirit."[47] Baptism is a rite of washing, cleansing and consecration. Following his own baptism and anointing by the Spirit as the Christ, the messianic Son of God, Jesus embarked on a mission to baptize the people of Israel with the Holy Spirit. The stories of expelling unclean spirits, cleansing lepers, forgiving sins, teaching what makes a person clean, cleansing of the temple and Jesus' dying on the cross show us different aspects of this ministry of cleansing, restoration and consecration. It finds expression in allusions to the Spirit in relation to the kingdom and Jesus' mission (Mt 12:18, 28; Lk 4:14, 18; 11:20), and in the preaching of Peter which tells "how God anointed Jesus of Nazareth with the Holy Spirit and with power; how he went about doing good and healing all who were oppressed by the devil, for God was with him" (Acts 10:38; cf. 2:22). If we were able to explore the Gospels' presentation of Jesus, we would see how the evangelists present God's personal presence in Jesus his Son, through his Spirit, Word and Wisdom, and how the emerging incarnational theology finds expression in John's declaration: "And the Word became flesh and lived among us, and we have seen his glory, the glory as of a father's only son, full of grace and truth" (Jn 1:14). The activity of the historical Jesus marks a new, decisive phase in God's purposes to consecrate, reclaim and restore Israel, and then the rest of humanity.

Thesis B represents the other side of the coin, an alternative way of looking at the same phenomena. It is bound up with an interpretation of the Torah with regard to prophets who seek to lead people astray (Deut 13:1-8; cf. Mt 27:64; Lk 23:2; Jn 11:47-48). The prophet who performs signs and wonders in order to lead people astray is not only to be disregarded. He is to be killed, so that the evil may be removed from Israel. My thesis argues that when the authorities saw Jesus performing miracles and giving teaching which differed from their understanding of the Torah, they quickly concluded that Jesus was the kind of prophet described in Deuteronomy 13, and that appropriate steps should be taken to remove him. This thesis explains the significance of the charge that Jesus was casting out demons by Beelzebul (Mk 3:29; Mt 10:25; 12:24; Lk 11:15; cf.

Jn 7:12; 8:48). Similar attitudes can be found in the Dead Sea
Scrolls. The prescription for dealing with the sign-working prophet
who leads astray is repeated in the Temple Scroll (11Q Temple 54:8-
18). The Beelzebul charge is paralleled by the Damascus Rule which
prescribes that those who teach apostasy under the influence of Belial
should be judged by the law relating to those possessed by a ghost or
familiar spirit (CD 12:2-3; 4QDc 3 1:18-19; cf. Lev 20:27). Although Jesus parried the charge by showing its self-defeating character, the episode marked the beginning of the conflict that led to the
cross. I see the Gospels as written to defend Jesus against the charges
of being a deceiver by setting forth the true nature of his mission and
person. What the opponents blasphemously denounced as Satanic
activity is, in fact, the manifestation of the Holy Spirit in and
through Jesus (Mk 3:28; cf. Mt 12:31-32; Lk 12:10).

3.3. The Two Poles of Christology

Christology has two poles: the historical Jesus and our ongoing human experience. We need to pay attention to both. I shall begin this
final section with some thoughts on the latter. The problem with Anselm's approach is that it works out a Christology without reference
to Jesus and the Holy Spirit. Nevertheless, it suggests a context for
Christology by exploring the human condition. It does so by asking
how sin affects our relationship with God, and directs us to those
aspects of Christology that meet this need. Today we have many
Christologies: Feminist, African-American, Asian, African, Hispanic,
Third World and so on. Each of them seeks a Christ that answers a
situation. But all too often they provide still more examples of the
face seen at the bottom of the well. But even here there is both gain
and loss. For in a sense, the process of looking down the well is like
the hermeneutical circle. We understand the meaning of a text in relation to its parts. But there is also the reciprocal relationship between readers and text by which readers bring to the text experiences
which enable them to see things that otherwise would not be seen.
In turn the text throws new light on our situation. But we need to be
careful, and learn to disentangle insights from agendas.

Anthony C. Thiselton warns of the importance of distinguishing
between sociocritical hermeneutics and sociopragmatic hermeneutics:

> If Latin American hermeneutics, black hermeneutics, and femi-
> nist hermeneutics seek to evolve a genuinely liberating critique
> of injustice and oppression, in which uses of biblical texts in the
> interests of oppressors are unmasked, it becomes essential to dis-

entangle those strands within them which utilize socio-critical theoretical models from others which crumble and collapse into socio-pragmatic systems of hermeneutics. Socio-contextual pragmatism can achieve nothing beyond the attempt to fight oppressors with the oppressors' own oppressive weapons. Whoever is the most militant, the most articulate, the most manipulative, the most self-confident (sometimes even the most supposedly pious) appears to win this rhetorical power struggle.[48]

What applies to hermeneutics applies to Christology. At its best, a sociopragmatic Christology which pays scant attention to the historical Jesus is no more than a picture painted on water or in air, a figment of its creator's imagination without substance. At its worst, such a Christology functions as a tool of manipulation in a rhetorical power struggle. But a sociocritical Christology can be a means not only of gaining new insight into Christ from a perspective other than our habitual ones. It can also be a means of challenging ourselves and our culture to repentance, faith and discipleship.

Earlier I was critical of Kähler's famous dictum about the real Christ being the Christ who is preached. But one more thing needs to be said. The knowledge of Christ is never a matter of pure historical reconstruction. Nor is it a matter of getting at a figure *behind* the texts, but knowing Christ *in and through* the texts. The value of the kind of historical work that I have noted in discussing the "third quest" of the historical Jesus is rather like getting to understand the rules of a game so that one can appreciate the game better. Back in 1973 I saw my first game of baseball. I had just arrived from England on my first visit to America and was eager to enter the American experience by seeing "the national pastime" for myself. So I went to see the Chicago Cubs play the Pittsburgh Pirates. As someone who understood something about cricket (though I was never any good at it), I could just about make out what was going on. But I was baffled by the seemingly endless number of innings, and by what one had to do to stay in or get out. Only much later did I begin to understand the rules and appreciate the game. The same is true about the Gospels. We shall not understand what is going on—or worse, we shall impose our wrong interpretations on what we read—unless we gain an understanding of the history represented in the text and its significance.

A few months back I read a review in the *Los Angeles Times* of a new biography of the painter Henri Toulouse-Lautrec. The reviewer admired the author's research but felt that there were many questions that readers would have to answer for themselves. He concluded: "Think of this biography as a do-it-yourself Toulouse-Lautrec kit and you'll like it fine."[49] In a sense the Gospels are like that. They are not exhaustive biographies in the modern sense, but do-it-yourself kits which need to be made into something. In order to do this, we need historical understanding. But the Gospels also call for personal response. There is a price to be paid. Those who pay it will find themselves drawn into another world, the world of the historical Jesus, which turns out to be the realm of redemption as the horizons of that world fuse into the horizons of our modern world.

Notes:

[1] *Cur Deus Homo* 1.4 (Eugene R. Fairweather, ed., *A Scholastic Miscellany: Anselm to Ockham*, Library of Christian Classics 10 [London: S.C.M. Press; Philadelphia: Westminster Press, 1956], p. 105).

[2] Ibid.

[3] "For I do not seek to understand in order to believe, but I believe in order to understand [*credo ut intelligam*]. For this too I believe, 'that unless I believe, I shall not understand'" (*Proslogion 1*, in *A Scholastic Miscellany*, p. 73).

[4] *Cur Deus Homo* 1.5, 9, 11–15, 19–25; 2.6–14, 18.

[5] Anselm claimed in his preface that he had proved "by necessary reasons (Christ being put out of sight, as if nothing had ever been known of him) that it is impossible to be saved without him" (*A Scholastic Miscellany*, p. 100).

[6] W. V. O. Quine and J. S. Ullian, *The Web of Belief* (New York: Random House, 2nd ed., 1978).

[7] In my sketch of Anselm's argument I omitted some of his more dubious points, e.g., the discussion of why the number of angels who fell is to be made up from among men (*Cur Deus Homo* 1.16-18).

[8] R. P. C. Hanson, *The Search for the Christian Doctrine of God: The Arian Controversy, 318–381* (Edinburgh: T. & T. Clark, 1988), pp. 109–10, 562–72.

[9] *Against Praxeas* 29–30.

[10] Jürgen Moltmann, *The Crucified God* (London: S.C.M. Press; New York: Harper & Row, 1974).

[11] W. Pannenberg, *Jesus—God and Man* (London: S.C.M. Press; Philadelphia, Westminster Press, 1968), pp. 33–37.

[12] Ibid., pp. 21–30.

[13] A. Schweitzer, *The Quest of the Historical Jesus: A Critical Study of Its Progress from Reimarus to Wrede,* reprint with new introduction by James M. Robinson (New York: Macmillan, 1968). Schweitzer gave his original German work the more prosaic title *From Reimarus to Wrede: History of Research into the Life of Jesus* (1906). I have given my own assessments in *Jesus in European Protestant Thought, 1768–1860* (1985; reprint Grand Rapids, Mich.: Baker Book House, 3rd printing, 1995), and "Historical Jesus, Quest of," in Joel B. Green, Scot McKnight and I. H. Marshall, eds., *Dictionary of Jesus and the Gospels* (Downers Grove, Ill./Leicester, England: InterVarsity Press, 1992), pp. 326–41.

[14] Ibid., p. 238.

[15] In 1901 Wrede and Schweitzer published on the same day books dealing with the messianic secret (*The Quest of the Historical Jesus*, p. 330). Wrede's was entitled *The Messianic Secret* (Cambridge and London: James Clarke, 1971). Schweitzer's was entitled *The Mystery of the Kingdom of God* (London: A. & C. Black, 1914). The German word *Geheimnis* may be translated either by "secret" or by "mystery." The scholarly world endorsed Wrede and neglected the comparatively unknown Schweitzer who proceeded to write *The Quest of the Historical Jesus* to vindicate himself.

[16] *The Quest of the Historical Jesus*, p. 403.

[17] George Tyrrell (*Christianity at the Cross-Roads* [London: Allen & Unwin, {1909} 1963], p. 49), summing up his fellow Catholic Modernist's critique of Harnack. In *What Is Christianity?* (London: Williams & Norgate, 1901), Harnack had identified the essence of Christianity as Jesus' teaching about the kingdom of God, God the Father and the infinite value of soul, and the higher righteousness and the commandment to love. Loisy's critique appeared in *The Gospel and the Church* (1902; reprint with introduction by B. B. Scott [Philadelphia: Fortress Press, 1976]).

[18] Schweitzer had a long fascination with Nietzsche and his cult of the genius. He saw his own philosophy based on reverence for life as a superior version of Nietzsche's concern to live life to the full (*The Philosophy of Civilization*, trans. C. T. Campion [London: A. & C. Black, 3rd ed., 1946], pp. 174, 176). Schweitzer, who with his piercing eyes and flowing mustache bore a striking resemblance to Nietzsche, went on to live out his creed through his heroic career as a missionary doctor in West Africa, interspersed with virtuoso organ tours in the Western world and writing wide-ranging books on music, literature, theology and civilization.

[19] For an account and apologia see James M. Robinson, *A New Quest of the Historical Jesus and Other Essays* (Philadelphia: Fortress Press, [1959] 1983).

[20] Cf. Alister McGrath, *The Making of Modern German Theology: From the Enlightenment to Pannenberg* (Oxford: Blackwell, 1986), p. 234.

[21] *The So-Called Historical Jesus and the Historic Biblical Christ* (1896; Philadelphia: Fortress Press, 1964), pp. 66–67.

[22] Ibid., p. viii.

[23] Paul Tillich, *Systematic Theology* (Digswell Place: James Nisbet), 2:107–35. In *On the Boundary: An Autobiographical Sketch* (London: Collins, 1967), p. 49, Tillich admits that he owes his historical insights into the New Testament to Schweitzer's *The Quest of the Historical Jesus* and Bultmann's *The History of the Synoptic Tradition*. "The foundation of Christian belief is the biblical picture of Christ, not the historical Jesus. The criterion of human thought and action is the picture of Christ as it is rooted in ecclesiastical belief and human experience, not the shifting artificial construct of historical research" (p. 50). For discussion see George H. Tavard, *Paul Tillich and the Christian Message* (London: Burns & Oates, 1962), and more briefly Colin Brown, *Philosophy and the Christian Faith* (Downers Grove, Ill.: InterVarsity Press, 1968 and reprints), pp. 191–200.

[24] Cited from the version used in Morning Prayer II in *The Book of Common Prayer . . . According to the Use of the Episcopal Church* (New York: Seabury Press, 1979), p. 96.

[25] *Jesus Christ for Today's World* (Minneapolis, Minn.: Fortress Press, 1994), pp. 3–4.

[26] See (e.g.) James H. Charlesworth, *Jesus Within Judaism: New Light from Exciting Archaeological Discoveries* (New York: Doubleday, 1988); James H. Charlesworth, ed., *Jesus and the Dead Sea Scrolls* (New York: Doubleday, 1992); Joel B. Green and Max Turner, eds., *Jesus of Nazareth: Essays on the Historical Jesus and New Testament Christology, Studies in Honor of I. Howard Marshall* (Grand Rapids, Mich.: Eerdmans; Carlisle: Paternoster Press, 1994); Marcus J. Borg, *Jesus in Contemporary Scholarship* (Valley Forge, Penn.: Trinity Press International, 1994; James H. Charlesworth and Walter P. Weaver, eds., *Images of Jesus Today*, Faith and Scholarship Colloquies 3 (Valley Forge, Penn.: Trinity Press International, 1994); Bruce Chilton and Craig A.

Evans, eds., *Studying the Historical Jesus: Evaluations of the State of Current Research,* New Testament Tools and Studies 19 (Leiden, Netherlands: E. J. Brill, 1994).

[27] See (e.g.) Robert W. Funk, Roy W. Hoover and the Jesus Seminar, *The Five Gospels: The Search for the Authentic Words of Jesus, New Translation and Commentary* (New York: Macmillan/Polebridge Press, 1993); Burton L. Mack, *A Myth of Christian Innocence: Mark and Christian Origins* (Philadelphia: Fortress Press, 1988); Mack, *The Lost Gospel: The Book of Q and Christian Origins* (San Francisco: Harper, 1993); J. Dominic Crossan, *The Historical Jesus: The Life of a Mediterranean Jewish Peasant* (San Francisco: Harper, 1992); Jeffrey Carlson and Robert A. Ludwig, eds., *Jesus and Faith: A Conversation on the Work of John Dominic Crossan* (Maryknoll, N.Y.: Orbis Books, 1994).

[28] *Cynics and Christian Origins* (Edinburgh: T. & T. Clark, 1992), p. 147.

[29] *Christ and the Cynics: Jesus and Other Radical Preachers in First-Century Tradition,* JSOT Manuals 4 (Sheffield: Sheffield Academic Press, 1988). See the critique by C. M. Tuckett, "A Cynic Q?" *Biblica* 70 (1989): 349–76. There is a much stronger case for seeing affinities with proverbs and maxims found in Jewish literature. See Gustaf Dalman, *Jesus-Jeshua: Studies in the Gospels* (London: S.P.C.K., 1929), pp. 225–31.

[30] Richard Horsley, "Jesus, Itinerant Cynic or Israelite Prophet?" in Charlesworth and Weaver, eds., *Images of Jesus Today,* pp. 68–97. The alleged parallel with Cynic lifestyle in Lk 10:4-6 would preclude Cynic practice by its prohibition of carrying a bag and staff and of greeting. The emphasis of Jesus' followers on Christian community is contrary to the Cynic ideal of self-sufficient independence.

[31] In Carlson and Ludwig, eds., *Jesus and Faith,* p. 97. The comment comes at the conclusion of a paper on "The Quest of the Historical Jesus: Origins, Achievements, and the Specter of Diminishing Returns" (pp. 83–99).

[32] *Theology Today* 52/1 (1995): 17–28. Kee notes that "the serious flaws in [Crossan's] are cleverly covered up by appeal to purely conjectural sources and stages in the development of the Jesus tradition" (p. 23). Thus, apocalyptic is seen as part of the later editorial redaction of Q which should not be attributed to Jesus himself. Elsewhere, Ben F. Meyer refers to the "ideological interests" that motivate this style of research on Q and the so-called "Q community" (*Reality and Illusion in New Testament Scholarship: A Primer in Critical Realist Hermeneutics* [Collegeville, Minn.: Michael Glazier, 1994], p. 186). For a very different approach see David Catchpole, *The Quest for Q* (Edinburgh: T. & T. Clark, 1993).

[33] *A Marginal Jew: Rethinking the Historical Jesus,* 1, *The Roots of the Problem and the Person,* 2, *Mentor, Message and Miracles* (New York: Doubleday, 1991, 1994).

[34] *The Death of the Messiah: A Commentary on the Passion Narratives in the Four Gospels,* 2 vols. (New York: Doubleday, 1994).

[35] *Christian Origins and the Question of God,* 1, *The New Testament and the People of God* (Minneapolis, Minn.: Fortress Press, 1992). Four further volumes are projected.

[36] For fuller accounts see my discussion in *Dictionary of Jesus and the Gospels,* pp. 336–41; Luke Johnson, *The Misguided Quest for the Historical Jesus and the Truth of the Traditional Gospels* (San Francisco: HarperSanFrancisco, 1995); and Ben Witherington III, *The Jesus Quest: The Third Search for the Jew of Nazareth* (Downers Grove, Ill.: InterVarsity Press, 1995).

[37] See (e.g.) Geza Vermes, *Jesus the Jew: A Historian's Reading of the Gospels* (London: Collins, 1973), *Jesus and the World of Judaism* (London; S.C.M. Press, 1983), *The Religion of Jesus the Jew* (London: S.C.M. Press, 1993); Donald A. Hagner, *The Jewish Reclamation of Jesus: An Analysis and Critique of Modern Jewish Study of Jesus* (Grand Rapids, Mich.: Zondervan, 1984).

[38] See (e.g.) Sean Freyne, *Galilee, Jesus and the Gospels: Literary Approaches and Historical Investigations* (Philadelphia: Fortress Press, 1988); Lee I. Levine, ed., *The Galilee in Late Antiquity* (New York and Jerusalem: Jewish Theological Seminary of America, 1992); John J. Rousseau and Rami Arav, *Jesus and His World: An Archaeological and Cultural Dictionary* (Minneapolis, Minn.: Fortress Press, 1995); Ernst Bammel and C. F. D. Moule, eds., *Jesus and the Politics of*

His Day (Cambridge: Cambridge University Press, 1984); Richard A. Horsley, *Jesus and the Spiral of Violence: Popular Resistance in Roman Palestine* (San Francisco: Harper & Row, 1987); Martin Hengel, *The Zealots: Investigations into the Jewish Freedom Movement in the Period from Herod I Until A.D. 70* (Edinburgh: T. & T. Clark, 1989).

[39] *Jesus and Judaism* (Philadelphia: Fortress Press, 1985); cf. Sanders, *The Historical Figure of Jesus* (London: Allen Lane/Penguin Press, 1993).

[40] *The Charismatic Leader and His Followers* (Edinburgh: T. & T. Clark; New York: Crossroad, 1991).

[41] *Jesus and the Constraints of History* (Philadelphia: Westminster Press, 1982).

[42] *The Aims of Jesus* (London: S.C.M. Press, 1979); *Critical Realism and the New Testament* (Allison Park, Penn.: Pickwick Publications, 1989); *The Mission of Christ and His Church: Studies in Christology and Ecclesiology* (Wilmington, Del.: Michael Glazier, 1990). See also above, n. 32.

[43] *Jesus and the Spirit: A Study of the Religious and Charismatic Experience of Jesus and the First Christians as Reflected in the New Testament* (London: S.C.M. Press, 1975); *Christology in the Making: A New Testament Inquiry into the Origins of the Doctrine of the Incarnation* (London: S.C.M. Press, 2nd ed., 1989).

[44] *The Partings of the Ways Between Christianity and Judaism and their Significance for the Character of Christianity* (London: S.C.M. Press; Philadelphia: Trinity Press International, 1991).

[45] *Miracles and the Critical Mind* (Grand Rapids, Mich.: Eerdmans; Exeter, England: Paternoster Press, 1984), pp. 293-325; "Synoptic Miracle Stories: A Jewish Religious and Social Setting," *Foundations and Facets Forum* 2/4 (1986): 55–76; "Trinity and Incarnation: In Search of Contemporary Orthodoxy," *Ex Auditu* 7 (1991): 83–100. I have given my interpretation of NT Christology in "Person of Christ," in G. W. Bromiley, general editor, *The International Standard Bible Encyclopedia* (Grand Rapids, Mich.: Eerdmans, 1986), 3:781–801. I further explored this question in my Hensley Henson Lectures at the University of Oxford on "The Question of Miracles and the Quest of the Historical Jesus" (1993). The lectures will be published in due course.

[46] The prophecy is widely assumed to refer to Pentecost, and to be the same as Acts 1:5 and 11:16. But to see the difference we simply have to ask, "Who is saying what to whom?" In Acts it is the Lord addressing the disciples. In the Gospels it is John addressing the crowds who have come for baptism. The Gospels give no account of Pentecost. The traditional interpretation of John's prophecy has to assume that Jesus' ministry was an interlude prior to the fulfillment which occurred only posthumously. I see Pentecost as the consecration and empowering of the disciples to continue the ministry of Jesus in the power of the Spirit. It marks the beginning of the ongoing mission of the church.

[47] All scriptural quotations in this article are taken from the New Revised Standard Version of the Bible, copyright the Division of Christian Education of the National Council of the Churches of Christ in the United States of America.

[48] *New Horizons in Hermeneutics* (Grand Rapids, Mich.: Zondervan, 1992), p. 27.

[49] Peter Schjeldahl reviewing Julia Frey, *Toulouse-Lautrec: A Life* (Viking), in the *Los Angeles Times,* 26 February 1995.

Part II: Biblical and Exegetical

6

The Dance Between God and Humanity

Bruce K. Waltke

IT SEEMED FITTING IN THIS TRIBUTE TO PROFESSOR J. I. Packer to write an article pertaining to "knowing God." More specifically, this article aims to help Christians to know God in addressing wrongs through an analysis of the dance between God and humanity as presented in Proverbs 15:30–16:15, with a special focus on 15:30–16:3.

This essay will first present a translation of the text with a focus on isolated exegetical details, then develop its argument within a clearly defined literary unit, and finally offer an exposition of 15:30–16:3 involving theological reflections.

Introduction

Accredited theological reflection on Proverbs depends on an accurate exegesis of every detail of isolated proverbs and, if they are deliberately arranged into meaning-rich contexts of larger, unified blocks of proverbial material, on their literary contexts. If, however, the proverbs are only a random, haphazard accretion of isolated sayings, then each is an entity in itself and has no other richer meaning gained from its surrounding literary context.

Historically most commentators have occasionally noted groupings in the proverbs literature of chapters 10–29, but for the most part the larger context created by such groupings has been ignored in the interpretation of the isolated proverb. In 1962 U. Skladny[1] set the stage for most subsequent discussion regarding the question of the arrangement of the proverbs into contexts. Skladny, by using analyses of form, content and style and employing statistics to quantify his findings, further delineated smaller subcollections: A (Prov 10–15), B (Prov 16:1–22:16), C (Prov 25–27) and D (Prov 28–29). This analysis conformed in part with the obvious editorial notices of the book's structure in 10:1; 22:17; 25:1; 30:1. William McKane,[2] R. B. Y. Scott[3] and C. Westermann[4] deny there is a context in the defined literary units sentence literature. However, in 1968 H. J. Hermisson[5] carried Skladny's analysis a step further by trying to discern thematic and poetic unities in Collection A. In 1972 G. E. Bryce[6] by using certain methods of French structuralism showed that Proverbs 25:2-27 constitutes a literary unit. In 1978 B. W. Kovacs found Collection B, which he begins at 15:28, as the embodiment of a consistent worldview.[7] In 1979 R. N. Whybray showed that an editor deliberately chose the place of the Yahweh ("LORD") sayings in 10:1–22:16.[8] In 1984 R. C. Van Leeuwen[9] by structuralism, poetics and semantics convincingly demonstrated that the proverbs in Collection C are arranged into larger literary compositions. In 1985 B. V. Malchow[10] proposed that Collection D is an intricately arranged collection serving as "A Manual for Future Monarchs." The recent commentaries by O. Ploeger,[11] A. Meinhold[12] and D. A. Garrett[13] have attempted to interpret individual proverbs within larger literary units. Meinhold succeeds best in this enterprise, but there is still much work to be done.

Since 1968 rhetorical critics have developed the discipline of poetics. Their indefatigable efforts and numerous publications have shown that biblical writers, by which is meant also collectors, editors and/or redactors, artistically gave unity to their work through such techniques as inclusio (i.e., marking off a literary unity by matching the end with the beginning), janus (i.e., linking sections together with a piece of literature that looks both back and forward), key words that stich the work together, synonyms, paronomasia (i.e., all sorts of sound plays often connected with sense), repetition of grammatical forms, structural patterns often in connection with form criticism, chiasms (i.e., reversing the structure), acrostics, etc.

Part II of this essay attempts to show that Solomon[14] used these techniques to give 15:30–16:15 unity.

I. A Translation
15:30 The light of the eyes[15] makes the heart glad,
         good news revives the whole person.[16]

15:31 The ear that listens to life-giving correction[17]
dwells among the wise.

15:32 The one who flouts instruction is one who despises his life,[18]
but the one who hears correction is one who acquires sense.[19]

15:33 The instruction[20] of wisdom[21] is the fear of the LORD,
and humility [comes][22] before honor.[23]

16:1[24] To a human being belong[25] the plans of the heart,[26]
but[27] from the LORD [comes][28] the answer of the tongue.[29]

16:2 All the ways of a person[30] [are] pure[31] in his own eyes,
but the LORD is the one who weighs motives.[32]

16:3 Commit[33] to the LORD your works,
and[34] your thoughts will be established.

16:4 The LORD works[35] all things to their counterparts,[36]
even the wicked for[37] an evil[38] day.[39]

16:5 Everyone who is haughty[40] is abomination to the LORD;
be sure of this,[41] he will not go unpunished.

16:6[42] Through[43] love and faithfulness sin is atoned for,[44]
and through the fear of the LORD is the turning aside from
evil.

16:7 When[45] the LORD[46] takes pleasure in[47] a person's ways,
he compels his enemies to surrender to him.

16:8 Better a little with[48] righteousness
than[49] a large income through injustice.

16:9 The heart of a human being plans[50] his way,
but the LORD directs[51] his[52] step.

16:10 An inspired verdict is on the king's lips,
in giving a judgment[53] his mouth is not unfaithful.

16:11 A just[54] balance and hand-scale[55] belong to the LORD,[56]
all the weights in a pouch[57] are his work.

16:12 To do[58] wickedness is an abomination to the king,
because a throne is established through righteousness.

16:13 Righteous[59] lips find the favor of kings,[60]
and he[61] loves whoever speaks[62] upright things.[63]

16:14 The wrath of the king[64] is the messengers[65] (*sic*) of death,
but a wise person pacifies it.

16:15 In[66] the light of a king's face[67] is life,
and his favor is like a cloud[68] of spring-rain.[69]

II. The Argument

The pericope consists of three parts sections: an introduction (15:30-

33), the main body of YHWH ("LORD") proverbs (16:1-9) and a conclusion of royal proverbs (16:10-15).

Introductions to literary units in 10:1–22:16, as obviously in 1:8–9:18 (see 1:8, 2:1; 3:1, etc.), pertain to the wise who accept wisdom and/or honor their parents, which entails accepting wisdom (cf., e.g., 10:1; 12:1; 13:1; 16:16). Although each of the four gnomic sayings of the introduction in 15:30-33 can apply in isolation to many different situations, together they also function as an introduction to the carefully arranged proverbs that follow in 16:1-15. Though written in the form of maxims, these introductions praising wisdom aim to encourage the son/disciple to embrace the teaching and to adjust his life by them. These four proverbs are knit tightly together into a coherent unit by a series of "catchwords": the anatomical features, "eyes" (v. 30a), "bones" (v. 30b) and "ear" (v. 31); the root *šmʿ* "to hear," represented by the noun *šᵉmûʿâ* ("news/report") (v. 30a) and the participle *šomaʿat* ("the ear that hears") (v. 31a); its compounds, *šomaʿat /šomēʿa tôkaḥat* ("hears correction") (vv. 31a, v. 32b); the noun *mûsār* ("instruction") (vv. 32a, 33a); and *ḥᵃkāmîm/ḥokmâ* ("wise/wisdom") (vv. 31b, 33a). The introduction and main body are linked by the catchword "LORD" (15:33a; 16:1b).

The main body (vv. 1-9), which is treated more fully below, coheres by the catchword "LORD" in either verset *a* or *b* of every verse, apart from v. 8. The other half of each of its verses pertains to humanity, though expressed variously as a "human being" (vv. 1a, 9a), "a person" (vv. 2a, 7a), "you" (v. 3), "wicked" (v. 4b), "everyone" (v. 5) and implicitly (v. 6). Other rhetorical features unifying verses 1-9 are treated below.

The conclusion (vv. 10-15) coheres by the catchword "king," which occurs in every verse except 11, and by the topic of living within the wise king's rule. These six verses in turn consists of three couplets. The first, verses 10-11, coheres by the catchword "justice," *mišpat,* by the assonances of their initial words, *qesem* ("inspired verdict") and *peles* ("balance") and of their final words, *pîw* ("his mouth") and *kîs* ("pouch"), and by their theme (i.e., the LORD administers his just kingdom through his wise king). The second, the complementary antithetical pair, verses 12 and 13, is linked by "kings" (plural) in their versets *a,* which stand out against the singular form, "king," in verses 10 and 14, and by the stock in trade antonyms "abomination" and "find favor" (vv. 5 and 7) and "wickedness" and "righteousness." Both proverbs illustrate the practice of justice (cf. vv. 10-11) by the wise king's evaluations: negatively with reference to the actions of the wicked (v. 12), and positively with reference to the speech of the righteous (v. 13). Chiastically the verses begin and end with his moral tastes: "abhors" and "loves." The third, the antithetical pair, verses 14-15, brings the unit to a climatic conclusion by contrasting the king's wrath, which heralds death, with his favor, which heralds life. The same contrast is found within one proverb in 19:12. The last two couplets are linked by the catchword "favor" (the first word in v. 13a and in v. 15b).

Verses 1-9 present the LORD and humanity as engaged in a dance. Humanity forms and God performs. The inclusio, verses 1 and 9, binds this part into a whole through synonyms and clearly sounds its theme: the LORD's sovereignty over human activity. The hearts of human beings arrange their thoughts, the LORD effects their answers (v. 1); the hearts of human beings plan their course, the LORD fixes their steps (v. 9). Note the catchwords "heart" (*lēḇ*) and "human being" (*'āḏām*) in their versets *a,* and "the LORD" in their versets *b.*

Verses 1-7 consist of two units (vv. 1-3 and 5-7), connected by verse 4, a janus verse. The first unit presents the LORD's sovereignty over human initiative, and the second, the LORD's sovereign justice over human morality. The term "janus" derives from the double-headed Roman god of doorways, who looks both back and ahead. The month of January, which looks back to the old year and ahead to new, also derives from this name. Verse 4a presents the LORD's sovereignty over human activity, matching verses 1-3, and verse 4b his justice regarding the wicked, matching verses 5-7.

In this essay, we can only exegete and reflect theologically in more detail upon verses 1-3. Suffice it to note here that verse 5 asserts in the most positive terms that the arrogant are an abomination to the LORD and will be punished. Because the proud fail by their impiety in their relation to God, they also fail by their unethical activity in their relation to humanity. As the biography of Cain shows, when humanity fails at the altar, it fails in the field. By contrast, verse 7 asserts that as for those who please the LORD, the Sovereign compels their enemies to surrender to them. Sandwiched in between these two verses, verse 6 gives instruction on how both to atone for past sins and to avoid future ones: namely, by covenant fidelity for the former (v. 6a) and by fear of the LORD for the latter (v. 6b). Verse 8, "a better-than proverb," stands apart, implicitly cautioning that the LORD's justice is not effected immediately. The several "better-than proverbs" (e.g., 15:16-17; 16:8, 19; 17:1; 19:22b; 22:1; 28:6) link righteousness with poverty and wickedness with wealth and so make it perfectly plain that piety and morality do not invariably lead in experience to social and physical benefits. Moreover, many proverbs recognize the failures of justice. "There are many sayings," says Van Leeuwen, "that assert or imply that the wicked prosper . . . while the innocent suffer"[70] (e.g., 10:2; 11:16; 13:23; 14:31; 15:25; 18:23; 19:10; 21:6, 7, 13; 22:8, 22; 23:17; 28:15-16a, 27; 30:14). The very first pericope, 1:10-19, represents thugs sending an innocent person to Sheol. The calculus of the book of Proverbs equating virtue with life/prosperity and vice with death/impoverishment looks to a future that outlasts Sheol. Until then, "better a little with righteousness than a large income through injustice."

This interplay between humanity and God implies situations where wrongs must be righted. Humanity arranges its thoughts to address a problem, but the LORD answers (v. 1); they commit their deeds to the LORD, and he fixes them as part of his eternal plan (vv. 3, 9b). Be sure of this, the wicked will be judged (v. 5), and the righteous will triumph (v. 7). In sum, by representing the interplay between God and humanity, verses 1-9 present an "ABCDary" of addressing evil.

III. Exposition
Introduction (15:30-33)
The introduction consists of two quatrains (vv. 30-31 and 32-33). The first refers to "good news/report" (*šᵉmûʿâ*), as, for example, of the wise teacher (v. 30) and to the disciple's ear that listens (*šomaʿat*) (v. 31). The second pertains to "instruction" (*mûsār*): flouted or accepted (v. 32) and elaborated upon as "the fear of the LORD" to be humbly received (v. 33). It bears repeating: these proverbs are applicable to many situations (e.g., the "good news" of verse 30 may refer to any good report), but together they also function as an introduction to the following collection. "The good news" of verse 30 refers more specifically to the wonderful report that God dances with the pure in heart!

The Good News Heard (vv. 30-31)
The favorable effects of good news: gladness and refreshment (v. 30). "The light of the eyes," literally, "the luminaries of the eyes," connotes vitality and joy.[71] The Old Testament repeatedly links light with life (Job 3:16; 33:28) and symbolizes life and good fortune by it (see Prov 4:18; 6:23; 13:9; 16:15). These proverbs associate light and life with wisdom, suggesting that shining eyes belong to the wise

(15:13a). His bright eyes "makes the heart (of the one observing him [e.g., the son/disciple]) glad." Verset *b* shows that the wise messenger's joyful and vital shining eyes complement his "good news." The noun glossed "news" occurs about thirty times in the Old Testament and refers to a verbal report of a recent event. Although in the historical books and prophets it is mostly used of "bad news" about battles—notable exceptions being the message the Queen of Sheba heard about Solomon (1 Kings 10:7) and glad news about the Servant's suffering to bring salvation to all (Is 53:1), in Proverbs it refers to the peace that good news reports have upon one. According to Y. Ratzhavi[72] the expression here and in 25:25 (cf. Is 52:7) reflects a blessing formula like that at the beginning of several of the Lachish letters, upon the one who hears the tidings of good (i.e., peace). If the son/disciple responds to the good news of 16:9, for example, he will experience peace indeed.

As the shining eyes of the wise gladden the heart of the observer, so the messenger's good news refreshes (literally, "makes fat") the bones (cf. 23:5). The parallels "make glad" (*yeśammaḥ*) and "make fat" (*teḏaššen*) also occur in Sirach 26:13: "A wife's charms delight [*śimmaḥ*] her husband, and her skill puts fat on his bones."

The good effects of listening: abundant life and dwelling with the wise (v. 31). The proverb now shifts to the listening ear, implicitly admonishing the disciple to have an ear that readily permits itself to hear correction and to accept humbly its medicine in order to enter life (see 6:23) and to dwell forever within the honored company of the wise (cf. 15:12). The "good news" of v. 30 is also a corrective (v. 31) and "instruction" to make one wise (v. 32-33). "All Scripture is God-breathed and is useful for teaching, rebuking, correcting and training in righteousness" (2 Tim 3:16 NIV). "Teachability," says Crawford Toy, "is the key that unlocks the door of the sages."[73]

"Life" in this book refers to the abundant life in an unending relationship with God. In the book of Proverbs the noun "life" (*ḥayyîm*) occurs thirty-three times and the verb "to live" (*ḥāyâ*) four times. After analyzing its uses in wisdom literature, William Cosser draws the conclusion that "'life' in the Canonical Wisdom Literature sometimes has a technical significance, viz., the fuller, more satisfying way of living to be enjoyed by those who 'seek Wisdom and find her,' a sense which can be rendered in English by some such phrase as 'full life,' 'fullness of life,' 'life indeed.'"[74] The schools where wisdom was taught in Egypt were called "Schools of Life."[75] In biblical theology true life is essentially a relationship with God. According to Genesis

2:17, disruption of the proper relationship with the One who is the source of life means death. Wisdom is concerned with the proper relationship (2:5-8) and so with this life. God continues forever to be the God of the wise, delivering them from the realm of death (see Mt 22:32). Clinical death seems to be only a shadow along the trail in that living relationship (cf. Prov 11:7a; 12:28; 14:32; 15:24; 23:17-18; 24:15-16, 19-20). In the book of Proverbs life has the last word for the righteous, and death is the final end of the wicked.

"To dwell" glosses the poetic word "to spend the night" (*tālîn*), connoting that one is at home among the wise and stays close to the this source of life, ready to hear correction as the last thing before retiring and the first words upon awaking (cf. Is 50:4). The listening ear characterizes true Israel's relationship with God more than the seeing eye. In God's encounters with the Israel he is always heard, but rarely seen.

Instruction Admonished and Explained (vv. 32-33)

Instruction flouted or accepted (v. 32). Verse 32 implicitly instructs the son/disciple not to rebel against instruction/correction, but to hear and receive it, because it is a matter of either loving oneself or of hating oneself, of life versus death (see 8:36; 15:6, 10). J. Gerald Janzen showed the verb *prᶜ* glossed "flout" denotes the value-laden judgment of "flouting of and rebellion against, structures and constraints claimed (rightly or wrongly) to be foundational to the true and life-giving order."[76] In 4:15 the father admonished the son to flout "the false way masquerading as what is true and right,"[77] but here he cautions him not to rebel against the family's inherited wisdom (cf. 4:1-9). If the son does, he paradoxically also despises (i.e., "wants to have nothing to do with"[78]) his own life. By contrast, if he "hears correction," he "acquires sense" (literally, "heart")—that is, he gains the mental and moral capacity to live, as its parallel, "life," makes clear.

Instruction elaborated upon (v. 33). This instruction is an inalienable possession of wisdom and is equated with "the fear of the LORD," the essential religious ingredient for a relationship with God. As this writer argued elsewhere,[79] the "fear of the LORD" has a cognitive aspect (namely, the objective revelation of God) and an affective aspect (namely, the acceptance of that revelation out of awe for the Holy One). This notion constitutes a fitting transition to the main body, presenting the dance between God and people. Verset *b*, "humility," emphasizes the emotional aspect of "the fear of the LORD." Accepting this instruction has promise of eternal life (v. 31b) and of social gravitas and honor (v. 32b).

In sum, if the son/disciple accepts the good news/correction/ instruction, including the truths about to be set forth, he will find gladness (15:30a), refreshment (15:30b), life (15:31a), the wholesome company of the wise (15:31b), good sense (v. 32b), the fear of the LORD, the *sine qua non* of wisdom (v. 33a) and social honor (v. 33b).

Divine Sovereignty over Human Initiative (vv. 1-3)

The divine sovereignty over human initiative pertains both to the disciple's speech, "the answer [*ma'nēh*] of the tongue" (v. 1b), and to his "works" (*ma'sēh*) (v. 3). Sandwiched in between these sayings is a proverb asserting that the LORD evaluates the motives behind them (v. 2). According to verses 1-3 human beings form, but the LORD performs; they devise, God verifies; they formulate, God validates; they propose, God disposes. They design what they will say and do, but God decrees what will endure and form a part of his eternal purposes. The tune for the dance between God and human is struck in verse 1, "To humanity belongs . . . but from the LORD. . . ."

In other biblical theologies God takes the first step in the dance with humankind. According to the New Covenant, God changes the human heart of stone into a pliable heart of flesh that it may feel (Jer 36:26). The New Covenant superseded the Old in part because it is based upon better promises than the Old (Heb 8:6). In the New, God takes the initiative and promises to open the heart and imprint the law upon it, whereas in the Old, Israel took the initiative and promised to keep law written on rock (Jer 31:33; Acts 16:14; 2 Cor 3:1-3). In Paul's theology God also takes the first step: "It is God who works in you to will and to act according to his good purpose" (Phil 2:13 NIV). So also in Hebrews: "Jesus, the Pioneer and Perfecter of our faith" (Heb 12:2 NIV).

Proverbs, however, is not concerned with this invisible first step of God. Instead, it is written for the children of the covenant, disciples, and represents them as taking the lead.

With Regard to Speech (v. 1)

The human initiative (v. 1a). The human being primarily in view is the son, for the proverbs were written for him (cf. 1:1-9) and, according to 22:21, he must give good and effective answers. He is referred to as an *'ādām,* "human being," to differentiate him from divine beings and to connote that his potentialities and limitations are determined by God. Implicitly the son is addressing a wrong, and he needs to plan how to redress the grievance.

The noun glossed "plans" (*ma^{a}rkēh*)—note its alliteration with *ma^{a}śēh* and *ma^{a}nēh*—is unique, but its meaning, "arrangement," is not in doubt. The verb '*rk* denotes "to set things carefully in order" (like setting armies in array for battle [Gen 14:8] or laying up wood for sacrifice [Gen 22:9]) or "to produce a case (for justice)" (Job 13:18), or "to bring forth words" (Job 32:14). Its feminine bi-forms, *ma^{a}rākâ* and *ma^{a}reket,* denote respectively "a row" (mostly the strategic battle line) and the carefully arranged row or stack of bread set out on the sanctuary table. Since the heart is the agent producing the careful and orderly "arrangement," appropriate glosses would be "thought-through plans" or "arguments." Every effective writer and speaker whom this writer has known, including the one to whom this volume is dedicated, carefully thinks through what he has to say before uttering it or setting it down on paper.

The sovereign response (v. 1b). The good and effective answer, however, is a gift from the LORD. Helmer Ringgren[80] rightly restricts "answer" to "*eine richtige Antwort . . . das passende Wort* [A right answer . . . the fitting word]." Unlike the English gloss, "answer," the Hebrew noun entails only a true and right response to a circumstance, not merely a verbal "reply" (cf. NIV). The noun occurs six times with reference to a wise "answer" that matches the situation. Job's three friends replied to him, but Elihu rightly judged "they did not find a *ma^{a}nēh* answer [i.e., 'refutation'] for him in their mouths" (Job 32:3, 5; cf. Prov 15:23). An answer that hits the nail on the head is from the good and wise LORD.

In that light the son is free of ultimate responsibility in meeting the need he addresses, and all praise belongs to the Author of every good and perfect gift. The good and effective answer depends upon careful planning, weighing the arguments and arranging them, but also, above all, upon God's benediction. "These reflections," says F. Delitzsch, "seeking at one time in one direction, and at another time in another, the solution of the question, . . . are the business of men; but the answer which finally the tongue gives, and which . . . will be regarded as right, appropriate, effective, . . . is from God."[81] Disciples need to ponder their answer (15:28) and to subordinate themselves totally in faith to the LORD to make it effective in its style and substance. The many good things the wise accomplish with their tongues (12:18; 15:1, 2; 25:11-12) owe their success to God, not to themselves. Paul expressed this truth by an agricultural metaphor: "I planted the seed, Apollos watered it, but God made it grow. So nei-ther he who plants nor he who waters is anything, but only God, who makes things grow" (1 Cor 3:6-7 NIV).

With Regard to Motives (v. 2)

The proverb continues the theme of God's sovereignty over human activity and is linked with verse 1 by the catchword "LORD," by the synonyms for humanity in general, "human being" (*'ādām*) and "person" (*'îš*), and the human psyche in particular, "heart" (*lēḇ*) and "motives" (*rûḥôt*). The proverb contrasts a person's assessment of his actions with God's evaluation of his motives. The proverb does not teach that "men never condemn their own conduct" (*pace* Toy) or that there is basic conflict between the human and divine assess-ments, but rather, as Meinhold commented, that since people justify all their actions, conflicts of assessment will arise.[82]

The human evaluation (v. 2a). A person tends to assess "all [his] ways" (i.e., his conduct both with regard to speaking [v. 1] and to doing [v. 2]) as pure. When he becomes aware of their impurity, however, he must confess and renounce them and so obtain mercy (28:13). The word glossed "pure" in its four references to the cult refers to pure olive oil (Ex 27:20; Lev 24:2) and pure gold (Ex 30:3; Lev 24:7). In its seven occurrences in wisdom literature it refers to ethical purity. The metaphor "right" is used instead in the synoptic proverb 21:2. "In his own eyes," however, signifies that he is deluded in his evaluation of himself independently from God. The human being has an amazing facility for self-deception (cf. Jer 17:9) and employs the poor standard of measuring his conduct by his own opinion of right and wrong,[83] rather than by the high ethical stan-dards revealed in this book.

The divine evaluation (v. 2b). The LORD, however, weighs (i.e., gauges and evaluates) the person's motives by the standards of his own character, which are revealed in Scripture.[84] The metaphor de-rives from an ancient Egyptian belief that after death the human heart is weighed on a balance against Maat (Truth), represented by a feather.[85] Here, however, the evaluation takes place during the per-son's life. The word glossed "motives" is literally "winds," "breaths" (i.e., the dynamic vitality that moves a person [see 15:4, 15]), a synecdoche for a person's entire disposition (Ezek 11:19; 18:31; 36:26; Eccles 7:8, 9), the whole inner life (Job 7:4; Ps 78:8), includ-ing his opinions or desires (cf. Ezek 13:3), mind (Ps 77:6), will (cf. Prov 16:32), and motives (cf. 2 Chron 36:22). What human being can weigh winds (cf. Job 28:25; Prov 30:4)!

Since the final verdict as to the purity of motives belongs to the LORD, not to the doer, even though a person thinks himself pure, he must not praise himself or decide his reward beforehand but depend upon the LORD, who alone truly evaluates motives (Ps 19:12; 139:23-24; 1 Cor 4:5-6; Heb 4:12-13). Furthermore, if he cannot judge his own motives, how much more should he not judge others (Mt 7:1). The best a person can do is to commit all he does to the LORD (Prov 16:3) in order that his ways will be pleasing to him (cf. 16:7).

With Regard to Deeds (v. 3)

The proverb now, using the second person of direct address, turns to "your deeds" (*ma⁽ă⁾śêḵā*), admonishing the disciple to turn over the ownership of his planned righteous deeds to the LORD, that he may establish them permanently as part of his history that outlasts the temporary triumph of the wicked. Verse 2 cautions that the LORD is assessing the motives behind both our words (v. 1) and our deeds (v. 3). Verses 1 and 3 assume that the morally untarnished LORD finds them pure. Only pure words and deeds endure forever. When human motives are pure, the LORD integrates them into his fixed righteous order (cf. Prov 10:22; Ps 127). The faithful must not fret or worry about the effectiveness of their plans, or even about their purity, for that assessment and their achievements depend upon God, not us (Ps 22:9; 37:5; 55:23; 1 Pet 5:7). The best we can do is to resign ourselves to his assessment regarding their purity and to trust him to ratify or to veto them. Since only the LORD can bring our plans to fruition, their success can be credited only to him. The Egyptian sage Amenemope (22.7; 23.10), an approximate contemporary of Solomon, instructed: "Settle in the arms of the god." Secular man, who feels so confident in his own capability, paradoxically is plagued with fear. By contrast, pious people, who know God's sovereignty and their own limitations, live in prayer and peace.

The human commitment (v. 3a). This synthetic parallelism consists of a protasis, in the form of an imperative (3a) presenting the conditional situational, and an apodosis, presenting the consequence of satisfying the condition. The imperative glossed "commit" (*gōl*) literally means "to roll," for example, of rolling a heavy stone from a well's mouth (Gen 29:3, 8, 10). If we roll our burdens (i.e., our needs and concerns) "unto the LORD" (*'el YHWH*), then implicitly we roll them from upon ourselves (see Ps 22:9; 37:5). *Gol 'el* is onomatopoeic; one almost hears the rolling sound of the stone. Israel's sublime God can be trusted. Indeed, the proverbs were written to teach a life of faith (cf. Prov 3:5; 22:19). "Your works," to judge from the parallel "your thoughts," refers to a person's planned deeds (cf. Mic 2:1), not those performed (cf. Gen 44:15). That distinction, however, may be too fine. Whatever the disciple performs he entrusts to the LORD to transform it into an eternal work.

The divine establishing (v. 3b). The root glossed "thoughts" exhibits two basic semantic elements: calculation and planning, "to think out, conceive, invent."[86] In verse 9 the personal and subjective elements are emphasized by adding "heart." "The reckoning and planning is to be interpreted subjectively as an internal thought process."[87] The verb "will be established" is also a creation term. However, whereas "thoughts" refers to inner creations, "established" (*yikkonû*) refers to the outward and overt bringing of something into existence. The meaning of *kûn,* glossed "established/fixed," can be assessed from the synonyms following it in the famous representation of creation in Proverbs 8:27-29:

> When he fixed [*bahªkînô*] the heavens, I was there,
> when he inscribed [*bᵉhûqô*] a circle upon the face of the deep.
> When he made the skies firm [*bᵉʾammᵉṣô*] above,
> when he fixed fast [*baʿªzôz*] the foundations of the deep;
> ʲ when he set [*bᵉśûmô*] for the sea its limit
> —and the waters can not go beyond his command—
> when he marked out [*bᵉhûqô*] the foundations of the earth. . . .

The creative works of human beings will come into existence as planned and be as firmly secure within history as the elements of the cosmos which the LORD planned and effected (see 8:27-29). In this way human beings participate creatively in salvation history.

Conclusion

Here then is good news: the LORD establishes forever as part of his eternal plan the creative words and deeds of the pure in heart in their overcoming of evil. When the disciple trusts the Lord to dance with him he will find gladness, peace, refreshment, life, favorable space with the wise, good judgment, a relationship with God and social honor.

By learning the steps of this dance he also learns the "ABCDary" for correcting what is wrong:

A: Arrange your thoughts before your speak, then turn it over to him for your expression to be effective.

B: Beware of your motives; don't be so cocksure of your purity;

God alone evaluates them accurately.

C: Commit your deeds to the LORD; then you will participate creatively in the salvation history that endures forever.

It would take another essay to show that the LORD upholds his moral order (vv. 4-9) through his wise and just king (vv. 11-15). This ideal portrait of the king points to one who far excels failed Solomon, namely, the King of kings and Lord of lords, Jesus Christ.

Notes:

[1] Udo Skladny, *Die aeltesten Spruchsammulungen in Israel* (Göttingen, Germany: Vandenhoeck & Ruprecht, 1962).

[2] William McKane, *Proverbs: A New Approach* (Philadelphia: Westminster Press, 1970).

[3] R. B. Y. Scott, "Proverbs, Ecclesiastes: Introduction, Translation and Notes," *Anchor Bible* (Garden City, N.Y.: Doubleday, 1965).

[4] Claus Westermann, "Weisheit im Sprichwort," in K. H. Bernhardt, ed., *Schalom: Studien zu Glaube und Geschichte Israels, A. Jepsen Festschrift*, Arbeiten zur Theologie 1/46 (Stuttgart, Germany: Calwer, 1971): 73–85.

[5] H. J. Hermisson, *Studien zur israelitischen Spruchweisheit* (WMANT 28; Neukirchen-Vluyn: Neukirchener, 1968).

[6] G. E. Bryce, "Another Wisdom 'Book' in Proverbs," *Journal of Biblical Literature* 91 (1972): 145–57.

[7] B. Kovacs, "Sociological-Structural Constraints upon Wisdom: The Spatial and Temporal Matrix of Proverbs 15:28–22:16" (Ph.D. diss., Vanderbilt; Ann Arbor, Mich.: University Microfilms International, 1978).

[8] R. N. Whybray, "Yahweh-Sayings and Their Contexts in Proverbs, 10:1-22,16," in *La Sagesse de l'Ancien Testament: [travaux presenté au Colloquim Biblicum Lovaniense XXIX]*, ed. Maurice Gilbert et al. (Louvain: Leuven University Press, 1979), pp. 153–65.

[9] R. C. Van Leeuwen, *Context and Meaning in Proverbs 25-27*, SBL Dissertation Series 96 (Atlanta, Ga.: Scholars Press, 1988; Ph.D. dissertation, University of St. Michael's College, 1984).

[10] Bruce V. Malchow, "A Manual for Future Monarchs," *Catholic Biblical Quarterly* 47 (1985): 238–45.

[11] Otto Ploeger, *Sprueche Salomos (Proverbia)* (*Biblischer Kommentar Altes Testament* 17/5; Neukirchen-Vluyn: Neukirchener Verlag, 1984).

[12] Arndt Meinhold, *Die Sprueche: Teil 1, Sprueche Kapitel, 1–15,* Zuercher Bibelkommentare, ed. Hans Heinrich Schmid, Siegfried Schulz and Hans Weder (Zürich: Theologischer Verlag, 1991).

[13] Duane A. Garrett, *Proverbs, Ecclesiastes, Song of Songs,* New American Commentary 14, ed. E. Ray Clendenen et al. (Nashville, Tenn.: Broadman Press, 1993).

[14] For an accredited defense and definition of Solomonic authorship of Proverbs 1:1–24:34 see K. A. Kitchen, "Proverbs and Wisdom Books of the Ancient Near East: The Factual History of a Literary Form," *Tyndale Bulletin* 28 (1977): 69–114.

[15] The reading of the Septuagint (LXX), *theōrōn ophthalmos kala,* "the eye that sees well," suggests to D. Winton Thomas ("Textual and Philological Notes on Some Passages in the Book of Proverbs," in *Wisdom in Israel and in the Ancient Near East: Presented to Harold Henry Rowley,* Supplements to *Vetus Testamentum* [Leiden, Netherlands: E. J. Brill, 1969], pp. 286–87) the

reading *mar'eh-'enayim*, not *me'or 'enayim* of the Masoretic text (MT). He interprets the retroverted reading to mean "the pleasure of looking at" (see Eccles 6:9). Since the parallel "good tidings" requires something seen and enjoyed, not the looking at something with pleasure, he repoints the form as a *hophal* participle, *mor'eh*, obtaining the rendering of the whole verse: "a fine sight cheers the mind as good tidings make the bones fat." Thomas, however, neither evaluates the paraphrastic nature of the LXX nor explains from a text critical viewpoint how the MT reading arose. The LXX may be yet another interpretation of the unique MT.

16 Literally, "makes the bone fat."

17 Literally, "correction of life," a genitive of effect (Bruce K. Waltke and M. O'Connor, *An Introduction to Biblical Hebrew Syntax* [Winona Lake, Ind.: Eisenbrauns, 1990] [hereafter WOC], paragraph [hereafter not noted] 9.5.2c).

18 Or "himself." Traditionally, "his soul." *Nephes* essentially means "passionate vitality" (see Bruce Waltke, *Theological Word Book of the Old Testament,* ed. R. Laird Harris, Gleason L. Archer Jr. and Bruce K. Waltke [hereafter *TWOT*] (Chicago: Moody Press, 1980), 2:587–91).

19 Literally, "heart." The daghesh in *leb* shows the close connection with the preceding word (cf. WOC 1.5.4e). The LXX reads *agapai psychēn autou,* "loves himself," to create a suitable antithesis to "hate himself" (see 19:8).

20 The emendation of Perles (cited by Ploeger, *Sprueche,* p. 179) and of Humbert (cited by Berend Gemser, *Sprueche Salomos in Handbuch zu Alten Testament* [Tübingen, Germany: J. C. B. Mohr/Paul Siebeck, 1963], p. 69) and accepted by J. Fichtner in *Biblia Hebraica Stuttgartensia* (Stuttgart, Germany: Deutsche Bibelgesellschaft, 1984; hereafter BHS), *musad* "is the foundation [of wisdom]" should be rejected because it destroys the catchword connection with verse 32 (see exposition).

21 *Hochma* is probably a genitive of inalienable possession (i.e., something intrinsically proper to it) (WOC 9.5.1h).

22 The preposition entails a verb of motion (WOC 11.4.3d).

23 The LXX *kai archē doxēs apokrithēsetai autei,* "and the highest honor will correspond with it," may have pointed *'nwh* as *'anūhā* (Ant. J. Baumgartner, *Étude critique sur l'étate du texte du Livre des Proverbes* (Leipzig: Imprimerie Orientale W. Drugulin, 1890), p. 151.

24 The original LXX lacks the first three verses, perhaps because of the poor state of its Vorlage.

25 Literally, "belonging to a human being are."

26 A genitive of instrument (WOC 9.5.1b, d).

27 Or, "and" (cf. KJV).

28 See note 8.

29 Also, a genitive of instrument, a metonymy for agent.

30 Genitive of authorship (WOC 9.5.1c).

31 *Zak* is singular to agree with collective *kol*. The adjective is derived from the root *zkk*, a biform of *zkh* (see KBL³ 258).

32 Literally "spirits/winds." Targum (Tg.) and Syriac (Syr.) probably read *'orhôt* (*'wrhyh*) and interpreted *tkn* to mean "direct," "order," "establish."

33 Syr., Tg., Vulgate (Vg.) read *gal,* "reveal/disclose," imperative *qal* of *glh,* not *gol,* imperative *qal* of *gll.* Against the versions note *glh* in *qal* never occurs with *'el.* Moreover, "a fatal objection to this emendation is the *scriptio plena* in Ps. 37:5 (*gwl*) . . . ; also the sense of Ps. 22:9" (William McKane, *Proverbs: A New Approach* (Philadelphia: Westminster Press, 1970), p. 497). Although McKane has many excellent comments, his new approach to Proverbs is essentially wrong.

34 The *waw* with the nonperfective after the imperative signifies purpose or result (WOC 39.2.2a).

35 Gnomic perfective (WOC 30.5.1c) in this gnomic literature, probably not "made" or "has

made."

[36] G. R. Driver (Review of M. Dahood, *Proverbs and Northwest Semitic Philology*, in *Journal of Semitic Studies* 10 [1965]: 113) argues *lamma'ᵃnēhú* is a mixed form, consisting of *lᵉma'ᵃnēhú* (preposition *lᵉma'an* + pronominal suffix), "for his own sake," and *lamma'ᵃneh* (preposition *l* + the noun *ma'ᵃneh*), "for a purpose/ answer." This is unlikely because *lema'aneh* is otherwise unattested, the antecedent *kōl* calls for a suffix (cf. McKane, p. 497), and the double determination (i.e., an article with a determined genitive [here a suffixed pronoun]) is unexceptional in West Semitic (Mitchell Dahood, *Proverbs and Northwest Semitic Philology* [Rome: Pontificium Institutum Biblicum, 1963], p. 36; WOC 13.6b, p. 157, n. 40; cf. *Gesenius' Hebrew Grammar*, as edited and enlarged by E. Kautsch and A. E. Cowley [Oxford: Clarendon Press, 1910], p. 127i). The article probably protects the term against the unique reading *lᵉma'ᵃnēhú* (so Vg. *propter semet ipsum;* "for himself" [KJV], see 15:24; i.e., for the LORD's own glory; to vindicate his name [2 Kings 19:34; 20:6; Is 43:25, 48:11]). Tg. and Syr. understood the expression to mean "to those who respond to [i.e., obey] him."

[37] Or, "to," parallel to "to its counterpart."

[38] Attributive genitive.

[39] With this verse the LXX closes its own series of proverbs.

[40] Literally, "high of heart." The absolute form is *gabēah*.

[41] Literally, "hand to hand;" the idiom thoroughly perplexed the ancient translators.

[42] LXX may have this verse after 15:27.

[43] Causal *b* (WOC 11.2.5e).

[44] *yᵉkuppar* is *pual* and perhaps resultative, "to make atoned," though a denominative function cannot be excluded, "to make a ransom" (WOC 24.4a). The verb in all its uses is never used for picturing an actual process but always with regard to the result attained (Ernst Jenni, *Das hebraeische Pi'el* [Zürich, 1968], p. 240).

[45] Temporal *b* with the infinitive construct.

[46] Genitive of agency.

[47] The Hebrew verb, "to accept favorably," can take a direct object or be transitive via *b*. The English idiom requires the preposition (WOC 10.2.1c).

[48] *Beth* of conmitantiae (WOC 11.2.5d).

[49] A positive comparative *min* (WOC 14.4d).

[50] Resultative *piel* (WOC 24.3).

[51] Two-place *hiphil* (WOC 27.2a,b).

[52] Genitive of inalienable possession.

[53] And, "against justice."

[54] An attributive genitive.

[55] A construct override construction with these two closely related nouns (WOC 9.3b). In that light there is no need to emend the text as in BHS or with Toy to omit "just" in verset a (i.e., first half of bi-cola). The unusual grammar, though not singular (*pace* Toy), mislead Jerome: "Weight and balances are judgments of the LORD," which ill-suits the parallel (Toy).

[56] Against Toy, who emends "LORD" to "king," Oesterley cites Amenemope 17: "The Ape sits by the balance, his heart is in the plummet; where is a god as great as Thoth, who invented these things and made them."

[57] Genitive of location.

[58] The infinitive construct functions as subject of the clause and takes "wickedness" as its object. The LXX, Tg. (see Healey) and Vg. agree in reading *'ōśēh* "the one who does wickedly," making clear that the wickedness of others, not the king himself, is in view. The Syr., however, reads "The kings who do wickedness are abominable," and the Zamora text of the Targum also independently interprets it as the king's own wickedness.

[59] Attributive genitive. There is no difference in meaning between feminine *ṣᵉdāqá* (v. 12) and masculine *sedeq*.

[60] Two MSS, LXX, Syr. and Tg. read "king," probably to harmonize with singular subject of verset b (i.e., second half of bi-cola). Vg. rightly retains plural, which links verses 12 and 13.

[61] The syntactic disagreement between the plural subject and singular verb is common in Hebrew poetry.

[62] For qal participle of *dbr* see WOC, p. 410, n. 39. The LXX *logous de* (Heb. *dᵉbārîm*) and Syr. *wmlt'* (*udᵉbar*) pointed the form as a noun, not a participle. This facilitating reading conforms better with *yᵉsārîm*, which normally means "upright people" (so Tg. and Syr., not LXX). Vg. reads with MT.

[63] The adjective used as a substantive (8:6; Dan. 11:10; see BDB, p. 449 entry 3c). The substantive form *mêphārîm* is found in four medieval codexes, probably to prevent the normal meaning "upright people."

[64] Genitive of inalienable possession.

[65] Form is dual.

[66] Spatial *b* (WOC 11.2.5b).

[67] The LXX reads *huios* for Heb. *ben*.

[68] An alternative construct form (cf. Is 18:44 (KBL³ 730).

[69] Genitive of species (WOC 9.5.3g). Tg. uniquely reads "in a clear sky."

[70] Raymond Van Leeuwen, "Wealth and Poverty: System and Contradiction in Proverbs," *Hebrew Studies* 33 (1992): 29.

[71] Aalen, *Theological Dictionary of the Old Testament*, edited by G. Johannes Botterweck and Helmer Ringgren (hereafter *TDOT*) (Grand Rapids, Mich.: Eerdmans, 1974), 1:158.

[72] Yehdah Ratzhavi, "Clarification of the Blessing Formula in the Lachish Letters," *Beth Mikra* 33 (1987/1988): 454–55 (Hebrew).

[73] Crawford H. Toy, *Critical and Exegetical Commentary on the Book of Proverbs* (Edinburgh: T. & T. Clark, 1977), p. 317.

[74] William Cosser, "The Meaning of 'Life' (*Ḥayyîm*) in Proverbs, Job and Ecclesiastes," *Glasgow University Oriental Society Transactions*, 15 (1955): 51–52.

[75] Causse, *Les disperses d'Israel*, p. 115, cited by Cosser, p. 52.

[76] J. Gerald Janzen, "The Root *prʿ* in Judges v. 2 and Deuteronomy xxxii 42," *Vetus Testamentum* 39 (1989): 405. He errs in following Gerhard's von Rad identification of wisdom as the created order. This common error among academics has been refuted by Elizabeth Faith Huwiler, "Control of Reality in Israelite Wisdom" (Ph.D. diss., Duke University, 1988), especially pp. 68–69.

[77] Ibid., p. 406.

[78] H. Wildberger, *Theologische Handwoerter Buch zum Alten Testament* (hereafter *THAT*) (München: Chr. Kaiser Verlag; Zürich: Theologischer Verlag, 1971), 1:882.

[79] Bruce K. Waltke, "The Fear of the LORD: The Foundation for a Relationship with God," in J. I. Packer and Loren Wilkinson, eds., *Alive to God: Studies in Spirituality Presented to James Houston* (Downers Grove, Ill.: InterVarsity Press, 1992), pp. 17–33.

[80] Helmer Ringgren und Walther Zimmerli, *Sprueche/Prediger* (Göttingen, Germany: Vandenhoeck & Ruprecht, 1962), p. 68.

[81] Franz Delitzsch, *Biblical Commentary on the Proverbs of Solomon*, trans. M. G. Easton (Grand Rapids, Mich.: Eerdmans, 1970), 1:334.

[82] Meinhold, *Sprueche*, p. 265.

[83] Cf. Kenneth T. Aitken, *Proverbs* (Philadelphia: Westminster Press, 1986), p. 247.

[84] *TWOT*, 2:970.

85 See James B. Pritchard, *The Ancient Near East in Pictures Relating to the Old Testament,* 2nd ed. with supplement (Princeton, N.J.: Princeton University Press, 1969), plate 639, p. 210.

86 *TDOT,* 5:230.

87 Ibid., p. 233.

7

Grace and Truth:
The Progress of
the Argument of
the Prologue of
John's Gospel

William J. Dumbrell

IT IS A VERY GREAT PLEASURE TO BE ABLE BY THIS essay to honor the ministry of Jim Packer, who has taught us all over the years the reality of "knowing God."

❖ ❖ ❖

John 1:1-18 is conventionally called the Gospel's Prologue, or in traditional terms, the summary of the content of the drama to follow, and the verses function in exactly this way, conveying the concerns of the gospel and indicating its emphasis. Though frequently scholarship has evaluated the Prologue independently of the Gospel, this is clearly hermeneutically incorrect. The Gospel of John concerns the intrusion into an implacably hostile arena of the Son of God and the conflict which ensued as Jesus the divine agent effected the divine intention to repair the breach between heaven and earth. Essential to the purpose of the Gospel is the divine origin of the Son. The Prologue argues for this in a movement beginning in verse 1 and culminating in verse 18.

The literary form of the Prologue to St. John's Gospel is important in the establishing of emphasis and purpose. The Prologue is a ring composition throwing verses 11-13 into prominence by its chiastic structure,[1] but with the inclusio formed by verses 1-2 and 18, placing the main emphasis upon the beginning and end of the material.[2] Of the whole, verses 1-2 and 18 show us Jesus in his relationship to God, which enables him to save; verses 3 and 17 indicate his role in the economy of salvation; verses 4-5 and 16 show the participation of humanity in the salvation revealed in Christ; verses 6-8 and 15 the testimony of the forerunner; verses 9-10 and 14 the response to the saving presence of Christ negatively and positively treated; verses 11, 12, 13 the significance of the Incarnation as the centerpiece of the Prologue.[3] The total movement of the Prologue is in two stages: firstly, verses 1-13, where we move from preexistence to the Incarnation and its results, and then a further movement from verses 14-18, which is designed to underscore the theological significance of the historical ministry of Jesus of Nazareth. My aim will be to suggest that the climax of the Prologue, as the ring construction indicates, is verse 18, in which the vital nature of the contrast between Mosaic and the Advent era, under discussion in verses 16-17, is underscored.

A major question of debate is the interpretation of verses 1-2 and their relationship to verse 18. It is often suggested that the anarthrous *theos* at John 1:1 should be translated "divine" (a view first advanced by Origen) and that the absence of the article concentrates attention on the nature of the Logos and not on his person and thus *theos* was used with qualitative force. Omission of the article is frequently explained by E. C. Colwell's rule, but the application of the rule is contested. The presence or the absence of the article in predicate nouns is not a matter of definiteness or indefiniteness but of usual word order, since definite predicate nouns as a rule in Greek are anarthrous.[4]

Apart from the force and translation of the corresponding 1:18, where following the major witnesses and reading *monogenēs theos,* in view of John 20:28 it is overwhelmingly probable that John 1:1 describes Jesus as God, with John 20:28 thus serving as a theological inclusion before the appendix of John 21. The position of anarthrous *theos* before the copula in verse 1c indicates that *theos* is the predicate in the neat way that the language has of making this distinction, and its anarthrous form further testifies to the general identity between the Logos and God but not their equation.[5] So far as John 1:18 is concerned the true text is probably the P66 and P75 reading

"monogenēs theos" (the P75 reading is *"ho monogenēs theos"*), as is recognized by many of the modern versions.[6] Moreover in John 20:28
Jesus unquestionably is being described as God, though Theodore of
Mopsuestia, in a way that recognized some modern sectarian differences, saw this only as an exclamation of gratitude to God! With
John 20:28 forming a virtual inclusio with John 1:1, a statement of
Jesus' deity occurs at the beginning of the Gospel, again, at the point
of transition from the Prologue to the earthly ministry, 1:18, and in
the final statement of faith which sums up all that Jesus was, 20:28.

In John 1:1 we have first the assertion of the preexistent *logos,*
where in the third clause of verse 1 the climax is reached and the Logos is God. The thought of the second clause moves on to the relationship in proximity of God and the Logos. It is clear, moreover,
that the Logos motif is brought in here to describe Jesus, the subject
of the Prologue, not that Jesus is being made to fit a preexisting
motif. The Logos acts as a mediator at creation (1:3), and the Prologue goes on to present Genesis 1–2 as recaptured in the Incarnation. He reveals God to man (1:8) and can for this reason be called
the light (1:5, 9). He mediates the divine gifts of life to man (v. 4),
the right to become the child of God (v. 12), grace (v. 16) and
knowledge about God (v. 18).

When we ask why Logos was used to describe the preexistence
relationship of the Son to the Father and not Sophia or Torah, two
reasons suggest themselves. First, we may look at the limitations of
the personifications of Wisdom and Torah arrived at by the Jewish
background to the New Testament. The wisdom background of the
first two sentences of John 1:1 is agreed, since Wisdom (Prov 8:23
JB) lays claim to preexistence: "From everlasting I was firmly set,
from the beginning, before the earth came into being." Claim is also
laid by Wisdom as well to proximity to God (Prov 8:30 JB): "I was
by his [God's] side, a master craftsman, delighting him day by day,
ever at play in his presence." Wisdom may also be described as "a
pure emanation of the glory of the Almighty. . . . She is a reflection
of the eternal light, untarnished mirror of God's active power, image
of his goodness" (Wisdom 7:25 JB). The proximity of Wisdom to
God is also claimed as it is in the second sentence for Logos (Prov
8:30; Wisdom 9:4; Sir 1:1). But there is no direct parallel in the wisdom literature to verse 1c that the Logos was God. The same high
claims were made for Torah, but of neither could it be said that Wisdom or Torah was God as it is in the third sentence, the climax of the
first two verses, of the Logos as God. Nor could it be said that Wis-

dom and Torah were uncreated, for indeed of Wisdom it is said in Proverbs 8:22-23 that she is the first of God's creations, who then becomes the companion of God. Wisdom may have existed in the heavens before the world was formed and shared the responsibility for the orderly character of creation, but she is still a creature, a personification in the Old Testament of God acting wisely. But the Logos is clearly a person, a member of the Godhead, not a personified principle as in the case of Wisdom and Torah.

Second, the emphasis in the Prologue is upon the revelation of God brought by Jesus. It is argued that the Logos motive commended itself as crossing national boundaries. It was used as a philosophical term in Greek thought as early as Heraclitus. Logos was the eternal principle of order in the universe in Stoicism, while in Philo Logos was a technical term designating, among other things, the Logos as the mediator between God and the world.[7] But when all that is said and those connections are made, Logos as a principle of order does not explain the Prologue use, though the possible point of contact with current thought would obviously have been a plus.

The consensus, however, is that any consideration of the Logos thought takes us back to the *dᵉbar Yahweh,* the word of God in the Old Testament, which enshrined God in his word. The Hebrew word *dābār* could refer to an active force, the dynamic creative power of God (Is 55:11; Ps 33:8; Gen 1:3). But it is important to note that the Word in the Old Testament was both creative and revelatory. Philo himself in his interpretation of Genesis 1:3 moves from the uttered word of God to the concept of the Logos.[8] It is in this sense of God immanent in his word that the Logos motif ties together the notion of preexistence and revelation.

Proceeding with the text, it is commonly recognized that *en archē* in John 1:1-2 renders *bᵉrē'šît* in Genesis 1:1 as in the LXX. The term *theos* in John 1:1-2 alludes also to Genesis 1:1-2. The central terms *phōs* and *skotia* in John 1:4-5 are taken from Genesis 1:2-5 ('*ōr* and *ḥōšek*). These words from Genesis 1:1-5 in John 1:1-5 are then interpreted by paraphrasing expansions. It seems that some of the words in 1:1-5 are thus interpretive replacements for words and phrases in Genesis 1:1-5 and that the term *ho logos* looks like the replacement for *eipein ho theos* LXX in Genesis 1:3, since the identification of *logos* and light in John 1:9 seems to draw on Genesis 1:3. The words "created the heavens and the earth" (NRSV) in Genesis 1:1 seem to be replaced by a formula in John 1:3 for creation: "all things came into being through him, and without him not one thing came into being"

(NRSV). Genesis 1:1-5, which completes the first day of creation, is reflected in John 1:1-5, which is a basic exposition of Genesis 1:1-5, throwing into prominence the association of the *logos* with creation in the beginning.[9]

Verse 4 then logically follows to document the appropriateness of the Logos as later incarnate, as John 1:4 goes behind the coming of light in Jesus (v. 9) to present a cosmic dimension of what becomes later a revelation to Israel. The verse deals with the ideas of life and light in relation to Logos and humankind in historical experience from creation to the Incarnation. The perspective is broader than being a reference to redemptive history, but it is relevant in this connection to mention that persons in biblical history saw the Logos/ Christ prior to his Incarnation.[10] "Abraham rejoiced that he would see my day" (Jn 8:56 NRSV), the vision of Isaiah 6 is interpreted as a vision of the preexistent Logos (Jn 12:41), while John 5:37b perhaps refers to Sinai, and again, to a vision of the Logos.

The thought of verse 5 also follows in logical progression, with the Logos in his preincarnate ministry (v. 5) as the revealer of God to humankind. He can, for this reason, be called the light (1:5, 9), but the sorry witness of history had been the general rejection of light. So the powerful presence in the world of the Logos as light had not been suppressed, supplanted or overcome.[11] The aorist itself of "overcome" is probably constantive and thus summarizingly referring to the general attitude of humankind up to John's day, or it may be temporal and thus refer to the Incarnation or the Fall. This continuation of this activity of divine illumination is stressed by the present tense of *phanei*.

In verses 6-8 advance preparations for the Incarnation are set in train as the light, *to phōs*, a common figure biblically for divine revelation, of verses 4-5 is understood from the viewpoint of the appearance of Jesus of Nazareth. Verses 6-8 provide for John's witness to Israel of the reality of the Incarnation and its significance while the continuing emphasis upon the concept of light that it continued to shine in darkness (v. 5), provides ground for further reflection in v. 9 of the developed role of the Logos in general revelation. As M. D. Hooker points out, the John the Baptist material (verses 6-8, 15) does not disturb its contexts but carries the thought forward.

The translation of verse 9 is difficult and much debated. The participle *erchomenon* is best, in the flow of thought in the Prologue, taken as referring back to the predicate *anthrōpon* (with the NIV). The participle without the article thus expresses what happens simultaneously with the verb. The translation is thus: "He (Logos) was the true light, which enlightens every human being as he enters the world." The assertion of the universal power of the Logos to give light and life to all (v. 4) provides the warrant for this verse. If taken with the imperfect verb, the participle *erchomenon* presents a periphrastic imperfect and must then be regarded as a particular comment upon John 1:6-8 and refer to the Incarnation.

The function of verse 9 not only seems to be to provide comment on verses 6-8 but also to provide comment of a more general character, and thus to link up with verses 1-5 and to summarize them, rather than being limited to the Incarnation itself. It is stressed in 1:9 as in verse 4 that John as the primordial light/Logos had a universal importance and a universal role which was particularly to be seen in the Incarnation. He enlightens every human being and provides the point of contact for the message of salvation. "The parallel between creation and redemption becomes totally clear. What the Logos should have been for humans according to the plan of creation, he became in fact for believers in the historical mission."[12] The cosmic dimension of the background to the Incarnation, together with the fact of the Incarnation, are thus bound together in verse 9. The point being made is that the general availability of truth for all on this level of revelation throws into clear relief the enormity of the rejection of the Logos in verses 10-11. This rejection was by those to whom, in addition to this general illumination, the oracles of God were committed!

The thought model for this coming of light seems to be provided by the frequent association of law with light in Judaism. Torah is that which gives light in Jewish sources. Torah is also life, and both of these concepts are connected with Logos. At the law giving on Sinai, Moses brought the primordial light down from heaven,[13] and further background is provided by functions ascribed in Jewish thought to Wisdom and Torah.[14] In the rabbinic commentary *Bereshith Rabbah* (*Genesis Rabbah* 3:3), *dābār* is interpreted as light, as God's spoken word. As the law giving of Moses was for all humans, so in John the light shines for every human when it comes. Likewise the coming of Torah made it possible for Israel and the world to walk in the light.[15] Wisdom of Solomon 18:4 remarks that the law's light was to be given to the world.

In John 1:10-11 it is said that the Logos came to his own property. He came to the world which he had created. The Greek word *kosmos* (world) is most often construed negatively in the Gospel of John as the organized world in opposition to Jesus, yet it is also the sphere of Jesus' saving ministry. The relationship of the Logos to the world was that of ownership, even prior to the Incarnation. But the Creator and owner who came was not received (v. 10). In John 1:3 it was stated that "all things came into being through the Logos." This is repeated in verse 10: the cosmos came into being through him. This is seen as a background for the cosmos's representative rejection of him through whom it came into being. In verse 11 the historical appearance of Jesus is stated: "He came to what was his own [*ta idia*] and his own people [*hoi idioi*] did not accept him." The debate whether *hoi idioi* refers to the world at large or to Israel seems to miss the point.[16] Israel is rather to be seen as the center of the world and therefore represents the world. A motif from the Wisdom tradition is reflected here, as stated in Enoch 40:1-2: "Wisdom went out in order to dwell among the sons of men, but did not find a dwelling; Wisdom returned to her place and took her seat in the midst of the angels."[17]

While the nation as a whole, his own, had rejected him, there had been a moderately favorable response (v. 12). Some within Israel, where his ministry had been confined, had received him, but their moderate number seems indicated by the "to all who received him" of verse 12. The fact that John reflects upon the totality of the ministry of Jesus is indicated by the aorist of "received" of verse 12. The new community to which John is referring came into being during the development of the Gospel. It is a plausible working hypothesis that the remainder of the Prologue will tell us how this community came about and what was its nature. But equally clearly the nation, the former sons of God (Ex 4:22; Is 1:2) who rejected Jesus, were themselves rejected (Jn 12:37-43), and the relationship of sonship formerly borne by all Israel has now been transferred to the believers[18] as restored or remnant Israel, the purpose of the Gospel elaborated at 20:31.

Verse 13 functions to rule out any human cooperation in the supernatural rebirth of faith to which verses 12-13 refer. All natural analogies are ruled out. Members of the new community were born not from "bloods," not by the participation of the parents in conception, not of the will of the flesh, not by natural propagation, not by the will of man, the impulse of the husband in the married relationship, not by any particular or general human decision, but from God. Their birth was incarnational and not by human generation.

The *kai* of verse 14 links the second half of the argument from verses 14-18 with the previous 1-13. The progression of the tripartite verse 14 is from preexistence to proximity to God to deity itself. Wisdom motives are in the first two elements but not in the third. In verse 1 the use of *logos* bore upon the deity of the Logos; in verse 14 it is his Incarnation which is in view. The repetition of the term *logos* provides the calculated linkage and thus by its restatement indicates to us the theological significance of the Incarnation. The Logos, pre-existent before creation, and the Logos' epiphany as Jesus the Son, is presented in a way that corresponds to the thought model applied to the Torah, that it existed before creation and was revealed at Sinai. The relation between Logos and Torah will be the subject of verse 17 and will be the point to which the argument is moving, as the very heavy allusions to the context of Exodus 32–34 will indicate.

When it is said that the word became "flesh" (Greek *sarx*), a word that has been rejected as having any part in the impulse to bring about the Incarnation of the Word (v. 13), it means that there is a unity between, on the one hand, the One who was before creation and through whom all things came into being and, on the other hand, all humanity—achieved in the woman-born historical person Jesus of Nazareth. A particular point is being made by the use of *sarx* which would have been missed by the more general *anthrōpos*. The Logos at the Incarnation took on humanity in all its weakness and frailty. John is not saying more here, as Paul often does, that the *sarx* is also the vehicle of humanity broken by the Fall. *Sarx* in the Johannine use as here is a neutral term, but a term which encapsulates all the human limitations as bound by time and transitoriness.

"Became" (v. 14) indicates the reality of the Incarnation since it provides and presupposes background. The *egeneto* states the crude, cold fact of the Incarnation, but on the other hand, it is assumed by the verb that the Logos maintained his identity in the new vehicle, since it was the Logos who became flesh and who tabernacled, as subject. The Logos was not thus absorbed by the *sarx,* but directed it, expressed himself through it, triumphed over its limitations and finally carried humanity to the right hand of God. As has been pointed out, we are on the verge of the doctrine of the two natures here. The Logos became flesh without sacrificing his essential divine nature, since his continuing reflection of that is intended by "we beheld his glory" as a statement of the new community's reaction, while in the word *flesh* the docetic assertions, apparent in the Asia of St. John's time of writing that the Logos descended upon a human but left him before the crucifixion to return to a spirit existence, are also rebutted. It was his incarnate existence now in Israel which re-called God's indwelling of his people through the symbols of the exodus. With this statement the Prologue reaches a climax whose content is virtually represented in verse 18, and the Gospel thereafter is an exposition of 1:14.

Reference is also made within verse 14 to the "tabernacling of the word,"[19] and clearly in the mind of John "dwelt among us" lays claim for Jesus to have exercised in his ministry a parallel function to that of the tabernacle/temple in the history of Israel. In this second part of the Prologue the mind of St. John is moving, with tabernacle, name, glory, giving of the law, grace and truth, in Exodus 32–34 thought forms, and we remind ourselves that material relating to the erection of the tabernacle and its ministry amounts to over one-third of the material in the book of Exodus. The theology of the book of Exodus is at pains to point out that the tabernacle was a symbol of God's ru-lership over and presence within Israel. The goal of the exodus was related to the effective worship of Yahweh, which must be begun as soon as the immediate destination of the exodus had been reached, namely Mount Sinai, the mountain of God, the mountain of God's appearance to Moses in Exodus 3:1.

Just as soon as the covenant providing for Yahweh's kingship over Israel had been concluded and Israel had accepted it, the instructions leading to the construction of the tabernacle had been given by God to Moses. By the requirement of the tabernacle's building to be in conformity to the pattern revealed on the mountain itself (Ex 25:9), the ancient Near Eastern concept of the deity as the true builder of the temple and the temple[20] as the earthly palace of the heavenly king and thus the symbol of the final authority of the deity over the city state/empire concerned, was being expressed in Israel. At a later stage in Israel's temple theology, the temple at Jerusalem, the replacement for the tabernacle, becomes the point of reference for the world in the last days, the center from which Yahweh's world rule would ema-nate not only for Israel but for the Gentile nations who would come in, in pilgrimage, to derive their framework for national control from the Torah to go forth from Jerusalem. Not only thus was the temple the highest point of political authority in Israel as the divine palace, but it was also the center to which the world would be referred for revelation needed for the regulation of world society. Jesus is, by al-lusion to the Exodus account which we have in verse 14, to be the parallel to this theological apparatus of the Old Testament. It be-comes very soon evident in John's Gospel, for which the Prologue is a theological summary, that Jesus is the new and replacement temple (2:19-22) of the new age, the structure to succeed and compound in his person all Jewish institutions, and he is also the point of divine reference for Israel and the world. Jesus will, in the course of his ministry, effectively destroy the old apparatus and in Jerusalem by his cross and resurrection erect the new tent.

The Exodus 33–34 notes of 1:14 are confirmed in "we have seen his glory" (NRSV), for the Prologue will draw, as the presentation continues, a comparison between Jesus and Moses to make clear the absolute superiority of Jesus in the comparison. The mention of glory is now logical, since glory and tent were associated in the exodus in the appearance of the heavy dark cloud (the Hebrew *kāḇóḏ*) which appeared first to Israel in Exodus 16:10, and which thereafter was linked to the exodus guidance and to the tabernacle (Ex 40:34-38) and the temple (1 Kings 8:11). But "we beheld his glory" has a further particular contribution to make to the context. The reader, by the Exodus overtones of the phrase, is invited to compare, in a Gospel where Jesus' superiority to Moses is so often emphasized, the experience of those who received Jesus and saw his glory with the experience of the greatest Israelite of the Old Testament, Moses, whose request to see the glory of God was denied.

After the grievous national sin of the construction of the golden calf (Ex 32), God refused to go with Israel to Canaan and gave Israel over to superintendence by an angel (Ex 33:2). The intercession of Moses occurs only after his special relationship with God is given attention (33:7-11). The promise given to Israel as a whole in Exodus 3:14 is now restricted to Moses alone (33:14). In view of the heavy burden of responsibility laid upon him, Moses now requests a vision of the divine essence, the divine glory (33:18), in a theophany to correspond to what all Israel had received at the enactment of the covenant and at the giving of the Ten Commandments (chaps. 19–20). Moses' request is denied (cf. 33:19) since no man, not even Moses, can see God and live (33:20). But Moses is recessed in a cleft in the rock so that when the divine glory passes by he will be protected (33:22). However, he had received the name (33:19; cf. Jn 1:12) and with this the right to call upon God in worship as Israel's representative and as, virtually, its replacement at this stage. The name given for access was a revelation of the general character of God to whom prayer and worship might be directed, but the glory of God, a knowledge of the inner essence of God, the ability to see God in person, was never granted in the Old Testament.

John makes it clear that what the community saw of Jesus was an intimate picture of the divine nature, for the general statement "we beheld his glory" is further filled out and elaborated by the detail that this was the glory as[21] of the unique[22] Son of the Father, one bearing the entire essence of the Father and coming directly[23] from his presence, and whom to see is to see the Father. The community had looked directly into the face of deity and had seen the fullness of his being and character as John reflects upon the reality of Jesus' ministry. But this also meant that they had encountered the tangible reality which undergirded the covenant relationship with Israel and provided for its continuance. John is not thinking of the epic points in the Gospel where the inner nature of Jesus could have been seen as reflecting the essence of the divine nature, nor even of the crucifixion itself which commonly in John is the time when Jesus is glorified, nor the signs done by Jesus in his public ministry (cf. 2:11). He is thinking of the ongoing contract which the ministry of Christ, though especially his suffering, prompted (cf. Jn 12:23-24). *Plērēs,* "full," the indeclinable adjective, probably refers to Logos, as the major statement of the verse, not to "glory," since glory is the reflection of the Logos, though *doxa,* the new thought in the verse, binds, by its repetition, both halves of the verse together. Since Logos resumes the presentation of John 1:1-5, not it but the manner of the indwelling, as the indwelling of the Logos among "us," i.e. Israel, is the important new point being conveyed by the verse, and such an indwelling was "full of grace and truth."

Grace and truth may refer to the *ḥesed wᵉᵉmeṯ* (loyal love and truth) of Exodus 34:6, a reference to the divine revelation given by God himself at the second giving of the covenant to Israel.[24] But on the other hand, it could refer to the communication of the divine revelation to Moses, grace found by Moses in God's sight in Exodus 33:12, 13, 16 and 17, and to Moses as the receptor of grace and mercy in Exodus 33:19.[25] Since *charis* is not picked up in the body of the Gospel as a Johannine item, perhaps because of its Pauline specialization, the use of it here is designed to direct us to the Exodus Old Testament context.

Clearly the accent, in the combination of grace and truth, is on grace since grace alone is resumed in verse 16. Ignace de la Potteries has argued for grace and truth as a hendiadys with the meaning of the gift of truth or the gift of revelation,[26] but the thought of the passage moves in a different direction to his proposals. The implication of verse 14 is that we are dealing with the content of revelation rather than the fact of revelation,[27] which makes a hendiadys less probable. As A. T. Hanson points out, de la Potteries' suggestion fails to do justice to the entire context of John 1:14-18—particularly, we might add, to verse 18.

The human witness to the preexistence of the Incarnate Word is then appropriately noted in verse 15 before a further major advance in the argument is offered in verse 16, which contrary to a recent spirited advocacy[28] is from John and not from the Baptist. So the assertion in verse 14 that the unique Son was full of grace and truth is confirmed by the community experience (v. 16). To have received of the fullness of his deity[29] as the community of faith had, and grace for grace (*charin anti charitos*), was, in view of the use of *lambanō* ("receive" in v. 12), to have received sonship. We are also directed by the term to the description of the divine nature in the Old Testament as full of grace (Ps 5:7; cf. Ps 106:45; of mercy Ps 51:1; 69:16), which would carry the implication that Jesus as full of grace (and truth) would be the bearer of the divine nature.

A number of meanings have been suggested for the phrase *charin anti charitos* in verse 16. D. A. Carson surveys options[30] and finds that the most popular modern interpretation is that *anti* here means "upon" or "in addition to,"[31] and hence the rendering "grace upon grace" (NEB, RSV) and "one blessing after another" (GNB, NIV). Carson himself argues that the most convincing interpretation is that which takes *anti* in its most common form as "instead of." Carson (with others) contends that the matter at issue in *anti* is replacement of the Mosaic law by the grace and truth coming through Jesus Christ. C. K. Barrett, however, suggests that grace did not come by Moses[32] and thus we cannot speak of the grace of the Gospel replacing the grace of the law. But this is a misunderstanding of the nature of the Old Testament, where salvation came to Israel in a context of grace, and the law was the interpretation of the nature of the life required within the covenant to maintain the relationship. J. S. King[33] suggests that the options reduce themselves to three: (a) replacement: love (in the New Covenant) in place of love (in the Sinai Covenant); (b) accumulation: grace upon grace; and (c) correspondence: grace for grace. The most natural choice seems to be a combination of (a) and (b), namely that as against the great movement in grace to Israel at Sinai, divine grace climaxed in this revelation of the Son.[34]

But John is drawing further upon the extensive experience of the Christian church. The Mosaic covenant and its interpretation by the

Torah, its amplification by Torah, is rightly seen as a movement of great grace, a gracious gift from God, but it is now replaced by the greatest gift, the grace and truth embodied in the new revelation of Jesus Messiah. Carson[35] makes the further point that S. Pancaro's position on references to law as depreciatory in John[36] cannot be sustained for the contexts such as "your law" (8:17; 10:34) which are simply an indication by Jesus in the contexts of the sharing of common ground. Carson notes, as others also suggest, that the law cannot be replaced since Scripture cannot be broken (10:34).[37]

True, with the death of Jesus, as Paul argues in Galatians 3, the Mosaic covenant ended as a special Jewish dispensation which had had significance up to the coming of Jesus, but to say that the Mosaic covenant has ended does not necessarily mean that the components with it fall into desuetude. Indeed, it can be fairly argued that the elements of the Ten Commandments as coming into force with creation are all in place prior to Sinai and that Sinai was not the initial delivery of the law, obedience to which is generally demanded, but its articulation as part of the covenant apparatus with which Israel is then bound.

The question of the particular circumstances under which the law was first delivered is an important issue here. The law, the Torah, given within covenant conclusion at Sinai, is the basis for the comparison which is being made with the new revelation of Jesus himself. Here we need to remember the details of this giving of the law. In verse 17 Moses is presented as a mediator "through" whom the law was given. Law, though a divine entity (*edothē*), actually came by Moses. The grace of Jesus, however, came to Israel unmediated. And we must ask, in what sense was the divine law given "through" Moses? Certainly not in the initial delivery of the law in Exodus 20. True, the divine theophany singled Moses out at the first delivery of the law, but the people were to hear when God spoke with Moses (Ex 19:9). The whole point of the first delivery of the covenant regulations in Exodus 20 was their immediacy and thus the individual responsibility to covenant under which the Israelites were placed as a consequence. While the case law (Ex 21–23) was mediated through Moses, this was clearly because of its lesser and derivative character. It is only after, and as a result of, the national sin of the golden calf that Moses becomes not only the mediator with God for Israel of the Torah but also the covenant carrier when the promise given to Israel at Exodus 3:14-15 is transferred to him in Exodus 33:14.

The distinction between Moses and Israel was then firmly established by the incident of the shining face of Moses in Exodus 34:29-35. In this passage Moses, with unveiled face, stands before Yahweh on the mountain and receives for Israel the renewal of the covenant on two new tablets. From the access which Moses enjoys in speaking with Yahweh, his face shines. Israel, as a result, is afraid to speak to Moses. Moses reassures them and addresses them with the details of the second covenant conclusion. When Moses had finished communicating the details of the revelation, he veiled his face, apparently as a measure of the distance that was now set between him and Israel on the matter of divine access. Israel was never thereafter in the Old Testament to obtain the direct reality of divine communication which had occurred for them in Exodus 19–20. The spiritual atrophy of Israel between Exodus 20 and Exodus 34 is thereafter in the Old Testament witnessed by the ongoing fact of mediation at the priestly and prophetic levels, a mediation which is finally and divinely given up at the Incarnation. So by reference to the incident of the giving of the law through Moses, where the *dia* underlines the mediatory role of Israel's Old Testament experience, the reception of the Torah within the framework of a broken, and yet renewed, covenant is being referred to. To these regulations and expectations the nation was never able to rise.

Thus, in verse 17, which explains verse 16, we do have a contrast. But it is not a contrast between law and grace, but rather between the significance of one revelation and another. The grace of God in the giving of the law after the national fracture of the covenant was indeed gracious and this is expatiated upon personally in God's dealings with Moses in Exodus 33:12-23 and in the context of Exodus 34:1-10. But as unexpected and unanticipated as that had been, and despite the great benevolence of God in forgoing extreme national punishment of Israel—and instead meeting them at the urgent point of their national need—the Exodus context by its provision for mediated experience for Israel then and thereafter provided no comparison with what God had now done in the issue of grace and truth.

The phrase "grace and truth" speaks for an immeasurably greater step taken in the history of religious experience, a new advance in divine revelation which far exceeds what was perhaps the greatest moment of Israel's national experience. The final granting of the Sinai covenant after the virtual national rejection of Israel by Yahweh was entirely a moment of grace, but it was, by its mediatory character, against the direct revelation of Exodus 20, a revelation which set the conditions for what was to be for the nation only an indirect knowledge of the deity throughout the Old Testament through constantly appointed mediators.

The Prologue rises to a crescendo with the incarnational response in verse 18 to verse 1. In terms of textual probability the better attested reading of *monogenēs theos* is to be adopted over *monogenēs hyios* in verse 18.[38] The flow of the Prologue, particularly in verses 14-17, encourages us to see verse 18 as the explanation of verse 17, as a result of which we come to the real meaning of what is grace and truth, and to the point of the entire Prologue itself. We now see the grace and truth of the final revelation directly, in the flesh, as verse 18 introduces what is to follow in the Gospel. The stark truth of the Incarnation was that in Jesus of Nazareth deity could be, and was, visibly encountered. In the ordinary situations of Palestinian life, in the tensions of a messianic ministry, in the series of resolute actions which took Jesus to the cross, the unveiled majesty of God was to be seen. John ends the Prologue with a theological flourish. Grace in this new revelation was a personal encounter which the new community had had with its founder; it was a meeting with the Incarnate God face to face; it was a view of the majesty of God. Truth was the communication of this grace, the revelation of its significance[39] as Jesus expounded[40] the meaning of this grace in revelation. He, John concludes, as the total outpouring of God's grace, had then made God known; in a full and final revelation he had revealed the truth of God.

So verse 17 does provide a comparison, but not between the law and its replacement: it is a comparison between the nature of revelation in the Testaments. The revelation to Moses had been an astounding event in the history of religion. God had chosen Israel as his special people and planned to use them to reach the world at large. And in spite of their obvious unworthiness and their manifest sinfulness, he had persevered with that choice, albeit from Sinai on by the hands of mediators. The people of his choice had shown their unworthiness by their constant series of failures in the Old Testament period. But, nevertheless in a revelation which had transcended all that had gone before, the Logos had come to them as unto his very own, but they had rejected him. To the Logos who had become flesh as the manifested unmediated glory of God, in the last move of all by God to his people, Israel, the response had been negative. But in and through the cosmic conflict which characterized the ministry of Jesus, and for which the light and darkness motifs of the Prologue provide background, some had received him. By the Incarnation they had seen deity revealed, and to those who believed on this basis and whose faith, though faltering, had survived the fact of the cross and seen the significance of his resurrection, Jesus had given the power to become the sons of God—the replacement for national Israel, the remnant of Israel, the restored people of God. Through them God would be pleased to reach out and to carry the message of the Word who had become flesh to the ends of the earth. The logic of the presentation of the Prologue has been progressive, culminating in verse 18, and the theological flourish of this verse concludes this great introduction to this epic of world literature.

Notes:

[1] R. A. Culpepper, "The Pivot of John's Prologue," *New Testament Studies* 27 (1980–1981): 1–31. For Culpepper the chiastic structure of the Prologue pivots on verse 12c.

[2] On the approaches to the structure of John 1:1-18 see Jeff Stanley, "The Structure of John's Prologue: Its Implications for the Gospel's Narrative Structure," *Catholic Biblical Quarterly* 48 (1986): 241–63.

[3] M. Vellanickal, *The Divine Sonship of Christians in the Johannine Writings* (Rome: Pontifical Biblical Institute, 1977), pp. 149ff.

[4] B. M. Metzger, "On the Translation of John 1:1," *Expository Times* 63 (1951–1952): 125ff., summarizes and evaluates Colwell.

[5] Ed L. Miller, "The *Logos* Was God," *Evangelical Quarterly* 53 (1981): 72.

[6] Apart from the superiority of Greek witnesses, *monogenēs theos* is the Revised Version margin reading of 1881, where the marginal readings usually refer to the judgment and preferences of the revisers which was overruled by the conservatism of the day.

[7] Ed L. Miller, "The Johannine Origin of the Johannine Logos," *Journal of Biblical Literature* 112/3 (1993): 447–49.

[8] P. Borgen, "Logos Was The True Light," *Novum Testamentum* 14/2 (1972): 120.

[9] P. Borgen, "Observations on the Targumic Character of the Prologue of John," *New Testament Studies* 16 (1970): 288–95.

[10] N. A. Dahl, "The Johannine Church and History" in W. Klassen and G. F. Snyder, ed., *Current Issues in New Testament Interpretation* (New York: Harper, 1962): 130–36.

[11] *Katalambanō* would normally mean "to seize," and thus to seize the mind, therefore "understand." But at John 12:35, where the verb is again used in the Gospel meaning "overcome," "overtake" is required by that context as well as here in John 1:5.

[12] Rudolf Schnackenburg, *The Gospel According to St. John* (New York: Crossroad, 1990), 1:244.

[13] Borgen, "Logos Was the True Light," p. 124.

[14] Torah particularly in Jewish thought took on the role of the giver of light which Wisdom had played in creation—Schnackenburg, *Gospel According to St. John*, 1:253. Note Ps 119:105; Prov 6:23; Is 26:9; Wisd 18:4; Ecclus 24:27; cf. *Test Levi* 14:4, and note the rabbinic periphrasis for man as "one who comes into the world."

[15] P. Borgen, "The Targumic Character of the Prologue of John," *New Testament Studies* 16 (1970): 288–95.

[16] P. Borgen, "Creation, Logos and the Son: Observations on John 1:1-18 and 5:17-19,"

Ex Auditu 3 (1987): 93.

[17] John Ashton, "The Transformation of Wisdom: A Study of the Prologue of John's Gospel," *New Testament Studies* 32/2 (April 1986): 168.

[18] At John 11:52 the phrase "children of God" occurs in the ironic prophetic utterance of Caiaphas as a description of the new people of God who are a replacement for the national Israel that the context rejects. At John 8:39 the term *tekna* further occurs, where the tekna are the possessors of true freedom and the true descendants of Abraham, and not the Jews.

[19] The Greek verb concerned, *skēnoō*, is cognate with the noun *skēnē* used in the LXX for the tabernacle as pitched.

[20] On temple building as a task for deity see B. Halpern, *The Constitution of the Monarchy in Israel* (HSM 25) (Missoula, Mont.: Scholars Press, 1981), pp. 19–31.

[21] *As* is not an adverb of comparison here but one of identity of essence.

[22] The derivation of *monogenēs* is recognized as stemming from *monos*, only, and *genos*, kind. See D. A. Fennema, "John 1:18 'God the Only Son,'" *New Testament Studies* 31 (1985): 126.

[23] As the preposition (*para*) seems to denote.

[24] LXX translated *ḥeseḏ* by *charis* freely in the later books though it is Hebrew *ḥen* in Exodus 34:6. This does not entirely preclude a reference to the text here. But what is clearly involved is a reference to the general context of Exodus 33–34.

[25] M. D. Hooker, "The Johannine Prologue and the Messianic Secret," *New Testament Studies* 21/1 (Oct. 1974): 53–55.

[26] In E. E. Ellis and E. Graesser, eds., *Jesus und Paulus* (Göttingen, Germany: 1975), "Charis paulinienne et Charis johannique," pp. 256–82.

[27] A. T. Hanson, "John 1:14-18 and Exodus 34," *New Testament Studies* 23 (1976): 90–101.

[28] Particularly by Elizabeth Harris, *Prologue and Gospel: The Theology of the Fourth Evangelist* (Sheffield, England: Sheffield Academic Press, 1994), pp. 26–62.

[29] *Pleroma* in accordance with Old Testament usage will mean the fullness/riches of the divine life. Schnackenburg, *Gospel According to St. John*, 1:275.

[30] D. A. Carson, *The Gospel According to St. John* (Leicester, England: Inter-Varsity Press, 1991), p. 131.

[31] M. J. Harris, *New International Dictionary of New Testament Theology*, ed. Colin Brown (Exeter, England: Paternoster, 1978), 3:1179–80.

[32] C. K. Barrett, *The Gospel According to St. John* (London: S.P.C.K., 1958), p. 168.

[33] "The Prologue to the Fourth Gospel: Some Unsolved Problems," *Expository Times* 86 (1975): 373.

[34] Zane C. Hodges, "Grace After Grace: John 1:16," *Bibliotheca Sacra* 135 (1978): 40.

[35] Carson, *Gospel According to St. John*, p. 332.

[36] *Law in the Fourth Gospel* (*Supplement to Novum Testamentum* 42; Leiden, Netherlands: E. J. Brill, 1975).

[37] Carson, *Gospel According to St. John*, pp. 132–33.

[38] The extremely audacious phrase of John's *monogenēs theos* probably excited early sensitivities. It is very difficult to credit a change in the text from *monogenēs hyios* to *theos*, though the movement the other way would have been early and attractive.

[39] Truth in this context means something like "divine revelation." Schnackenburg, *Gospel According to St. John*, 1:272.

[40] *Exēgeomai* = lead, explain, interpret. J. P. Louw argues for "declare." Bultmann argued for "reveal," for 1:18 sums up what the Logos does, says and is. Harris, *Prologue and Gospel*, summarizes these opinions and herself argues for "communicates 'divine things.'" For her, correctly, 1:18 is the climatic statement of the Prologue (pp. 109–15).

8

Paul Doing Theology for the Corinthians: Second Corinthians

Paul Barnett

Have you been thinking all along that we have been defending ourselves to you? We have been speaking in the sight of God as those in Christ; and everything we do, dear friends, is for your edification. (2 Cor 12:19) [1]

I T IS A PRIVILEGE, INDEED, TO JOIN WITH OTHERS IN thanking God for the continuing ministry of J. I. Packer. As a younger man I was profoundly and permanently shaped by such classics—as they have become—as *"Fundamentalism" and the Word of God*, *Evangelism and the Sovereignty of God* and *Knowing God*. It has been no disappointment, as it sometimes is, in the nature of things, to come to meet the man, as I have done in recent years. He is in person the embodiment of what he has exhorted us to be, a gracious and humble man of God who loves his Savior and who continually gives himself in the service of the people of God.

❖ ❖ ❖

It is instructive to sit at the elbow of the apostle Paul to watch him "doing theology for the people of God." This has been my privilege for the past several years as I have labored in writing a commentary on the text of Second Corinthians. So astonished have I been at the subtlety of his thought in the nuances of the text, and on the other hand, of its sheer theological power, that, on occasions, I have felt constrained simply to stop writing that I might thank God for his minister Paul.

Let me share some reflections on Paul as "theological craftsman," as revealed in Second Corinthians.[2]

Historical Circumstances

Before looking at the letter let me clear the ground in regard to historical matters. In the mid-fifties, Paul had made a second visit to Corinth, a visit occasioned by pastoral emergency. Upon return to Ephesus he wrote a follow-up letter, often called the "Severe Letter," borne to Corinth by his envoy, Titus. Soon afterwards he left Ephesus, traveling via Troas (near the mouth of the Dardanelles) to Macedonia, where he was eventually reunited with Titus.

Titus's reports to Paul about the circumstances of the Corinthian church, from which he had just come, provoked Paul to write this present letter. Second Corinthians is Paul's response to Titus's reports. What, then, did Titus report to Paul in Macedonia? There was some "good news." The Corinthians had eventually disciplined the man who had wronged Paul during that second visit (2 Cor 7:12). The church must now forgive the offender (2:5-11).

The greater part of Titus's report, however, was "bad news." This came in two categories. First, there were criticisms of Paul. His previous visit was deemed to be ineffective and he had not returned as promised, but had sent a harsh letter instead. It was being said of Paul in Corinth, "His letters are weighty but his bodily presence is weak and his speech is beneath contempt" (10:10—my translation). Paul was being seen as a "man of flesh" (1:12, 17), whose seeming unending sequence of misfortunes marked him out as incompetent in ministry (2:14-16; 3:5-6).

The second category of "bad news" related to recent negative developments in Corinth which Titus reported and which Paul addresses in the letter.

1. The collection for the Judaean churches, established by Titus during the previous year, had lapsed (8:6, 10; 9:2).

2. Moreover, Titus reported, Paul's insistence on self-support by working was a continuing source of unhappiness (cf. 1 Cor 9:1-23), not least that he showed no sign of changing his policy (11:7-11; 12:13-16a). Some, however, suspected that he did receive money "craftily," by an indirect route through his coworkers, to gain some

moral advantage (12:16b-18; cf. 4:2; 7:2).

3. More seriously, however, was Titus's report that, despite his second letter (canonical First Corinthians) and the second ("painful") visit, a section of the church remained entangled in the cultic and immoral life of the city (6:14–7:1;12:2–13:2).

4. The worst development, however, was that in recent times the Corinthian congregation had welcomed a group of Jewish Christian "false-apostles" whose influence threatened to destroy altogether Paul's relationship with the Corinthians (2:17–3:2; 5:11-13; 10:12–12:13). In the seven years of Paul's association with them this was by far the most serious problem which has arisen.

Our canonical Second Corinthians is the response of Paul, apostle and theologian, to these current difficulties within the Corinthian congregation, as reported by Titus to Paul in Macedonia.

Shape of the Letter
The letter falls into two parts. The first part is apologetic, defending and explaining himself in regard to past misunderstandings (1–7). Thus in 1:1–2:13 he offers an explanation of his much criticized non-return. This leads into a lengthy theological excursus defending his "sufficiency" as a minister of the new covenant, calling on the Corinthians to "be reconciled to God" (5:20), but, equally, to "widen" their "hearts" to him (6:11-13).

The second part is corrective, written to secure action in advance of Paul's impending final visit to them (8–13).[3] He encourages them to complete the collection (8–9), to recognize as "false apostles" those who have now come to Corinth, arguing that the "superiority" of his sufferings in ministry marks him out as a true and "better" minister of Christ (10:12–12:13). Finally, he calls on them to break with sexually immoral behavior (12:20–13:2), associated as it probably was with the local temple cults (6:14–7:1).

The "bridge" between the two halves of the letter is 7:2-4. His expressions of warm confidence in them, together with remarks about his and Titus's joy (7:13-16), pave the way for the letter-bearer Titus's ministry to the Corinthians, as the applicatory second part of the letter begins in earnest in 8:1.

Paul could have said all this to the Corinthians in a few pages. It is part of his theological method that he does not do so. Rather, he allows the sometimes petty and to a degree unrecoverable details of Titus's report to set the agenda for the magnificent body of teaching we find in this letter. The sheer weightiness of his argument and the density of the theological texture indicates that here is a letter to be read again and again. Moreover, that the letter is addressed not only to the church in Corinth but also to "all the saints who are in the whole of Achaia" (1:1; cf. 1 Cor 1:2), a large province, supports the notion that this is no mere occasional letter, to be read once, then put to one side (cf. Col 4:16).

Why Paul Needed to Defend His Legitimacy in Ministry

This is a long, and at many points complex, epistle. Is there a controlling idea that, once understood, serves as a key which unlocks the meaning of the letter?

In our view, Paul's defense of his legitimacy as a "minister of the new covenant"/"a minister of Christ" (3:6; 11:23), is the controlling theme of Second Corinthians. Directly or indirectly, great tracts of the letter are devoted to it (1:1–7:16; 10:1–13:14). Indeed, apart from the section relating to the collection (chs. 8–9), it could be argued that Paul's legitimacy in ministry is either directly to be read out of the text throughout or to be read between the lines.

Why does he need to offer this defense? Here we are driven to conjecture. In our reconstruction of the circumstances in Corinth at the time of Titus's report to him Paul's ministry had come under the criticism of both the indigenous Corinthians and the newly arrived Jewish missionaries. The local people regarded him as inadequate on account of the ineffectual second visit, which was followed, not by the promised return visit, but by a harsh letter.

For their part the Jewish Christian newcomers also saw Paul as deficient, as the following reconstruction suggests.

On arrival in Corinth, they challenged Paul's teaching to the Corinthians on a number of matters, in particular, his fulfillment-eschatology (1 Cor 15:3-4) and his separation of those "baptized into Moses" (1 Cor 10:2; "them"—10:6) from "us . . . upon whom the ends of the ages have come" (1 Cor 10:11). As Jews who were also Christians, they reject Paul's inference of the supersession of the old covenant, asserting it to be still operative.

Paul's claims to be an apostle, which are based on having "seen" the glorious Lord, the man of heaven (1 Cor 9:1; 2:8; 15:49), would demand that he should be, in some sense, a "glorious" figure, as Moses, who had seen the glory of the Lord at Mount Sinai.

According to popular Jewish belief at the time, Moses' glory was thought to be undiminished throughout his life.[4] This was taken to be a sign of the continuing efficacy of the Mosaic covenant; Paul's fulfillment eschatology which effectively discontinued the Mosaic dispensation is seriously erroneous. Paul's sufferings, which are well-known, reveal him to be anything but glorious, bringing his "fulfillment" preaching into question. By contrast the Jewish missionaries asserted their "superiority" over Paul, in particular based on their claims to "visions and revelations from the Lord" which transported them to Paradise where they heard words unable to be uttered (cf. 12:1-5). The evidence for these mystical heavenly revelations was their ecstatic speech (cf. 5:11-13).

Not least these Jewish Christians claim that Paul's preaching about Jesus as a crucified Messiah effectively "veils" his gospel from Jewish audiences (4:3), for whom such a message would have been offensive (cf. 1 Cor 1:23).

Paul responds to these criticisms of weakness and inadequacy, emanating as it appeared to be from both local Corinthians and Jewish-Christian newcomers, in particular, in two extended passages. The first is in 2:14–4:15 and the second is in 10:1 to the end of the letter.

Within these extended passages are found two extraordinary passages of considerable complexity. The first, 3:1-18, is Paul's midrashic-style exposition of Exodus 34:29-35. Here Paul contrasts the old and new covenants in terms, on one hand, of their respective brightness of glory, and on the other, of the veiling of the people under the former covenant, and their unveiling under the new covenant.

The second is the so-called "Fool's Speech" (11:1–12:13), in which he answers those who claim their "superiority" over him, parodying his "superiority" by cataloging his "weaknesses" sustained in ministry. If the first literary form is distinctly *Jewish*,[5] the second is distinctly *Hellenistic*.[6]

The veil-midrash on one hand and the "Fool's Speech" on the other serve to symbolize, respectively, that Paul was both Hebrew and Hellenist. More fundamentally, however, the thorough Christological permeation of these forms—whether the midrash or the "Fool's Speech"—reveals the profound degree by which Saul of Tarsus had been converted in heart and mind to Jesus as Messiah and to his Spirit who had now come.

Legitimacy in Ministry: The Key to Second Corinthians

Paul's defense of his ministry throughout the letter are conditioned by a barrage of criticism from Corinth, whether by local detractors or newly arrived "superlative" apostles, as he calls them, or by some alliances of both local and visiting opponents.

1. He is "an apostle of Christ by the will of God" (1:1) as the Corinthians should know; "the signs of the apostle were wrought among [them] . . . signs, wonders and mighty works" (12:12).

Undergirding this confidence is God's historic call of him, as indicated by his use of verbs of aorist tense to point to the moment of that call. It is God who has made Paul *competent*[7] as minister of a new covenant (3:6) and, in a probable reference to the Damascus event, he says that "God made his light *shine*[8] in our hearts . . ." (4:6). Twice he writes of "the authority the Lord *gave* . . ."[9] (10:8; 13:10). He speaks of "the field which the God *assigned* . . ."[10] (10:13).

In a number of passages Paul makes a studied connection between the present tense, reflecting his ongoing ministry, and the aorist tense pointing to the moment when that ministry began. Having "been *convinced* [at or soon after the Damascus christophany] that one died for all" Paul *"persuades* men . . . [*being*] compelled by Christ's love" (5:14, 11).[11] Again referring to his commission in the past, he writes, "God *gave* us the ministry of reconciliation . . . *committed* to us the message of reconciliation"[12] (5:18-19). This he contrasts with his ongoing ministry *"representing* Christ . . . God *making* his appeal through us. We [*continue to*] implore you . . . *working* with God we [*continue to*] to urge you . . ."[13] (5:20; 6:1). Three times Paul uses the present tense "we [*continue to*] speak"[14] to characterize an ongoing ministry which arose from God's unique and specific call to him to do so (2:17; 4:13; 12:19; cf. 13:3).

Mindful of the impact within him of the Damascus event he solemnly asserts that "the truth of Christ is *in* [him]" (11:10), referring almost immediately, and by contrast, to *"false* apostles" who disguise themselves as "apostles of Christ" (11:13). Paul "speaks [the word of God] . . . from God" (2:17). He is the true apostle of Christ.

2. It is not Paul, but the Lord [Christ], who commends his ministry (3:3; 10:18). Paul appeals to the Corinthians' experience of the Spirit of the living God in their hearts (3:3, 18; 5:5; 13:14), which is theirs in consequence of his preaching in their midst (1:19-22; cf. 11:4), whereby they are a "temple of the living God" (6:16). Since this is the Spirit promised in fulfillment of the new covenant (Jer 31:31-35; Ezek 36:26-27), this is now the era of the "ministry of the Spirit" (3:8) and Paul is a minister of the new covenant, "made competent" for it by God (3:5-6; cf. 2:16). That the Corinthians have the Spirit, that Christ Jesus is "in" them, a matter they can "prove" (13:5-

6), is evidence that Paul is a minister of the new covenant. Paul is not "incompetent" in ministry, but "made competent" by God. The presence and activity of the Spirit in them shows that he is not self-commended, but is commended by the Lord (10:18).

3. But yes, he is "inferior" to the "superlative" apostles. Fools boast and Paul will boast of the foolishness, even the madness, of—of all things!—"weaknesses." Many times in the letter (1:8-11; 4:8-11; 6:3-10), but especially in the "Fool's Speech" proper (11:23–12:10), he will point to afflictions and sufferings sustained in the course of his ministry. The repeated sufferings-catalogs (*peristaseis*) show that, unlike the "superlative" apostles, there is no triumphalism with the true apostle of Christ (2:14). But nor was there with the Christ who was "crucified in weakness" (13:4). Paul's sufferings replicate, extend into history, "share" the "sufferings of Christ" (1:5; 2:15; 4:10-12; 12:10), showing that he is, in fact, a "better minister of Christ" than the "superlative" apostles (11:23).

The climax of those "weaknesses" was the "weakness" of the "thorn for the flesh . . . the messenger of Satan" (12:7-9). Paul had experienced a "vision and revelation" from the Lord, which had transported him to paradise where he had heard words which he was not permitted to utter (12:1-6). God's "gift" of this unidentified and protracted "weakness," however, pinned him to the earth in humility and dependence on the Lord to whom he prayed. The inference is clear. Through their "visions and revelations" the newcomers are uplifted in religious pride; they are, in Paul's grimly ironical words, "superlative" apostles. In the unremoved "thorn" Paul exercises his ministry in humility and patience, lacking power of his own, utterly dependent on the Lord, who himself had prayed three time in Gethsemane and who had been powerless at Golgotha. *God's* power is made perfect in weakness.

For Paul, Christ in his sufferings is the model for his ministry. It is "on account of Jesus"[15] that Paul is the Corinthian's "slave" (4:5), that he is continually "handed over to death" in the course of his ministry (4:11). It is "on behalf of"[16] Christ that he comes as envoy pleading, "Be reconciled to God" (5:20) and "on behalf of" Christ that he must be content with "weaknesses, insults, hardships, persecutions, difficulties" (12:10). Even his discipline of offenders in church is by the "meekness and gentleness of Christ" (10:1), although this was taken by them to be "weakness" (10:10). As Jesus' ministry was nontriumphal, so, too, was Paul's. Paul replicated the life but also, more particularly, the death of Jesus.

As the "minister" of the "minister," Jesus (11:23; Mk 10:45), Paul "lowers" himself in arduous labor of self-support to "elevate" them in salvation (11:7), is "spent for their souls" (12:15) and "though poor makes many rich" (6:10; cf. 8:9). The "superlative" apostles, by contrast, are lords who enslave and exploit (11:20).

Paul's ministry exercised in the weakness of suffering was, in fact, shaped by his message. His ministry was cruciform because he proclaimed the Crucified. Nonetheless, it was marked by resurrection power; God repeatedly delivered his servant from death (1:8-11; 4:7-8; 7:5-7; 12:7-9).

4. But, despite current allegations to the contrary, he is a man of holiness and godly sincerity (1:12; 2:17), who is true to his word (1:18), who has rejected deceit and guile (4:2) and who has not manipulated or cheated the Corinthians (7:2; 12:16-18). His life is an open book before God (12:19), and he trusts also before the Corinthians (4:2; 5:11), in the light of the coming judgment (5:10; 1:14; 1:23; 2:17).

Immediately after writing about the death and resurrection of Christ as the center of humanity and of history (5:14-17), Paul writes about God's institution of the diaconate of reconciliation (5:18–6:13). Paul calls upon the Corinthians to acknowledge him as God's ambassador, spokesman and coworker (5:20; 6:1). The call "Be reconciled to God" (5:20) follows from, and cannot be separated from, the call "open wide your hearts" to him (6:11-13).

It follows that Paul's ambassadorial ministry and the message of reconciliation entrusted to him was no afterthought, no *ad hoc* thing. The apostolate, as exercised by Paul, is to be regarded as much an article of faith as the reconciling death and resurrection of Christ upon which it depends and from which it flows.

Paul's Ministry Is Tied to the Eschatological Centrality of Christ
Paul ties the defense of his ministry, as marked by death (suffering) and resurrection (deliverance), to the death and resurrection of Christ, the centerpoint of humanity and of history (5:14-17). Throughout this letter Paul defends the legitimacy of his ministry on the grounds that it gives authentic expression to both the death and resurrection of Christ.

This is the reason the letter has so much to say explicitly and implicitly about the death and resurrection of Christ. Properly grasped it gives legitimacy to the pattern of Paul's life, which was under severe criticism in Corinth at that time.

Fundamental to Paul's thought is that "now is the day of God's salvation" (6:2). In this regard Paul focuses our eyes on Christ. Even the casual reader of this letter is immediately struck by the early appearing words, *"in him . . . through* [Christ]" (1:19-20) which point to the centrality of Jesus Christ. In Jesus Christ, the Son of God, God fulfills all the promises of God under the old covenant (1:18-20), thereby bringing that covenant to its appointed end (3:7-11). *Through* Jesus Christ, the church, which has been gathered by the apostolic word centered in him, utters its "amen" as it draws near to God in prayer and thanksgiving (1:20).

In a unique and cosmic event he has died and been raised for all, bringing the existing created order to an end (4:16-18; 5:17) and dividing history into "no longer" and "now" eons (5:15-16). The "day of God's salvation" has, indeed, dawned. The "new creation" has begun. The blessings of the end time—the righteousness of God, reconciliation with God, the Holy Spirit, at least by "deposit"—have come into the present, in Christ (1:20-22; 5:18–6:2).

Jesus Christ is called "Lord" and preached as "Lord" (4:5). On his great coming "day," all will be raised from the dead, all will be made manifest before his judge's tribunal (1:14; 4:14; 5:10). The church, like a virgin daughter, is pledged to her Lord for consummation on that day (11:2-3). Yet in his gracious incarnation, "rich" though he was, he made himself poor to enrich the impoverished (8:9). In his death, without sin though he was, he so embraced sin as to bestow the righteousness of God on all who belong to him (5:21). In "meekness and gentleness" of life (10:1) Jesus Christ was "slave" for his people, "handed over to death" for them (4:5, 11).

In Jesus Christ, God has gathered up the past and anticipated the future. All the promises of the past are fulfilled in him, all the blessings of the future are found in him. In the light of the eschatological centrality of Jesus Christ the message of the apostle to the wayward Corinthians is simple and direct, "Be reconciled to God . . . *now,* because now is the day of salvation" (5:20; 6:2).

Paul does not allow the reader's eyes to leave Jesus Christ.

The Hope of Glory
Whereas the doctrine of Paul the apostle as minister of the new covenant and of Christ, in this the day of God's salvation (6:2), is a strand running through the entire letter, his teaching on the hope of the glory of God is contained within the excursus on apostolic ministry (2:14–7:4). It appears in two passages, 3:12–4:7 and 4:14, 16–5:10,

which are both universal in application, but which, in both cases, flow out of passages which focused on Paul's ministry (2:14–3:11 and 4:7-13, 15).

1. Paul sees the glory of God as "permanent" (3:11), the ultimate goal (3:18), beyond the universal resurrection (4:14) and the universal judgment (5:10). This glory is eternal and weighty (4:17).

2. By contrast, until then, within this present eon, humans are blinded to God by the god of this eon, perishing, (4:3-4). Each is a mere earthen vessel (4:7), whose outer form is withering away (4:16) under the impact of "affliction" (4:17), a mere "tent" to be dismantled at death (5:1).

3. By the light of the gospel, however, God shines his light into human darkness, in the face of Jesus Christ (4:6). As one turns to the Lord there is the flash of inner illumination which anticipates the ultimate glory of God and the believer's conformity to the image of the Lord (3:16, 18). This present experience of glory corresponds with the present "deposit" of the Spirit in anticipation and promise of his fullness in the end-time (5:5).

4. Overwhelming though "such a hope" of future glory is, Paul does not minimize the dark realities of present existence. Those who are as still "in the body" are not yet "at home with the Lord" (5:6, 8). The intervention of death prior to the onset of the end-time will mean a time of nakedness, something that provokes a "burdened sighing." Beyond that the tribunal of Christ the judge faces each and every believer with its revelation of deeds done in the body and divine recompense for them (5:10).

5. It is likely that Paul deliberately emphasizes the painful realities of the present in this letter, to bring an appropriate sobriety to the Corinthians. It appears that they had an overrealized spirituality, with accompanying pride, based on the evident manifestations of the Spirit among them (1 Cor 1:7; 4:7-8; 14:36). Now, additionally, they have welcomed "superlative" apostles, who boast of "visions and revelations from the Lord" (11:5; 12:1, 11).

6. It may be no coincidence that Paul's sober portrayal of ministry in nontriumphalist terms, as sketched above, corresponds with his candid presentation of the dark realities of mortal existence. Apostolic ministry is exercised in the power of God, but in the midst of weakness. The future is laden with glory, but the present is, frankly, painful, and death is not to be romanticized. Christ was raised and lives in power, but only subsequent to his weakness of death. Only after death is there life. There is power, the power of God, but it rests

upon apostles and people not in power, but in weakness (12:7-9). And there is glory, which is glimpsed now through hearing the gospel (4:6), but it is not yet fully realized (4:17-18). The children of God walk by faith, not by sight (5:7).

Pastoral Ministry from Second Corinthians

Second Corinthians presents many inspiring texts and passages to the reader and teacher of God's Word. A quick survey reveals approximately eighty individual verses lending themselves to extended meditation and exposition, apart from the sixty or so constituent paragraphs of the letter. This letter is a rich quarry of precious metal for the edification of God's people.

But how are those who stand outside the ranks of the initial recipients of the letter to interpret and apply it to themselves?

The preliminary question for every reader and congregation is: does this writer have any claim over my thinking and behavior? If Paul's words lack a dominical authority this letter is of only relative interest, with no power in the conscience of individual or church. No issue in this letter is more important to resolve than this. The view taken here is to acknowledge the unique place of the apostle to the Gentiles, authorized as he was to edify the churches (10:8; 12:19; 13:10). This letter comes to us with the full weight of canonical Scripture.

Once this is recognized, the admonitions the apostle made to that church readily carry over to churches and their members in other places and other times. Throughout history churches have struggled with the interface with their secular environment, with a propensity to stray from revealed truth and lifestyle with an accompanying tendency to fragmentation and division. In this regard it is helpful for us to place ourselves in the Corinthians' shoes and be reconciled to the God who has reconciled us to himself, who is faithful to covenantal promise, who comforts the downcast and who raises the dead. Like the Corinthians, our churches and their members need to separate themselves from the dark seductiveness of the pagan cults. Let us remain focused on Christ, in whom we believe for our forgiveness and on whom our hopes rest. Let us, too, be encouraged that the Spirit in whom we have been sealed is transforming us from glory to glory (1:21; 3:18). May our churches seek the "mending" and the unity (13:9, 11) which only comes through the grace of Christ, the love of God and the fellowship of the Holy Spirit (13:14).

Second Corinthians will not permit narrow congregationalism.

The powerful appeal to complete the collection will not allow the Corinthians to regard themselves as the only island in the sea (8–9). Rather they must see themselves as part of an archipelago stretching across the world. It is, indeed, a test of their grasp of the gospel that they recognize the need for "equality" in material things among the far flung people of God (8:13-15), despite the distances involved and the differences of theological emphasis and tradition between the churches of the Pauline mission and the churches of Judea.

In one passage late in the letter Paul declares that he has not been defending himself, but speaking for the edification of the readers (12:19). It is likely that Paul is, in particular, pointing to passages about himself. Given the triumphalism of the "superlative" apostles and, indeed, the spiritual pride of the Corinthians, it is likely that Paul has in mind those passages about himself in which the non-triumphalist, "slave"-like character of his ministry has been set forth (e.g., 2:14-16; 4:1-15; 6:3-13). Above all, there is Paul's own example of one who might well have been inflated in pride through his extraordinary visions and revelations, but who was forced to learn the lesson of humility and deep dependence on the Lord in the thorn that was not removed (12:1-10). Here is edification for triumphalists and proud "Corinthians" of every generation.

What, then, of the more specialized reader whose vocation is missionary or pastor? Here we face the problem that Second Corinthians is, in particular, the apologia for Paul's person and for his apostolic ministry.[17] How, then—if at all—is the missionary or pastor able to apply to himself or herself passages which Paul originally related deliberately to himself?

The answer is that the ministry of the new covenant was not confined to the generation of the apostle, but *continues* until the Lord comes. To be sure, Paul as apostle stood uniquely as pioneer of that ministry, following hard on the Lord who commissioned him en route to Damascus. As revelator (4:6) Paul as apostle cannot be replicated and his insistence on self-support in ministry was peculiar to him (11:7-11; 12:13-17) and for unique reasons. Few are called on to suffer as he did establishing and caring for the churches.

Nonetheless, the greater part of his teachings about ministry stand as model and inspiration to subsequent generations of missionaries and pastors. His comments about ministry—that at its heart lie endurance and patience, sacrifice and service, love of the churches, fidelity to the gospel, sincerity before God, above all a rejection of triumphalism with its accompanying pride—remain throughout the eon to shape and direct the lives of the Lord's servants. Paul's ministry as sufferer and servant is precisely modeled on Jesus, and finds its legitimacy in the face of detraction and opposition for just that reason, as also must ours, if that is our calling. Thus Second Corinthians may be bracketed with the Pastoral Letters in its applicability to the work of those whose vocation it is to serve God as his ministers.

Notes:

[1] All biblical quotations are translations of the author.

[2] Although recent major commentaries (e.g., Furnish, Martin, Thrall) see the present letter as an amalgamation of previously independent letters, I regard it as a unity. Among other reasons, we find critical vocabulary not found in earlier letters of Paul scattered across the supposedly originally partitioned sections, e.g., the verb "commend" (3:1; 4:2; 5:12; 6:4; 7:11; 10:12, 18; 12:11). This is but one of a number of examples of the spread of hitherto unused vocabulary across the whole canonical epistle. See Introduction to the author's forthcoming commentary published by Eerdmans in the New International Commentary (NIC) series.

[3] This whole letter, but particularly its second part, will prepare the Corinthians for Paul's third and final visit (2:2-3; 9:4; 10:2; 11:9; 12:14, 20, 21; 13:1, 2, 7, 10).

[4] Thrall I:244 n.365 cites a Targum Fragment: "The splendor of [Moses'] face was not changed." See further Thrall I:243–44.

[5] Consistent with his assertion that he is a "Hebrew" (11:22), we note echoes from the liturgy of the synagogue in various benedictions (e.g. 1:3-11, 20; 11:31) and thanksgivings (e.g., 2:14; 9:15), and various asseverations arising from the OT (e.g., 1:12, 23; 11:10). His text is peppered with quotations from and allusions to the OT (e.g., 3:3-6, 16; 4:13; 5:12; 5:17; 6:1-2; 6:14–7:1; 9:6-8; 9:9-10; 11:2; 10:17; 13:1). The vocabulary and thought of Is 40–55 appears to underlay 5:14–7:1. The dualistic apocalypse arising from the division of the ages (4:16–5:10), hinged around the general resurrection (4:14; cf. 1:14; 5:10), arises from the religious culture of contemporary Judaism. On the significant place of apocalyptic in the thought of the apostle see J. C. Beker, *Paul the Apostle: The Triumph of God in Life and Thought* (Philadelphia, 1980, 143–63.)

[6] Increased awareness of Greco-Roman culture of the period indicates that Paul was familiar with, and prepared to express himself in terms of, that culture. It has been long understood that 2 Corinthians is written in educated *koine* in the format of a Hellenistic letter. More recently, however, similarities in Pauline epistolary layout and expression have been detected in (1) Hellenistic forensic political speeches, with, e.g., their *exordia* (cf. 1:12-15) and *encomia* (cf. 1:15ff), and (2) in the so-called *peristaseis*, whereby lists of sufferings and achievements, often stated contrastively (cf. 4:8-9; 6:3-10; 11:23-33; 12:7-10), are given (see e.g., Young and Ford, *Meaning*; Fitzgerald, *Earthen Vessels*, 148–201). The contrasts—negative and positive (2:17; 11:22-23a; cf. 10:12)—between himself and his opponents and the catalogues of weaknesses which serve to disclose a God-given power to overcome them (4:8-9; 6:3-10; 11:23b–12:10), and which legitimate his ministry in the face of rivalry, appear to have numbers of parallels within Hellenism, including Hellenistic Judaism. Attention has also been drawn to Paul's use of paradox (see Martin, 242–43), metaphor (see Martin, 242–43), invective (see Marshall, "Invective," 359–73), as well as comparison (see Forbes, "Comparison," 1–30). The "Fool's Speech" (11:1–12:13) probably remains the most striking example of Hellenistic cultural influence, which however, by his use of irony, he subverts.

[7] Gk. *hikanōsen*.

[8] Gk. *elampsen*.

[9] Gk. *edōken.*

[10] Gk. *emerisen.*

[11] Gk. *anthrōpous peithomen . . . hē . . . agapē tou Christou synechei hēmas, krinantas touto.*

[12] Gk. *tou theou . . . dontos hēmin tēn diakonian tēs katallagēs . . . themenos en hēmin ton logon tēs katallagēs.*

[13] Gk. *presbeuomen . . . hōs tou theou parakalountos . . . deometha . . . synergountes . . . parakaloumen . . . .*

[14] Gk. *laloumen.*

[15] Gk. *dia Iēsoun.*

[16] Gk. *hyper Christou.*

[17] Apart from the chapters devoted to the collection (8–9), the other major passages, despite their diversity, are united by the common theme of Paul's defense and exposition of his apostolic ministry. In this regard even the plural pronouns "we . . . us," with few exceptions, are expressive not of coauthors Paul and Timothy (1:1), nor of fellow-proclaimers Timothy and Silas (1:19), but of Paul alone, Paul as *apostle.* Thus the "we" who are, for example, "Christ's ambassadors . . . God's fellow workers" (5:20; 6:1), who "preach . . . Jesus Christ as Lord" (4:5; cf. 11:4), to whom God gave "the ministry . . . the word of reconciliation" (5:18, 19), is *Paul,* who worked "the signs of an apostle . . . signs, wonders and miracles" when present in Corinth (12:12). It was in *Paul's* heart that God shone his light that his apostle might reveal Jesus Christ to others (4:6), and it was he to whom the Lord gave his authority to edify the churches (10:8; 12:19; 13:10).

9

Prospects for the Pastoral Epistles

I. Howard Marshall

Politics, in the famous phrase of the British politician R. A. Butler, is "the art of the possible." It is therefore concerned less with ideals and more with what is expedient and may be achieved in practice by agreement and, if necessary, by compromise between people with different ideas and policies. Biblical and theological scholars, however, would argue against any kind of expediency or compromise and insist that it is the quest for truth and for truth alone which must inform our endeavors. It may be hazardous to deny that anything is totally impossible, but the point may come when one asks whether there are some beliefs that we wish to regard as true but which we are incapable of defending, let alone of persuading others of their truth. Are there some theological statements that we would like to regard as true but that are in fact impossible to maintain? Do we spend our time trying to defend impossible positions? Would it be wiser to defend other positions that come within the realm of possible truth? Are evangelical dogmas necessarily true?[1]

The evangelical dogma in question in this essay is the "truth" concerning the authorship of a subset of the set of letters purporting to be written by Paul. Seven of these letters are more or less universally accepted to be by one author who by definition is the historical Paul.[2] Within current critical scholarship it is now virtually taken for granted that the remaining six letters attributed to Paul are not his own compositions but rather "deutero-Pauline" writings and that the task of the interpreter is no longer to demonstrate this fact but rather to explore its implications.

The question arises: is an attempt to defend the Pauline authorship of the Pastoral Epistles (hereafter "PE") today a case of attempting the impossible or at least the highly improbable? What should be the scholarly agenda of evangelical students in the case of these letters, and in the case of the other so-called Deutero-Pauline letters? More precisely, is the "received tradition" about the authorship of these letters in fact "the truth," and should we attempt to defend it?[3] Have we to allow that the traditional solution is not within the range of the possible and cease to waste effort on defending the indefensible?

Discussion of the issue is complicated by the fact that very often a set of facts will be observed and interpreted differently by scholars who approach them from different angles, and it is very difficult to find the decisive evidence which will compel the universal adoption of one interpretation rather than another. Consequently, my survey of the factors regarding the character and authorship of the PE will inevitably be affected by subjective considerations.[4] Let us look at some of these points briefly.

Considerations Relevant to the Pauline Authorship of the Pastoral Epistles

A. *Language and Style*

1. Vocabulary. The first question is that of vocabulary and its implications for style. For many people the investigation by P. N. Harrison continues to be decisive. Three main points were developed. He demonstrated that the PE have a far greater proportion of words not found elsewhere even in a thirteen-letter collection of "Pauline" letters than any other letters in it.[5] He argued that the vocabulary as a whole was closer to that of second-century writers.[6] And he showed that the PE especially lack a great deal of the connective tissue found in the genuine letters.[7] Later scholars have confirmed Harrison's thesis. K. Grayston and G. Herdan adopted a more sophisticated mathematical approach than Harrison and confirmed his vocabulary argument.[8]

Other scholars have shown up some serious flaws in Harrison's methodology. D. Guthrie in particular refuted the argument that the vocabulary is a second-century one.[9] In a thesis that has been undeservedly ignored J. M. Gilchrist showed that many of Harrison's allegedly distinct arguments were variants of one and the same argument; Harrison is said to provide a "stage army" in which the same argument is served up several times in different forms.[10] More recently the Grayston/Herdan approach has been challenged.[11]

Nevertheless, the upshot of the debate is that the shape of the vocabulary is certainly different from that of the genuine Pauline letters.[12] The problem is how this fact is interpreted.[13]

2. Syntax. A related approach is the attempt to analyze the syntactical style of the letters by considering such factors as sentence length, the positioning of words, the relative proportions of nouns and verbs. Initial investigations in this area by A. Q. Morton were severely flawed, but they have been succeeded by more refined methods.[14] They have, however, been subject to considerable criticism.[15] Again, the impression which I gain is that there is a recognizable difference from the genuine letters.[16]

3. Rhetorical style. Linked with these two points is the more diffuse element of rhetorical style, the manner of composition and argument. An analysis of the structure of the letters shows that they are constructed in a different manner from the acknowledged letters of Paul. There is, for example, the lack of an opening thanksgiving in First Timothy and Titus (admittedly paralleled in Galatians). There is also the lack of personal material (except in Second Timothy). Less has been done in the way of analysis here, and therefore one is perhaps reduced more to subjective impressions. I am again left with the feeling that this is not the Paul that I know from the genuine letters.

The interpreter has to offer an explanation of this set of features. Some five types of explanation have been offered.

1. First, there is the straightforward conclusion that the PE are by an author other than Paul.

2. At the other extreme there is the claim that the differences from the acknowledged letters are minimal and well within the range of style of a single author, perhaps writing over a long period of time. I am uncomfortable with this argument for three reasons: it seems to me that the differences are considerable; the period of time is not sufficiently long; we do not have the evidence that an individual's style can alter to such a great extent.

3. A refinement of the previous explanation attributes the changes to the effects of old age on a writer. It is high time that this theory was abandoned. It is based on a false assumption, and it leads to an unhappy conclusion. There simply is no evidence that old age does have these effects in general or the specific effects seen in the PE. Moreover, while this explanation certainly saves the PE for "Paul," it is a different Paul from the earlier Paul who writes differently and whose thought may well have aged as well as his style of writing.

Consequently, a person writing an account of "the theology of Paul" would not be able to use the PE as a source for his thought in the same way as the earlier letters.[17]

4. There is the suggestion that the PE contain very considerable elements of "traditional material," and it is in effect the style of the tradition which we are observing.[18] Again, this argument is a peculiar one. It means assigning a very great deal of the content to tradition rather than to the author, so that again the PE are saved for the name of Paul at the cost of denying him a creative role in their composition. Moreover, it is not clear what exactly the relation of this "tradition" to Paul himself is. In any case, there is a stylistic and theological homogeneity in the PE which makes it difficult to separate tradition from composition.

5. Finally, there is the possibility that the details of composition are due to a colleague or "secretary" who was given a rather free hand. Here again the effect is to "rescue" the PE for Paul at the cost of denying that he himself produced their contents. They have his blessing but not his mind.

Nevertheless, to some conservative scholars these last three explanations are viable options in that they preserve the truth of the ascription to Paul, even though it is in effect a "different" Paul. In the last analysis, it is this preservation of the literal truth of the claim to authorship by Paul which matters for them, even if the result is that it is not the "real" Paul who is the author.

B. The Historical Setting of the Author

The letters do not give a lot of information to enable us to fix them in a specific setting, but there is sufficient material to suggest some possible scenarios which are not directly reflected in our other sources of information.

1. The traditional reconstruction works with the hypothesis of a period of activity after a putative release from his two years of imprisonment in Rome (Acts 28). This view has the undoubted advantage over its rivals of placing the three letters together in one period of time and thus accounting for their stylistic peculiarities as a group over against the other letters.[19]

2. Other attempts have been made to fit the PE into Paul's missionary career as recorded in Acts.[20] It may well be that theories of this kind cannot be refuted, since the record in Acts is sufficiently fragmentary to allow for all kinds of reconstructions. The great difficulty is that these three letters, which differ from the *Hauptbriefe* (i.e.

Paul's principal writings—Romans, First and Second Corinthians and Galatians) in linguistic and theological style but manifest a close unity among themselves, are interspersed over the same period of composition, and we are left wondering how and why the same writer could move so easily from one style to another.

3. Alternatively, it has been suggested that the PE, as we have them, are compositions incorporating fragments of actual Pauline letters, and when these fragments have been prized away from their present setting, it is possible to devise various hypothetical situations for each of them.[21] Here again there are few limits that can be set on the ingenuity of scholars. Thus arguments against the self-consistency of Second Timothy 4 and therefore against the historicity of the details can be met at the cost of allotting different fragments to different situations and allowing that the letters are secondary compositions.[22]

Whoever takes any of these lines has, then, still to reckon with the difficulty that the PE will then have been composed in or around the same time as the other, undoubtedly genuine letters of Paul with their different language and style. The problem is most acute for those who place the letters into the Acts scenario rather than at the end of Paul's life. They have to show how and why the thinking is different in this series of letters from that in the other series with which they are intertwined chronologically.

To be sure, there is a problem for the skeptics here. They have to explain the origin of these details. The older generation of scholars was prepared to accept that genuine fragments were embedded in pseudonymous letters. The contemporary trend is very much to regard the details as fictitious and to explain them as modes of conveying *paraenesis* (instruction) in veiled form: Paul is presented as an example to be followed, his opponents reflect current dangers in the church, and so on. But paraenetic purpose and authentic composition need not be mutually exclusive possibilities.

C. *The Recipients*

The difficulty perceived here is the nature and manner of the instruction given to colleagues of Paul who have worked with him for many years and should be in no need of what at times seems elementary instruction that should have been well-known to them. Conservatives have to fall back on the argument that this material is really meant, or is meant as much, for the congregations of Timothy and Titus, who will then know how their leaders are to behave and how they are to respond to them.

The pseudonymous solution is similar. These letters are really for the third/fourth-generation churches and their leaders, who are directly addressed under the guise of Timothy and Titus. The letters are cast as indirect instruction (by telling Timothy and Titus what to tell their congregations) as a means of showing how the leaders of the readers have their authorization and theology handed down to them from Paul. Scholars are getting ever more sophisticated in developing this point.[23]

But this type of interpretation, which has been used by conservative scholars to explain the alleged formality and impersonal character of the letters, overemphasizes the element of indirect address to the congregations. The letters are addressed to individuals and are concerned with how they are to exercise their ministry. This is clearest in the case of Second Timothy, which is essentially instructions for the personal life and witness of the church leader. But it has also been demonstrated that First Timothy is concerned primarily with the figure of "Timothy" himself, and the argument could be extended to apply to Titus also.[24] It follows that the letters are addressed primarily to church leaders, to the people appointed to lead local congregations, and they are in effect given the kind of instruction that Paul gave to his own colleagues, who in their turn appointed the readers as their colleagues. The people who would most easily identify with the named recipients are surely church leaders rather than members of the congregation, although the latter would overhear instruction and exhortation meant for themselves.

But this means that we are back with the problem that the letters are giving Timothy and Titus the kind of instruction with which they should already have been familiar and in a way that is surprisingly formal. The view that the PE are to be understood in terms of Paul giving instructions to his colleagues, and doing so in full view of the congregations who are also meant to read the letters, thus remains difficult.

D. The Opposition

Is the author attacking problems in Paul's lifetime (or foreseen by him for the future), or is he attacking problems of his own day under the guise of problems contemporary with Paul?[25]

To some extent the opposition described in the letters can be compared with other known and datable movements. Many scholars argue that it is characteristic of the early second century and identify it either with Gnosticism or with some form of asceticism.[26] Others will argue (and I tend to agree) that it is of a piece with the kind of opposition reflected in First and Second Corinthians or in Colossians.[27]

E. The Theological and Practical Instruction

That the actual content of the letters is different in character from that of the earlier Paul is not to be denied, even by those who would insist that what is said is in theological harmony with Paul. We then face two sorts of question.

1. The first question is whether the material on leadership and other aspects of church organization can fit into a scenario within the lifetime of Paul and is of a kind that he would have written.

Already in the acknowledged writings of Paul we have evidence of a development leading to the existence of "bishops and deacons" as local church leaders alongside at least two other groups of people. The first of these is people who had charismatic gifts to minister in various ways including prophesying and teaching and more "tangible" forms of ministry. The second is the group of people, like Paul himself and his colleagues, who were engaged in a church-planting exercise which included the after-care of new congregations. These three types of activity and personnel can be found at every stage in the early development of the church. In the PE there is little about charismatically endowed individuals other than those who hold some kind of official position (Timothy himself!). But the pattern could vary from place to place and time to time, and the question is whether the variant of it here is credible within a Pauline setting and indeed whether this is the best setting for it compared with other possibilities.[28]

2. The second question relates to the differences in theology and theological expression from the acknowledged letters of Paul. Here the issue is not whether the theology has shifted from that of Paul's earlier letters for that matter is beyond dispute (just as Ephesians and Colossians also show undoubted developments from the *Hauptbriefe*). The issue, rather, is the direction and manner of the shift: is it the kind of development that Paul himself might have experienced, or does it tend in other directions? That is to say, are the developments such as Paul might have produced himself, just as (for example) his use of the term *body* has developed from First Corinthians to Colossians, or are they more likely to be the work of somebody else?

A major factor here is how the theology of the letters is expressed in new ways. Over against the older critical position, which saw in the PE a rather tired, pedestrian theology which was a definite decline from the Pauline heights, there is good evidence to show that the PE represent a creative attempt to re-express Pauline theology in new ways for a new situation and to use fresh terminology to do so. It is striking how far the language and ideas of the PE find parallels in the Greco-Roman world and especially in Greek-speaking Hellenistic Judaism which had taken over much from the surrounding world.[29] The Christology is newly formulated in terms of epiphany, and the nature of the Christian life is expounded in terms of godliness and sobriety.[30] The reply can be offered that there is nothing here that Paul himself could not have done with his broad background in both Palestinian and Hellenistic Judaism; that may be true enough (we have little evidence to settle the issue of Paul's capacity for change), but the problem is why he has not adopted this medium in his earlier letters and above all why he has felt it necessary to re-express the nature of the gospel and the Christian life in letters ostensibly addressed to close colleagues. It would seem that the real audience is not Timothy and Titus. It would equally appear to be the case that the theological development is not due to Paul himself.

It is sometimes claimed that the differences from the earlier letters are due to the fact that here individuals are being addressed. In fact we have two types of difference, the "un-Pauline" style of theologizing and composition in the letters and the curious style in which colleagues of Paul are addressed. The latter is generally regarded as un-Pauline in that Timothy and Titus are given instructions of a character which is inappropriate if they really were Paul's companions.

F. The Picture of Paul

Finally, one of the major current arguments against Pauline authorship is the picture of Paul which is reflected or presented in the PE, a Paul who is put forward as a saint and martyr and as the sole apostle and authority for the gospel. A formidable case has been developed that Paul is deliberately presented as an example to be followed and as the person on whom the gospel depends. Succession from him and his message is vital for the continuance of the church. It is argued that the kind of statements attributed to Paul about himself are such as the historical Paul could never have made.[31]

We need, therefore, to ask how far the kind of presentation of Paul himself here is compatible with the self-portrait that emerges in his earlier letters and (again) how far it is likely that he would present himself in these terms to close colleagues. I have to confess to some unease with a Paul who writes in this way about himself.

G. Conclusion

The result of these half-dozen points is to show that direct Pauline authorship faces a number of objections of varying strength. Their effect is to lead most contemporary scholars to a comparatively late dating of the PE at the end of the first century or in the early years of the second century. My own view is that the doctrinal and ecclesiastical setting of the letters is compatible with composition during or immediately after the life of Paul, but that the way in which the thought is expressed, both linguistically and theologically, poses great problems. There is no great difficulty to my mind in the historical Paul having to deal with the kind of concrete situations envisaged in the PE and writing letters to his colleagues to advise them on what to do in the face of opposition and the need to consolidate the church situation. The problem is the way in which it is done, which seems to make it unlikely that he himself wrote in these terms to trusted colleagues. The difficulty is less acute with Second Timothy, although Paul might be thought to address Timothy like a public meeting.

Although the objections vary in strength, their cumulative effect is to cast very strong doubts on the traditional evangelical defense of direct Pauline authorship and to raise the question whether it really belongs within "the art of the possible." Are we defending the impossible, and do we need to adopt some other hypothesis?

The Problem of Pseudonymity

The reigning alternative hypothesis is that the letters were written later than Paul by some unknown person who was using Paul's authority to say what he believed that the church of his day needed to know.

Those who adopt this view may evaluate the PE in different ways. On the one hand, there is the straight view that the author has a theology which represents a decline from that of Paul into "early catholicism." It is extraordinary how persistent this view is. On the other hand, there is the more positive evaluation of the PE as an attempt to maintain Paulinism in a changed situation. These two types of judgment tend to be intertwined with one another, and it would be hard to find either of them in a pure form.[32] On the whole, the current tendency is to argue that the PE did a good job in their own day, even if they did not do it as well as Paul would have done.[33]

As it is currently held, this understanding of the composition of the PE is to be carefully distinguished from the way in which heretics created and used pseudonymous writings in order to promote their own false teachings. Proponents of this view would generally argue that the author of the PE had a profound reverence for Paul (witness the commendatory picture of Paul which the letters convey) and laid the utmost stress on the preservation of the "tradition" and the teaching given by Paul as the sole authority who is named. The letters are ostensibly concerned above all else to conserve and consolidate, to preserve the Pauline gospel and teaching as the right response to heretical teaching. In doing so, the risk was to ossify the Pauline teaching and to allow no further developments of it. At the same time, to be sure, there is a "shift" from Paulinism in that the stress on holding fast to the "deposit" represents a shift from the creative thinking of Paul and in that the author does reformulate Pauline teaching in various ways in response to the needs of his time and as a reflection of his own individual thinking.[34] Nevertheless, the overall aim is to bring Paul up to date and to preserve his influence for a new generation.

It would be difficult to condemn the motives behind such an exercise. The problems arise when we consider the method that is alleged to have been employed. The generally accepted explanation invokes the practice of deceptive pseudonymity. That is to say, the letters were written in such a way as to make people believe falsely that they were written by Paul, so that they would accept them as authoritative, apostolic writings. The later the letters were composed, the more likely it is that deliberate deceit was involved. They are pseudonymous in the sense that they were written by somebody other than Paul who was trying to deceive his readers into thinking that they were genuine writings by Paul (which had presumably been "lost" and had now been rediscovered).

Some scholars who hold that a deliberate attempt to deceive is a fact, attempt to play down the moral disquiet that this procedure may arouse for modern readers, especially for conservative Christians. One claim is that by the standards of the time it was not morally culpable and should not be assessed by contemporary morality. It was, we are told, a common practice in the ancient world, and there was no moral stigma attached to it.[35] It must not be judged by the literary conventions of the modern world.[36] Against this argument is the simple and incontrovertible fact that second-century orthodox

Christianity objected strongly to it, as practiced by heretics, and it is unlikely that first-century Christians differed on the matter.[37] According to L. R. Donelson, there are no examples of works that were known to be pseudonymous being accepted as authoritative.[38]

Or it is argued that the attribution of a writing to an earlier person was nothing more than a claim to continuity of teaching. R. Bauckham roots the procedure in Second Peter in "the conventions of a Jewish literary genre" which the later church no longer understood.[39] Evidently, it was conventional to supplement the writings of earlier authorities with material that stood in the same tradition. The authority of the pseudonymous author of Second Peter thus "lies in the faithfulness with which he transmits and interprets for a new situation, the normative teaching of the apostles. . . . The pseudepigraphical device is therefore not a fraudulent means of claiming apostolic authority, but embodies a claim to be a faithful mediator of the apostolic message."[40] Here there is a subtle shift from the bothersome issue which is not "claiming apostolic authority" so much as "claiming to be the apostle," and it is not obvious that the element of fraud has been eliminated so long as there was intent to deceive.

The same line is developed independently and in great detail by David Meade, who holds that the later writer was making a claim not to authorship but to standing in the same tradition, like the people who added their oracles to the writings of an earlier prophet in the Old Testament.[41] But this hypothesis does not get round the fact that there was intent to deceive, and the apparatus of pseudonymity was used to this end.[42]

Many conservatives still feel uneasy with this type of argument. The hypothesis that writings inspired by the Spirit of truth used deceitful methods is generally regarded as unacceptable. However, the weakness of the evangelical position is that it may appear to rest upon an *a priori* judgment based upon theological considerations about inspiration rather than being open to arguments based on the historical and literary evidence.

A better way forward is to explore the relationship of the theological judgment to the actions and thinking of early Christians. It is accepted that there was a high regard among early Christians and in the New Testament for truth and truthfulness. There is also a strong emphasis, not least in the PE themselves, on the importance of preserving the tradition without perverting it in any way. It can then be argued that the emphasis on truth, which lies at the heart of the evangelical doctrine of Scripture, was characteristic of the New Testament writers themselves and, further, that people so motivated would have been unlikely knowingly to write or accept deceptive, pseudonymous works. The composition of Christian writings and the intent to deceive would not have been compatible. The demonstrable clear attitude of the orthodox church to pseudonymity in the second century is a powerful confirmation of this thesis. Consequently, it can be argued on the basis of the early church's attitude to truth that the practice of deceptive pseudonymity is extremely improbable. In this form the theological argument acquires persuasiveness instead of being open to dismissal as irrelevant.[43] Is there, then, some alternative to deceptive pseudonymity which is free from the objections to which it is open?

Preserving the Pauline Tradition: An Alternative to Pseudonymity
Various theoretical possibilities can be noted.

1. An author may use another person as a secretary and delegate powers to them to write on his behalf, and then sign the letter as being in effect from himself. This type of theory has often been suggested for the PE, but it is open to the objections that it attributes to Paul a different procedure from that adopted in his other letters, that it requires one common amanuensis for all three of the PE (despite their different places and times of origin) and that no reference is made to a co-author in the letters.[44]

2. Again, it is permissible for the work of an author who has died to be posthumously edited and published for future generations, although in the modern world it would be normal for some indication of this fact to be made.[45]

3. It is not too great a step to a scenario in which somebody close to a dead person continued to write as he would have done. An incomplete work can be completed by somebody else, but again in a modern situation this would be made quite explicit.[46] There is a rather fluid boundary between this and the previous possibility, depending on how far the actual words of the deceased are utilized.

In none of these cases does the element of deceit arise. Later generations might forget the facts of the origin, in much the way in which Hebrews appears to have gained access to the canon, humanly speaking, because it was believed to be by Paul and not just because its contents commended it. But this is no argument against the legitimacy of the original enterprise.

We now ask whether some such a scenario is possible for the PE and can be positively defended rather than being a last, desperate, improbable possibility clutched at by conservative scholars. It is not a new theory, being upheld by such scholars as P. N. Harrison and B. S. Easton.[47] My concern here is to suggest that in some form it may contain the truth concerning the origin of the PE and that it can be defended against recent criticism.

A. One popular form of this theory has been the attribution of the PE to Luke. Despite the advocacy of this view by a number of scholars, it is indefensible on grounds of style and theology.[48]

B. Another suggestion is authorship by Timothy or Titus.[49] Timothy has also been claimed as the author of Colossians, written within Paul's lifetime. If correct, this would set a precedent. But the differences between Colossians and the PE are as great as between the PE and the Pauline corpus generally, so that the difficulties for the hypothesis that Timothy was responsible for both are on a level with the difficulties surrounding straight Pauline authorship. If Timothy were not the author of Colossians, this would free him for the PE. If we attribute Colossians to Timothy, then Titus becomes a candidate for authorship of the PE.

The theory requires that one person be the author of all three letters, since there are no perceptible differences in style between First Timothy and Titus that would require separate authorship. We are left with the puzzle of why Timothy writes letters addressed to himself and also to Titus (and vice versa).

Thus this theory is a possibility, but it is surrounded by a number of imponderable factors.

C. A remaining possibility is some other person whose identity is a matter of guesswork. The name of Tychicus has been suggested, and other persons mentioned in Second Timothy could also be mentioned.

So far no compelling evidence for any one particular person has emerged. We simply have the possibility of some person close to Paul who passed on to other people the kind of thing that Paul could have said had he been still alive and based his attempt on knowledge of the things that Paul did say.[50] However, our lack of ability to make a positive identification is no argument against a solution to our problem which deals acceptably with a number of problems.

1. It solves the moral problem in that there was no attempt at deceit. It thus provides a more probable context for post-Pauline authorship than theories which assume deliberate deception.

2. It places the PE close to Paul and means that their claim to his authority is more easily justifiable historically than would be the case

with later compositions.

3. It explains the elements which point to a possibly later date and setting than that of Paul's own life. At the same time, it recognizes that the concerns for the preservation of doctrine and the consolidation of church structures in existing congregations are exactly what would be expected from Paul himself as he foresaw the end of his own ministry and supervision. Strong support for this setting comes from R. A. Campbell in his work on the development of church leadership.[51]

4. It solves the problem of the personal references to other people in the PE. These are historical colleagues and opponents of Paul who are mentioned as examples of faithfulness or of disaster or in some cases as dangerous opponents who are still active. The later the letters are placed, the more difficult it becomes to account for these personal references.

5. The writing of orthodox works in the name of early Christians is most likely to have taken place soon after their deaths. It ceased thereafter. The orthodox Christian writings which survive from the end of the first century and the beginning of the second are without exception anonymous or are by persons whose names they bear; none of the writings of the Apostolic Fathers or the Apologists claim to be by figures of the past.[52] It is only in less orthodox circles that real pseudonymity arises.[53]

6. There is no elaborate attempt at creating verisimilitude. The writer does not imitate Pauline style closely, nor does he quote from Paul's acknowledged letters, although there are inevitable echoes of them. There is a lack of personal details of the kind that would create a (fictitious) setting that would favor authenticity. The personal details in Second Timothy are most probably drawn from actual Pauline notes. The material cited as "tradition" is not especially Pauline. On the contrary, the author was free to write in his own style. These points show that the author was not trying to deceive his readers into thinking that these were genuine Pauline works. If we have a hagiographical picture developed which does not correspond with what Paul would have said about himself, this is not a problem, provided that we recognize it for what it is, namely a picture of Paul as others saw him.

Implicit in our reconstruction is the assumption that the ostensible recipients "Timothy" and "Titus" are not the real recipients but are "types" of the people addressed. As we have noted already, the primary audience is church leaders in congregations in the Pauline mission area, and the secondary audience is these congregations themselves.

It is most reasonable to associate the letters with the congregations in the areas mentioned, Crete and Ephesus/Asia Minor. We know sufficient of the Asia Minor situation to recognize the likelihood of opposition to Paul there (cf. Acts 20), and placement of the letters close to Paul's lifetime leaves the field free for the activity of John at a still later date. But it is probable that the sort of problems which Paul encountered continued, and it is not at all surprising that the kind of doctrinal aberration found in Corinth crossed the Aegean Sea to Ephesus and found its way to Crete. In Paul's own lifetime the same opponents stalked around his mission field generally.

We can thus propose a general scenario in which the tendencies that can be detected in Paul's lifetime and especially toward the end of it continued and required the same kind of response as he would have given. In this situation somebody produced letters written in the name of Paul, addressed to his immediate helpers and with the implicit rubric: "These letters represent the kind of thing that I think that Paul would have to say to our churches today if he were still alive. Consequently, I have not simply repeated the actual things that he said, but I have had to think how he would have reacted to present circumstances." If Paul had in fact written letters (possibly Colossians and Ephesians) in his own lifetime in collaboration with others who had a major share in their composition, this could have afforded a precedent to encourage such further writing.

Despite some dissenters, the three letters are by one author. Differences between them are due to the different situations addressed rather than to differences in authorship or thinking. So much so is this the case that some scholars insist that they were composed as a corpus and intended to be interpreted as such. This is improbable. One of the weaknesses of the standard theory of pseudonymity is that it fails to develop a case for the composition of Titus alongside First Timothy unless Titus is a sort of "first attempt."

Conclusion

All that has been done here is to present the outline of a thesis which, it may be claimed, belongs within the area of "possible truth" and is therefore worthy of further investigation and refinement. Much remains to be done to demonstrate that placing the PE in close contact with Paul gives a much more convincing interpretation of them than is given by theories of their late, pseudonymous origin, and to deal with objections that may be raised to the theory.[54]

My proposal represents an attempt to "do biblical criticism" within the parameters of that general understanding of the nature of Scripture which has been so capably defended by Jim Packer, to whom many of us are indebted beyond measure for the way in which he offered a stalwart defense and convincing exposition of what we believed and still believe to be true but could not express anything like so well ourselves.[55]

From the point of view of evangelical theology with its high doctrine of biblical inspiration, the present proposal should raise no difficulties. One weakness in popular statements of the doctrine is the tendency to tie the work of the Holy Spirit to the exact moment of writing. B. B. Warfield was, however, careful to observe that there was a process which included the preparation beforehand by God of the right people to pen the right words.[56] The production of inspired writings could involve a process of preparation (e.g., Luke gathering his information) and the activity of several people (e.g., the task of the "witnesses and ministers of the word" who provided Luke with his information). Equally the editing of Paul's legacy and the attempt to set down what he would have said can be seen as tasks carried on under divine overruling to produce documents through which the Holy Spirit continues to speak to the church.

Notes:

[1] As a student of the New Testament I trust that I may be allowed to stretch the meaning of "doing theology" to include "doing biblical criticism;" doing theology is dependent on understanding and using the Bible, and any study which contributes to our understanding of what the Bible says or does not say is surely germane to the task of systematic theology.

[2] We can ignore for our present purpose problems regarding whether some of the letters are editions composed out of shorter pieces, and therefore possibly containing some non-Pauline materials and some editorial material.

[3] There are, of course, conservative scholars who do so: G. D. Fee, *1 and 2 Timothy, Titus* (Peabody, Mass.: Hendrickson, 1988); G. W. Knight III, *Commentary on the Pastoral Epistles* (Carlisle, England: Paternoster Press, 1992). See further T. C. Oden, *First and Second Timothy and Titus* (Louisville, Ky.: John Knox Press, 1989); L. T. Johnson, *1 Timothy, 2 Timothy, Titus* (Atlanta, Ga.: John Knox Press, 1987). For the most recent statement of the case against deceptive pseudonymity see P. H. Towner, *1-2 Timothy & Titus* (Downers Grove, Ill.: InterVarsity Press, 1994).

[4] An appropriate example can be seen in the 1995 Tyndale New Testament Lecture by Philip H. Towner, in which he shows that passages which express the ecclesiology of the PE can be interpreted rather differently depending on which overall perspective regarding the composition and date of the letters the scholar adopts. See "Pauline Theology or Pauline Tradition in the Pastoral Epistles: The Question of Method," *Tyndale Bulletin* 46/2 (1995): 287–314.

[5] The essential point is that the PE have a vocabulary of 902 words (including 54 proper

names), i.e., 848 ordinary words; 306 of the latter are not found in any of the ten Pauline letters. This proportion is much higher than for any other Pauline letter. Conversely, there are some 1635 ordinary words and 103 proper names which occur in one or more of the ten Pauline letters and do not appear in the PE. It is also argued that a number of words which are common to Paul and the PE are used with different meanings. These points are developed at some length in terms of words per page and *hapax legomena* without decisively affecting the main hypothesis. See P. N. Harrison, *The Problem of the Pastoral Epistles* (Oxford: Oxford University Press, 1921).

6 Harrison's argument is that of the 175 *hapax legomena* in the PE, 93 are found in the Apostolic Fathers and Apologists. Out of 131 other words which are not in the working vocabulary of Paul, 118 occur in the second-century authors. Conversely, of 634 words in the ten epistles of Paul which are not found in second-century authors, 595 of them are also not found in the PE. However, Guthrie showed that the former group of words are virtually all attested in the first century (many in the LXX), and therefore the suggestion that the PE could not have been written in the first century collapses.

7 Harrison argued that 112 "particles" which occur in the ten Pauline letters do not occur in the PE out of a total of 214 altogether. This appears to be a large number and suggests a comparative poverty of style in the PE. Guthrie disputed the figures but not entirely successfully.

8 K. Grayston and G. Herdan, "The Authorship of the Pastoral Epistles in the Light of Statistical Linguistics," *New Testament Studies* 6 (1959–1960): 1–15.

9 *The Pastoral Epistles and the Mind of Paul* (London: Tyndale Press, 1956).

10 J. M. Gilchrist, "The Authorship and Date of the Pastoral Epistles," unpublished Ph.D. thesis, Manchester, 1966, esp. ch. 2 (pp. 27–61).

11 T. A. Robinson, "Grayston and Herdan's 'C' Quantity Formula and the Authorship of the Pastoral Epistles," *New Testament Studies* 30 (1984): 282–88.

12 So rightly Fee, *Commentary*, p. 24.

13 See A. D. Forbes, "Statistical Research on the Bible," *Anchor Bible Dictionary* 6:185–206, esp. 185–93 on the NT, for a critical survey of recent studies.

14 A. Q. Morton and J. McLeman, *Paul, the Man and the Myth* (London: Hodder & Stoughton, 1966).

15 A. Kenny, *A Stylometric Study of the New Testament* (Oxford: Oxford University Press, 1986). See also K. Neumann, *The Authenticity of the Pauline Epistles in the Light of Stylo-statistical Analysis* (Atlanta, Ga.: Scholars Press, 1990).

16 Cf. N. Turner in J. H. Moulton, *A Grammar of New Testament Greek* (Edinburgh: T. & T. Clark, 1976), 4:101–5, who notes the undoubted differences and explains them partly by some Latin influence on Paul in Rome and in greater part by the use of a different amanuensis who was given a freer hand.

17 Conservative scholars in general are not happy with theories of development in Paul's theology which suggest that some of what is said in the earlier letters is superseded or contradicted by later material. Why, then, should they be happy with the theory of a senescent Paul writing the PE?

18 E. E. Ellis, "Traditions in the Pastoral Epistles," in C. A. Evans and W. F. Stinespring, eds., *Early Jewish and Christian Exegesis* (Atlanta, Ga.: Scholars Press, 1987), pp. 237–53.

19 This is the view of such scholars as D. Guthrie, *The Pastoral Epistles* (Leicester, England: Inter-Varsity Press, 1990); Knight, *Commentary*. For a full development see W. Metzger, *Die letzte Reise des Apostels Paulus* (Stuttgart, Germany: Calwer Verlag, 1976).

20 J. A. T. Robinson, *Redating the New Testament* (London: S.C.M. Press, 1976); J. van Bruggen, *Die geschichtliche Einordnung der Pastoralbriefe* (Wuppertal, Germany: Brockhaus, 1981).

21 This approach was taken by P. N. Harrison.

22 This is, of course, not an argument against this hypothesis, merely a statement of a conse-

quence that flows from it. If the hypothesis is correct, we must live with its consequences.

23 See, for example, M. Wolter, *Die Pastoralbriefe als Paulustradition* (Göttingen, Germany: Vandenhoeck und Rupprecht, 1988).

24 J. T. Reed, "'To Timothy or Not': A Discourse Analysis of 1 Timothy," in S. E. Porter and D. A. Carson, eds., *Biblical Greek Language and Linguistics: Open Questions in Current Research* (Sheffield, England: Sheffield Academic Press, 1993), pp. 90–118.

25 We can exclude the view that the opposition is a fictitious construction bearing little relationship to actual opponents of the author.

26 The former view is the critical orthodoxy. For the latter see D. R. MacDonald, *The Legend and the Apostle: The Battle for Paul in Story and Canon* (Philadelphia: Fortress Press, 1983); M. Y. Macdonald, *The Pauline Churches: A Socio-historical Study of Institutionalization in the Pauline and Deutero-Pauline Writings* (Cambridge: Cambridge University Press, 1988); F. Young, *The Theology of the Pastoral Letters* (Cambridge: Cambridge University Press, 1994).

27 P. H. Towner, "Gnosis and Realized Eschatology in Ephesus (of the Pastoral Epistles) and the Corinthian Enthusiasm," *Journal For the Study of the New Testament* 31 (1987): 95–124.

28 See especially R. A. Campbell, *The Elders: Seniority Within Earliest Christianity* (Edinburgh: T. & T. Clark, 1994), who places the developments in the PE close to the time of Paul.

29 It is remarkable how frequently Philo provides some of the closest parallels in language and thought.

30 I. H. Marshall, "'Sometimes Only Orthodox': Is There More to the Pastoral Epistles?" *Epworth Review* 20/3 (1993): 12–24.

31 See especially Wolter, *Pastoralbriefe*.

32 Cf. A. T. Hanson, *The Pastoral Epistles* (London: Marshall, Morgan & Scott, 1982): 48–51, esp. 50f.

33 Cf. Young, *Theology*, for a very positive presentation; see further Marshall, "Sometimes."

34 There are, of course, critics who insist that the result is very un-Pauline. L. R. Donelson, *Pseudepigraphy and Ethical Argument in the Pastoral Epistles* (Tübingen, Germany: J.C.B. Mohr, 1986), p. 60, is pretty scathing about the author's ignorance of Pauline thinking.

35 This view must be carefully distinguished from the view which says that writings were produced under false names but without any attempt to deceive, since the readers knew perfectly well who the real author was. For this view see further below.

36 "In short, if one had a cause which was important enough and a lie could assist, then it is 'permissible' to employ a lie" (Donelson, *Pseudepigraphy*, p. 19).

37 This point has been denied by D. G. Meade, who claims that there was a discontinuity between the first and subsequent centuries (*Pseudonymity and Canon* [Tübingen, Germany: J.C.B. Mohr, 1986], p. 206), but his arguments are quite unconvincing; see the forthcoming Aberdeen thesis of T. L. Wilder, "New Testament Pseudonymity and Deception."

38 Ibid., p. 11f.

39 *Jude, 2 Peter* (Waco, Tex.: Word, 1983), p. 162.

40 Ibid., p. 161f.

41 Meade, *Pseudonymity*.

42 As Meade has to allow (e.g., p. 121).

43 There may be circumstances in which the theological argument from inspiration is to be used. The Christian believer may have no easy reply to some of the standard arguments against theism and yet nevertheless persist in belief on the basis of considerations that could be dismissed as subjective. A firm belief in the divine inspiration of Scripture has often kept believers from adopting false views of its origin and veracity even when they could not immediately produce historical backing for their position.

44 See E. R. Richards, *The Secretary in the Letters of Paul* (Tübingen, Germany: J.C.B. Mohr,

1991). The view that Paul used a secretary in his other letters but wrote the PE himself (M. Prior, *Paul the Letter-Writer and the Second Letter to Timothy* (Sheffield, England: Sheffield Academic Press, 1989) is highly unlikely.

[45] For a rare example in the ancient world see the *Prologue to Sir.*

[46] The example of students attributing their works to the philosopher who taught them may belong here.

[47] Harrison, *Problem,* p. 12; B. S. Easton, *The Pastoral Epistles* (London: S.C.M. Press, 1948), p. 19. This view is traced back to F. C. Baur; see Donelson, *Pseudepigraphy,* p. 9.

[48] For earlier attempts and the fullest defense see S. G. Wilson, *Luke and the Pastoral Epistles* (London: S.P.C.K., 1979). Against this view see my review of Wilson in *Journal for the Study of the New Testament* 10 (1981): 69–74.

[49] See R. Bauckham, "Pseudo-Apostolic Letters," *Journal of Biblical Literature* 107 (1988): 469–94, esp. 492–94.

[50] It is unlikely that the author was using the extant letters of Paul as a conscious source; the echoes can be explained as reminiscences of what Paul said or wrote.

[51] *Elders,* pp. 176–79.

[52] The *Didache* of "the Twelve Apostles" claims no more than that its teaching "is in accordance with the witness and teaching of the apostles;" only in later documents are explicit pseudepigraphical claims to authorship by the apostles made. See P. Bradshaw, *The Search for the Origins of Christian Worship* (London: S.P.C.K., 1992), p. 104f.

[53] *3 Corinthians* and the *Epistle to the Laodiceans* are later, clumsy forgeries and do not affect the point.

[54] Lack of space prevents attention to these questions. But the purpose of the essay (in the eyes of the editors of the volume) was to set out an agenda! For example, there is the question as to why the author wrote his instruction in the form of letters to Timothy and Titus instead of addressing directly his intended audience. But this may well be due to the origin of the letters in circles which knew of Pauline instruction to these men and wished to carry on the tradition. It is then perhaps more likely that Timothy and Titus were still alive and had some share in the composition. These, however, are matters for further reflection.

[55] J. I. Packer, *"Fundamentalism" and the Word of God* (London: Inter-Varsity Fellowship, 1958). My position differs from that expressed in the appendix on "Pseudonymity in Scripture" (pp. 182–86) by claiming that there can be a nondeceptive type of writing in the name of Paul.

[56] B. B. Warfield, *The Inspiration and Authority of the Bible* (London: Marshall, Morgan & Scott, 1951), pp. 154–58.

Part III: Historical and Interdisciplinary

10

The Importance of Tradition for Modern Evangelicalism

Alister E. McGrath

ANYONE SEEKING TO HONOR JAMES I. PACKER IS confronted from the outset with a monumental problem. Where do you start? Packer has made landmark contributions to the evangelical discussion of the authority of Scripture and the theological basis of evangelism; he has championed the rediscovery of the Puritan heritage for the modern church; perhaps most importantly, he has demonstrated the inextricable link between theology and spirituality and in his *Knowing God* has provided evangelicalism with one of its most significant works of spirituality in the twentieth century.

My problem, therefore, was to single out one aspect of Packer's massive contribution to the intellectual and spiritual shaping of evangelicalism which could be explored in the compass of a single essay. In the end, I decided to focus on one theme which has recurred in Packer's writings: the importance of tradition for modern evangelicalism. This theme can be found in his first major publication, *"Fundamentalism" and the Word of God* (1958), and recurs throughout his writings subsequently. Perhaps the most concentrated discussion of the theme occurs in his 1992 essay "The Comfort of Conservatism," which represents one of the most lucid analyses of the role of tradition within evangelicalism.[1] I believe that Packer has identified a theme which is already of major importance, and will continue to be of relevance as evangelicalism continues its expansion into the next millennium. The present essay is therefore both an exposition of Packer's views on this theme, and an exploration of its significance for modern evangelicalism.

The Nature of Tradition

To speak of "tradition" is immediately to run into potential misunderstandings. For some writers, particularly within Roman Catholicism and Eastern Orthodoxy, "tradition" has considerable authority. Tradition would here be understood to designate a traditional doctrine or belief, which has binding force on account of its antiquity. Yet this can easily degenerate into an uncritical sentimentality. "We've always believed this" can simply mean "We've always been wrong." As the third-century writer Cyprian of Carthage pointed out, "an ancient tradition can just be an old mistake." Tradition is to be honored where it can be shown to be justified and rejected where it cannot. This critical appraisal of tradition was an integral element of the Reformation,[2] and was based on the foundational belief that tradition was ultimately about the interpretation of Scripture—an interpretation which had to be justified with reference to precisely that same authoritative source.

The word *tradition* is best defined primarily as "the process of passing on and handing down." It can be seen at work in the New Testament, particularly in Paul's handing on to the Corinthian believers the beliefs which were of foundational importance to him.

> Now, brothers, I want to remind you of the gospel I preached to you, which you received and on which you have taken your stand. By this gospel you are saved, if you hold firmly to the word I preached to you. Otherwise, you have believed in vain. For what I received I passed on to you as of first importance: that Christ died for our sins according to the Scriptures, that he was buried, that he was raised on the third day according to the Scriptures, and that he appeared to Peter, and then to the Twelve. (1 Cor 15:1-5)[3]

Here, Paul speaks of "passing on" what was of first importance to him. In a sense, evangelicals have been doing the same ever since: passing down from one generation to another the gospel of Christ and the ways in which they understood and applied it to their situations.

The idea of "tradition" is of particular importance to modern evangelicalism. Evangelicals have always been prone to read Scripture as if they were the first to do so. We need to be reminded that others have been there before us and have read it before us. This process of receiving the scriptural revelation is "tradition"—not a source of revelation in addition to Scripture, but a particular way of understanding Scripture which the Christian church has recognized as responsible and reliable. Scripture cannot be read as if it had never been read before. The hymnodies and liturgies of the churches constantly remind us that Scripture has been read, valued and interpreted in the past.

Evangelicalism, steeped in the heritage of the Reformation, has always been resolutely opposed to the introduction of any "human traditions" into matters of Christian doctrine. The Westminster Confession summarizes the evangelical consensus on this major issue:

> The whole counsel of God, concerning all things necessary for his own glory, man's salvation, faith and life, is either expressly set down in Scripture, or by good and necessary consequence may be deduced from Scripture; to which nothing at any time is to be added, whether by new revelations of the Spirit, or traditions of men.[4]

Yet this does not mean that the labors of previous generations of faithful Christians to understand and apply Scripture is to be ignored. "Tradition" is understood by Reformers such as Luther and Calvin as a history of discipleship—of reading, interpreting and wrestling with Scripture. Tradition is a willingness to read Scripture, taking into account the ways in which it has been read in the past. It is an awareness of the communal dimension of Christian faith, over an extended period of time, which calls the shallow individualism of many evangelicals into question. There is more to the interpretation of Scripture than any one individual can discern. It is a willingness to give full weight to the views of those who have gone before us in the faith, providing forceful reminders of the *corporate* nature of the Christian faith, including the interpretation of Scripture.

Tradition and the Interpretation of Scripture

As Packer pointed out in his earliest major writing, the Christian past provides a resource for the Christian present. As we seek to interpret Scripture and unfold its many treasures, we can learn from the wisdom of the past.

> The Spirit has been active in the Church from the first, doing the work he was sent to do—guiding God's people into an un-

derstanding of revealed truth. The history of the Church's la-
bour to understand the Bible forms a commentary on the Bible
which we cannot despise or ignore without dishonouring the
Holy Spirit. To treat the principle of biblical authority as a prohibition against reading and learning from the book of church
history is not an evangelical, but an Anabaptist mistake.[5]

Packer can therefore be regarded as stressing the importance of being
aware of the historic and corporate nature of the Christian faith. This
point is developed further in his 1992 essay "The Comfort of Conservatism," which points out the dangers of refusing "to affirm the
positive role of history and community in shaping one's understanding."[6] Everyone has "traditions," whether they recognize them or
not; the key question is "whether our traditions conflict with the
only absolute standard in these matters: Holy Scripture."

Clearly, the danger of accepting the importance of the past must
be acknowledged. There is a real danger that we may treat "as divine
absolutes patterns of beliefs and behavior that should be seen as human, provisional, and relative."[7] The way in which Christians have
behaved or thought in the past can easily become normative for future generations, even though these have no absolute divine sanction
whatsoever.

Up to this point, we have focused on doctrines; let us explore this
point by considering a traditional evangelical practice. Many evangelicals would regard it as quite unthinkable to have an evangelistic
meeting without a final "altar call." This tradition goes back only to
the middle of the nineteenth century, when it was introduced by
Charles Finney (1792–1875).[8] Yet the fact that many evangelicals
have accepted the tradition of "altar calls" makes those calls neither
sacrosanct nor godless. Tradition, in one sense, is neutral. As Packer
points out,

All Christians are at once beneficiaries and victims of tradition—
beneficiaries, who receive nurturing truth and wisdom from
God's faithfulness in past generations; victims, who now take
for granted things that need to be questioned. . . . We are all
beneficiaries of good, wise, and sound tradition, and victims of
poor, unwise and unsound traditions. This is where the absolute
"last word" of Scripture must sort out the wheat from the chaff.
Hence the apostle Paul's counsel: "Test everything. Hold on to
the good" (1 Thess 5:21).[9]

This approach has implications at every level, especially in relation to
the interpretation of Scripture.

For Packer, every traditional way of reading Scripture must, in principle, be open to challenge. As the study of church history makes clear, the church may sometimes get Scripture wrong. Thus the sixteenth-century Reformers believed that Scripture had been misunderstood at a series of critical junctures by the medieval church, and undertook to reform its practices and doctrines at those points. This, however, is a case of a tradition being criticized and renewed from within, in the light of the biblical foundations upon which it ultimately rests. The Reformers did not regard themselves as founding a new tradition; their concern was to reform a tradition which already existed, but which appeared to have become detached from its scriptural foundations.

Affirming the authority of Scripture ultimately entails recognizing that even its most prestigious interpreters can be mistaken on occasion and need to be challenged and corrected in its light. This principle is vigorously stated by the Lutheran Formula of Concord (1577):

> We believe, teach and confess that there is only one rule and norm according to which all teachings (*dogmata*) and teachers are to be appraised and judged, which is none other than the prophetic and apostolic writings of the Old and New Testaments. . . . Other writings, whether of the fathers or more recent theologians, no matter what their names may be cannot be regarded as possessing equal status to Holy Scripture, but must all be considered to be subordinate to it, and to witness to the way in which the teaching of the prophets and apostles was preserved in post-apostolic times and in different parts of the world. . . . Holy Scripture remains the only judge, rule and norm according to which all doctrines are to be understood and judged, as to which are good or evil, and which are true or truly false.[10]

As Packer states this point, "Scripture must have the last word on all human attempts to state its meaning, and tradition, viewed as a series of such human attempts, has a ministerial rather than a magisterial role."[11]

Evangelicalism has, at least in principle, accepted this emphasis on Scripture as the absolute authority in all matters of doctrine. Yet during the course of its history, evangelicalism has developed certain habitual or set ways of interpreting Scripture. These need to be checked out, rather than accepted uncritically. Furthermore, in more recent times charismatic individuals have arisen, demanding that we interpret critical passages *their* way, thus interposing themselves between evangelicals and Scripture. Such a development can be resisted, particularly through an appeal to the Reformation doctrine of the priesthood of all believers.

However, a more serious issue also focuses on this point and is perhaps best explored by posing a question. Should today's evangelicals feel under an obligation to repeat faithfully what yesterday's evangelicals believed, or the strategies which they adopted? Are, for example, evangelicals of the 1990s obligated to repeat the beliefs and practices of evangelicals back in the 1920s or 1950s? On first reflection, the answer might be: "Of course!" Yet a more cautious answer is required. For evangelicals of today to affirm uncritically what evangelicals thought and did in the past is to be trapped by a tradition. It does not matter whether the tradition in question is evangelical or not. The key point is that it is a tradition. The only viable answer is the following: "We shall affirm what our forebears believed and practiced where it is warranted by Scripture." At least in principle, we must recognize that our distinguished forebears may require gentle and godly correction—in precisely the same way as future generations may wish, with equal gentleness and godliness, to correct us in our beliefs and practices. This is a painful insight; it is, however, an essential and biblical insight.

For example, an evangelical group back in the 1920s might have felt that the most appropriate response to developments in the wider culture was for evangelicals to withdraw from the world and form separate communities. This approach could easily be defended on biblical grounds. Yet evangelicals in the 1990s are under no obligation to follow that strategy. In the first place, they might wish to challenge the biblical interpretation which led to that strategy, arguing that the need to be salt and light to the culture mandated engagement with, rather than withdrawal from, society. And in the second, they might argue that the 1920s strategy was entirely proper, given the situation of the time. But times have changed, and the strategy needs to change in consequence. What was an appropriately biblical response in the 1920s was not appropriate in the 1990s—not because Scripture had changed, but because the situation being addressed had changed, requiring a different approach if the same biblical principles were to be upheld.

The history of evangelicalism suggests that the success of the movement rests upon its willingness to correlate Scripture with the context in which it finds itself, rather than mechanically reaching backwards into evangelical history to draw out past correlations. The issue is that of applying Scripture to new and hitherto unexperienced contexts, rather than slavishly repeating interpretations of Scripture originally developed in order to address a very different cultural context.[12] David F. Wells comments thus on the task of evangelical theology:

> It is the task of theology, then, to discover what God has said in and through Scripture and to clothe that in a conceptuality which is native to our own age. Scripture, at its *terminus a quo*, needs to be de-contextualized in order to grasp its transcultural content, and it needs to be re-contextualized in order that its content may be meshed with the cognitive assumptions and social patterns of our own time.[13]

The same basic approach lies behind Packer's demand that we constantly return to Scripture, rather than rely upon what some sage of yesteryear happened to say about Scripture. It may indeed turn out that we have much to learn from that sage of the past; yet this cannot be presupposed. In all things, we must "test everything and hold on to the good."

Packer's approach is thus an antidote to traditionalism—that is to say, a nostalgic and backward looking approach to the Christian faith which "can quench the Holy Spirit and cause paralysis and impotence in the church"[14] by demanding that we blindly and uncritically repeat exactly what evangelicals did and said back in the 1950s, the 1920s, the 1820s or the 1730s—or whatever period in evangelical history happens to be regarded as a "golden age" by its supporters. Yet at the same time, he lays the foundation for *the critical affirmation and reappropriation of the past*. In other words, Packer sets out an approach by which what is wise, good and true from the past can be discerned and gladly and joyfully reappropriated by today's church. Rediscovering the historic and corporate dimensions of our faith makes the great treasures and resources of the Christian past accessible and available to the present, thus enriching the life and witness of modern evangelicalism. We are enabled, as Packer puts it, to "receive nurturing truth and wisdom from God's faithfulness in past generations."[15]

The Usefulness of Tradition

So why is this emphasis on tradition so significant? Why does Packer need to be heard on this point? The answer to this question is complex. Packer himself points to four major reasons why a recovery of tradition is important to evangelicalism.[16] It allows us to discover our historical *roots,* introduces a sense of *realism* concerning our own situation, provides *resources* for the modern church and acts as a *reminder* of yesterday's successes and failures, so that the church may learn from them. In what follows, I shall explore some of these points with reference to two specific issues: the need to counter radical individualism within evangelicalism, and the way in which the past can stimulate and inform our thinking today.

Tradition Is an Antidote Against Individualism

North American evangelicalism continues to be strongly individualist, with no real sense of historical "belonging" or rootedness. As such, it is radically prone to destabilization. Too often, the North American evangelical has been "a spiritual lone ranger who has proudly or impatiently turned his back on the church and his heritage"—a development which, for Packer, is "a surefire recipe for weirdness without end!"[17] Rediscovering the corporate and historic nature of the Christian faith reduces the danger of entire communities of faith being misled by charismatic individuals and affirms the ongoing importance of the Christian past as a stabilizing influence in potentially turbulent times. A similar lack of rootedness is characteristic of other western contexts, especially Australia.[18]

The importance of Packer's point can be seen in many ways. For example, in terms of the cultural history of North America, it is no accident that the most bizarre recent religious cults, as well as innovative approaches to Christianity, generally have their origins in California, where a deep sense of rootlessness prevails. In his important study entitled *The Evolution of Human Consciousness,* John H. Crook comments as follows on the rise of the "hippie" movement in California around the time of the Vietnam War:

> It is no accident that the impetus came largely from the immigrant state of California where traditional cultural values are perhaps most fragmented and a need for new roots is most pronounced.[19]

This deep sense of rootlessness is directly related to many of the destabilizing developments especially associated with Christian churches in this fragmented and unstable region. The rediscovery of tradition is an important means by which balance can be restored to churches which are lurching from one new teaching to another and longing for some stability and security.

A recognition of the importance of tradition is also of vital importance in resisting new teachings of highly dubious merit. For example, consider the following argument, which has emerged in some more radical evangelical circles.

Christians are under no obligation to celebrate the Lord's Supper. The command to "do this in remembrance of me" (Lk 22:19) was given to the apostles, not to us. It was something that they were asked to do, but which does not apply to modern evangelicals.

This teaching is clearly seriously defective. It is inconsistent with the New Testament witness; thus Paul clearly assumed that the Christians at Corinth were obedient to Christ's instruction (see 1 Cor 11:17-34). It makes nonsense of the Great Commission (Mt 28:17-20), in that the commission to "go and make disciples of all nations" was given to the apostles. On the basis of the logic of the teaching in question, this commission no longer applies to modern evangelicals. Even on the basis of these preliminary considerations, the teaching is thoroughly dubious.

But there is another argument, and it is an important one. In the past, Christians have never believed this teaching. It is a theological novelty. Whatever their differences over the Lord's Supper may have been, the great Reformers (Luther, Calvin and Zwingli) were adamant that Christians should celebrate the Lord's Supper as a vital and integral aspect of Christian life, worship and witness. Tradition thus acts as a safeguard against maverick lone rangers, who try to drag evangelicalism down their idiosyncratic doctrinal routes. It has been well said that heresy is as much about demanding additional beliefs as it is about denying central beliefs.

Tradition is like a filter, which allows us to identify suspect teachings immediately. To protest that "We have never believed this before!" is not necessarily to deny the correctness of the teaching in question. But it is to raise a fundamental question: *why* have Christians not believed this before? And, on further investigation, it usually turns out that there are often very good reasons for not accepting that belief. The past here acts as both as a resource and a safeguard, checking unhelpful and unorthodox doctrinal developments by demanding that their supporters explain their historical and theological credentials.

Packer's approach thus points toward the need for evangelicals to be aware of the great defining moments in the development of Christian doctrine. Why did the church renounce Arianism? Why did the church fight against those who rejected the full divinity of the

Holy Spirit? Why did Augustine repudiate Pelagius's doctrine of total human freedom and the Donatist view of the church? Why did Luther reject works-righteousness? These controversies are landmarks in church history, in that they brought to a sharp focus some central issues of biblical interpretation. And they remain relevant today, as modern evangelicalism struggles to gain a sense of stability and responsibility. Church history is no irrelevance; it is a means by which today's Christians can learn of the ways in which God's people have served him in the past, whether that service ended in success or failure. It is no accident that evangelicalism seems prone to replay the great doctrinal debates of the patristic period; too many evangelicals know nothing of the past, and are unaware of the great doctrinal debates of the patristic or Reformation periods, and their momentous implications.

Not only are evangelicals often ignorant of the distant past; they tend not to know their more recent family history. And through ignorance of that history, they are liable to repeat the mistakes of the past—the evangelical infighting, for example, which came close to extinguishing the movement in North America during the 1920s and early 1930s. There are skeletons in the evangelical family closet, some of which remain a burden to the movement. Knowing the family history is one way of avoiding past errors and preparing to face the future. "History repeats itself. It has to. Nobody listens the first time round" (Woody Allen).

Tradition Provides a Resource for Today

One of Packer's major contributions to modern evangelicalism lies in his emphasis on the importance of the Puritan heritage. In many ways, Packer's approach here represents a specific application of a more general truth—namely, that there are periods of great creativity and vitality in Christian history, which can nourish and sustain those who live in less happy times. "No age shows equal insight into all spiritual truths and all facets of godliness, but the explorer of tradition finds the wisdom of every age opening up for him to draw on."[20] The usefulness of his approach can be illustrated by turning to the past for illumination on other issues, where modern presuppositions need correcting. An excellent example is the way in which the Reformation offers us invaluable insights concerning the nature and place of theology.

It is clear that much modern academic theology is perceived as totally pointless, not just by the general public, but even by educated lay Christians. Yet the Reformation offers us a vision of a time when theology was directed towards the issues which concerned the Christian public. As a university teacher of theology at Oxford, I cannot help but notice the reaction of theology students to my lectures on Reformation thought. "We can understand what these people are talking about!" is a typical response from students who have been bewildered by the verbal prolixity (often, it has to be said, masking a conceptual shallowness) of the writings of some recent theologians. "They're dealing with real questions" is another response, grounded in a growing impatience with an academic theology which seems bent on pursuing questions of purely academic interest.

The issues which are today treated with what often approaches polite contempt by academic theologians were regarded as of vital importance by sixteenth-century writers—issues such as the nature of the true church, the proper relation of the church and state, the grounds of Christian assurance and a direct answer to the age-old question "What must I do to be saved?" These issues are still debated today. But they are largely debated outside the academy, in local church study groups, in university Bible studies and in many North American seminaries. The academy has become seriously isolated from the heartbeat of North American Christianity. Happily, this has happened to a far lesser extent in the United Kingdom. This anxiety is also reflected in the status of the theologian, to which we may now turn.

In the Middle Ages, theologians were often equally isolated from the community of faith. They were generally individuals, like the great Thomas Aquinas, who were based in the majestic monasteries of Europe. They were closeted within the confines of the monastic life, and wrote—when they wrote at all—for an audience of their fellow monks. It is rare—but happily, as the example of Thomas à Kempis reminds us, not totally unknown—to find a medieval theologian operating outside this context. In our own day and age as well, theologians have become increasingly detached from the communities which they are meant to serve. They have become more and more professionalized, isolated within academic theological faculties and becoming vulnerable to the charge of dwelling within ivory towers. Professionalization has tended to remove theologians from within the communities of faith and placed them within the narrow confines of the universities. Secularization has led to a separation of personal faith and academic life; the professional academic theologian need not have any commitment to the faith or life of the church.

The Reformation bridges the gap between these two unsatisfactory approaches to the function of theology and offers a working model to contemporary evangelicalism. The Reformers, however diverse their origins may have been, were individuals who were based in the cities of Europe, living within the communities which they served and sharing their faith. They were isolated by neither monastery nor university from the people who looked to them for guidance. Their task was to interpret and apply the gospel to the concrete situations in which they found themselves—above all, in relating to the lives of ordinary people. Perhaps one of the most important moments of the Reformation may be traced to 1520, when Luther made the momentous and dramatic decision to cease being a purely academic reformer, addressing academic issues and audiences, and instead to make a direct and passionate appeal to the religious hopes and faith of the German people. Luther became both a preacher and a pastor—and his pastoral concern and experience shows up, time and time again, in his theology. Luther read and interpreted the New Testament as one who believed that it was of vital and continuing relevance to the life of the Christian community (another stark contrast between the theologians of the Reformation period and much modern academic discussion). His is a genuine pastoral theology, a theology which addresses the needs and concerns of ordinary believers and those who seek to minister to them.

It is clear that there is a model here which has relevance and appeal for today. The Reformation offers a very different model, with a distinguished history of application within the Christian tradition. The theologian is one who is called to serve the community of faith from within. Part of that service is criticism of its ideas and outlooks—but it is a loving and caring criticism on the basis of shared Christian beliefs and commitments, rather than the modern criticism of the Christian community by academic "theologians" on the basis of secular beliefs and values, often radically agnostic or atheistic, which that community feels no pressing reason to share.

Luther argued forcefully that "it is the duty of every Christian to espouse the cause of the faith, to understand and defend it, and to denounce every error."[21] Luther's doctrine of the priesthood of all believers, linked with that of the material sufficiency of Scripture, leads him to this challenging conclusion: precisely because all believers are priests, all are charged with the responsibility of maintaining the true faith, against the distortions of those who, claiming to be their leaders, ought to know and act better. One modern interpreter of this doctrine is the famous Swiss theologian Karl Barth. For Barth, theology is far too important to be left to such people. It is a matter for everyone who believes and thinks about his or her faith. It is a matter for anyone who wants to think responsibly about God and the tasks and opportunities which faith in God brings.

> Theology is not a private subject for theologians only. Nor is it a private subject for professors. Fortunately, there have always been pastors who have understood more about theology than most professors. Nor is theology a private subject of study for pastors. Fortunately, there have repeatedly been congregation members, and often whole congregations, who have pursued theology energetically while their pastors were theological infants or barbarians. Theology is a matter for the Church.[22]

Packer himself is an excellent example of a serious theologian, with excellent academic credentials, who has chosen to take the needs and concerns of ordinary Christians seriously. In his publications and speaking ministry, Packer has shown himself to be a faithful and lucid representative of this Reformation understanding of the role and calling of the theologian.

Yet there is still another issue which merits attention and which the Reformers illuminate. What is theology? For most people, theology is about the academic study of theologians. Yet for Luther, "the proper subject of theology" is "a God who justifies."[23] We need to rediscover that theology does not mean "the study of theologians" but "the study of *God*." The academy has set a purely academic agenda for too long; it is time to redress that balance.

One result of a purely academic study of theology has been the emergence of an artificial division between theology and spirituality. Yet the Reformation points to a close link between theology and adoration. Packer himself provides a superb demonstration of the link between theology and spirituality in his best-known work, *Knowing God*. In a more recent article entitled "Introduction to Systematic Spirituality," Packer stresses the utter impossibility of separating theology and spirituality:

> I question the adequacy of conceptualizing the subject-matter of systematic theology as simply revealed truths about God, and I challenge the assumption that has usually accompanied this form of statement, that the material, like other scientific data, is best studied in cool and clinical detachment. Detachment from what, you ask? Why, from the relational activity of trusting, loving, worshipping, obeying, serving and glorifying God: the

activity that results from realizing that one is actually in God's presence, actually being addressed by him, every time one opens the Bible or reflects on any divine truth whatsoever. This . . . proceeds as if doctrinal study would only be muddled by introducing devotional concerns; it drives a wedge between . . . knowing true notions about God and knowing the true God himself.[24]

Packer's point is that a genuine experience of God makes the detached study of God an impossibility—a point appreciated by medieval mystical writers, who often spoke in rapturous terms of their experience and knowledge of God, and by Calvin, who stressed that true knowledge of God led to both obedience and adoration. The demand for "detachment" is like asking the lover to be neutral about the beloved. Commitment is not merely a natural outcome of an authentically Christian experience and knowledge of God; it is the substantiating hallmark of such experience and knowledge. This is an insight which the Reformers knew and cherished; it is an insight which the modern church needs to recover.

Conclusion

"Tradition allows us to stand on the shoulders of many giants who have thought about Scripture before us."[25] Packer here takes up an image, often used in the Middle Ages, to refer to the ministerial role of the riches of the Christian past. As the principle is stated by the medieval writer John of Salisbury:

> We are like dwarves sitting on the shoulders of giants. We see more, and things that are more distant, than they did, yet not because our sight is better than theirs, or because we are of greater stature than them. Rather, they raise us up, and by their great stature, they add to ours.[26]

Packer not merely provides a basis by which we may learn from the wisdom of the giants who have gone before us; he has become such a giant himself. I hope that he will accept this small tribute from a relative dwarf who has learned so much from him.

Notes:

[1] J. I. Packer, "The Comfort of Conservatism," in M. S. Horton, ed., *Power Religion: The Selling Out of the Evangelical Church?* (Chicago: Moody, 1992), pp. 283–99.

[2] See Alister E. McGrath, *The Intellectual Origins of the European Reformation* (Oxford: Blackwell, 1987), pp. 140–51.

[3] All scriptural quotations in this article are taken from the New International Version of the Bible, copyright the New York International Bible Society.

[4] Westminster Confession, I, 6; in E. F. K. Müller, ed., *Die Bekenntnisschriften der reformierten Kirche* (Leipzig, Germany: Böhme, 1903), 545.11–20.

[5] James I. Packer, *"Fundamentalism" and the Word of God* (London: Inter-Varsity Press, 1958), p. 48.

[6] "Comfort of Conservatism," p. 287.

[7] Ibid., p. 289.

[8] For a critical assessment of the theology that lay behind these "altar calls," see David L. Weddle, *The Law as Gospel: Revival and Reform in the Theology of Charles Finney* (London: Scarecrow, 1985).

[9] "Comfort of Conservatism," p. 289.

[10] *Epitome*, 1-8; in *Die Bekenntisschriften der evangelisch-lutherischen Kirche* 2nd ed. (Göttingen, Germany: Vandenhoeck & Ruprecht, 1952), 767.14–769.34.

[11] "Comfort of Conservatism," p. 288.

[12] For an excellent discussion of this point, see David J. Hesselgrave and Edward Rommen, *Contextualization: Meanings, Methods and Models* (Grand Rapids, Mich.: Baker Book House, 1989).

[13] David F. Wells, "The Nature and Function of Theology," in R. K. Johnston, ed., *The Use of the Bible in Theology: Evangelical Options* (Atlanta, Ga.: John Knox Press, 1985), p. 177.

[14] "Comfort of Conservatism," p. 283.

[15] Ibid., p. 289.

[16] Ibid., pp. 291–92.

[17] Ibid., p. 290.

[18] See the important analysis of Hugh Mackay, *Reinventing Australia: The Mind and Mood of Australia in the 90s* (Pymble, N.S.W.: Angus & Robertson, 1993).

[19] John H. Crook, *Evolution of Human Consciousness* (Oxford: Oxford University Press, 1980), p. 361.

[20] "Comfort of Conservatism," p. 292.

[21] Martin Luther, *Three Treatises* (Philadelphia: Fortress Press, 1970), pp. 21–22.

[22] Karl Barth, "Theology," in *God in Action* (Edinburgh: T. & T. Clark, 1936), pp. 39–57; quote at pp. 56–57.

[23] WA 40 II.328.17, "Theologiae proprium subiectum est homo peccati reus ac perditus et Deus iustificans ac salvator hominis peccatoris. Quicquid extra hoc subiectum in Theologia quaeritur aut disputatur, est error et venenum." The issues which this quotation raises are enormous. See the classic study of Ernst Wolf, "Die Rechtfertigungslehre als Mitte und Grenze reformatorsicher Theologie," *Evangelische Theologie* 9 (1949–1950): 298–308.

[24] James I. Packer, "An Introduction to Systematic Spirituality," *Crux* 26/1 (March 1990): 2–8; quote at p. 6.

[25] "Comfort of Conservatism," pp. 288–89.

[26] John of Salisbury, *Metalogicon* iii, 4.

11

James I. Packer's Contribution to the Doctrine of the Inerrancy of Scripture

Roger Nicole

MAY I BEGIN WITH A PERSONAL TRIBUTE TO MY brother in Christ, Jim Packer: On this your seventieth birthday, dear Jim, I salute you and congratulate you. You have not spoken or written in vain. My prayer is that, if the Lord should tarry, he will sustain you and your dear wife for many more years to come. May he enable you still to sound the clarion of inerrancy and carry on in a Spirit-filled ministry to your dying day. I offer the following in profound appreciation and affection.

❖ ❖ ❖

The doctrine of Scripture has been a subject of primal importance for evangelicals in the twentieth century, and rightly so, because the whole content of evangelical theology is predicated on the fundamental conviction that the Bible is the Word of God. The subject of inspiration therefore deserves ever-renewed study in order to ascertain what the Bible teaches on this as well as other topics. Then exposition, definition, application and vindication demand our concentrated effort. Three of the major defenders of plenary inspiration in the first half of this century had died in the early twenties (A. Kuyper in 1920, H. Bavinck in 1921 and B. B. Warfield in 1921 also). These were men of gigantic stature both in Christian commitment and in scholarship. A remarkable concentration of orthodox attention to the *theopneustia* characterized the second half of this century. It is here that the contribution of James I. Packer is situated.

As far as I am able to ascertain Dr. Packer first broke into print in 1952 with two articles on Puritan teaching, followed by one article on Richard Baxter in 1953. In 1954 in the second edition of the *New Bible Commentary,* edited by E. F. Kevan, A. M. Stibbs and F. Davidson (London: Inter-Varsity, 1954), he contributed a masterly introductory article on "Revelation and Inspiration." This occupied fourteen columns of small print and manifests the mastery that the author had already achieved at this early date. The emphasis is placed on the concept of revelation, to which more than ten columns are devoted. Inspiration then is summed up in three and a half columns. We note the following statement at the very start of Packer's career as a theological teacher:

> If the words of Scripture are God breathed, it is almost blasphemy to deny that it is free from error in that which it is intended to teach and infallible in the guidance it gives. Inerrancy and infallibility cannot be proved (nor, let us note, disproved) by argument. Both are articles of faith.[1]

We note the close connection of inerrancy and infallibility at a time when other evangelical scholars in the British Isles were accustomed to proclaim infallibility but also to regard the word *inerrant* as the object of discussion in North America only with no relevance in Great Britain!

The precise chronological order of books and articles may be culled from the annexed bibliographical listing. It is not necessary, therefore, to comment here on every contribution. In 1957, however, there was a bolt of lightning, precursor of coming thunder, in Packer's review of A. G. Hebert's *Fundamentalism and the Church of God.* Hebert had exhibited a serious misunderstanding of the evangelical stance on inspiration and of the implications of his own generally evangelical views for a proper doctrine of Scripture. The review appeared in *The Christian Newsletter* (4, no. 3, July 1957, pp. 37–40).

In 1958 came the thunder in the form of the volume *"Fundamentalism" and the Word of God* (London: Inter-Varsity and Grand Rapids, Mich.: Eerdmans, 191 pp.). How well I remember it: I had bought the small volume for $.95. When other members of the family had retired for the night, I started reading at 10:00 P.M. thinking that I might spend an hour or so with the book. I could not lay it down, however: each new chapter had an irresistible appeal, and I finally went to sleep at 4:00 A.M. having devoured this from cover to cover! Here was indeed a masterly piece of work, and I seldom had in my hands a book with which I could agree so thoroughly.

In the first two chapters Packer was taking to task a number of authors who were laboring under drastic misunderstanding and consequently misrepresentation of fundamentalism (A. G. Hebert, Alan Richardson and Michael Ramsey). These were men of considerable repute, but Packer exposed in plain view the short-circuiting of their approach. It was a case of David hitting three Goliaths with his sling! And this David had access to Goliath's sword: he had a D.Phil. from Oxford University!

The chapter on "Authority" goes to the heart of the issue: "Where is the supreme court for the Christian?" Is it the Bible acknowledged as the Word of God (evangelicalism), the church's canons and traditions (traditionalism) or some faculty lodged within humanity itself (subjectivism, liberalism)? Packer demonstrates that Jesus and the apostles, followed by the early church, stand unambiguously for the authority of the Word.

In the next chapter, the longest in the book, Dr. Packer undertakes to ascertain the precise character of the Old Testament, to which our Lord and the apostles appealed as having divine authority. He rejects "dictation" as being erroneously ascribed to evangelicals and "accommodation" as wrongly endorsing the idea that Jesus and his disciples shared in the faulty views of their contemporaries and gave expression to them in the New Testament. Packer insists that it is by the control of divine providence that the New Testament was written, a factor that can ensure the inerrancy of the text without involving a cancellation of the agency and personality of the human writers. Here the accusation of Docetism leveled against the evangelical view boomerangs in showing rather the Nestorianism of the critics!

Dr. Packer makes a careful analysis of the way in which Christ and the apostles use the Old Testament and introduce their quotations of it: it is apparent that they viewed the whole of it as vested with divine authority, even in its wording and most minute detail. It is this section that provides the most convincing argument for the plenary verbal organic inspiration of the whole Bible. Both *infallible* and *inerrant* properly characterize the Scripture. *Infallible* does not mean merely "which cannot deceive or mislead" but also, primarily, "incapable of error"; when this sense is recognized (as implied in the confessions of faith until 1900) it is practically synonymous with *inerrant*. If a distinction is pressed, *infallible* would indicate "no potential for error" and *inerrant* "no actuality of error." *Infallible* is the stronger word, although quite a few people think that the reverse is true!

All this, of course, applies to the text itself, not to human interpretations of the Bible that may fail to elucidate the true and full sense of any Scripture. Correction of one's interpretation must always remain a possibility, especially if it appears to contradict our understanding of another passage. Any interpretation to be acceptable must relate in a natural way to the text and fit into the total scriptural teaching.

A brief chapter on "Faith" follows, showing that our confidence in the divine character of Scripture is not grounded on arguments, even though some arguments are very strong, but rather in a perception and confidence wrought in us by the Holy Spirit.

In a superb chapter entitled "Reason," Dr. Packer carefully delineates the place of human reason in our relationship to Scripture. He skillfully avoids the shoals of rationalism, which covets God's place in that it demands everything to be subject to its own judgment, and of irrationalism, which demeans and flouts a God-given faculty that is an element of the image of God in humanity. Human reason is needed to *receive* a revelation of God that is expressed in verbal fashion, to *apply* this revelation and integrate it with the rest of our knowledge and with our own situation in time and space, and finally to *communicate* it to others. The conflict is not between faith and reason, but between a faith grounded in the Word of God and the overbearing demands of a sinful reason that ambitions to occupy God's place (Gen 3:4).

In the last chapter before his "Conclusion" J. I. Packer deals with "liberalism," exposing the fallacies of "old" as well as "new" liberalism. It discounts the authority of Christ, manifests spiritual impenitence, denies God's rule over his world and presupposes a fundamentally wrong apologetics. Here Goliath's sword finishes what the slung stone had begun (1 Sam 17:51). This book is a veritable classic. It enjoyed three printings in its first year and many more since.

In 1960 at the Oxford Conference of Evangelical Churchmen, J. I. Packer presented a lecture on "The Origin and History of Fundamentalism" in which he analyzed certain features which had made Fundamentalism objectionable. He advocated the Augustinian equation "What Scripture says, God says" as together "the foundation, stumbling block and strength" of evangelicalism. He also showed how liberalism, the school of Biblical Theology, so-called, and Barthianism fell short on this count by insisting that some parts of the Bible are tainted by human error.

In 1961 at the International Conference for Reformed Faith and Action held in Cambridge, Dr. Packer delivered a lecture on "The Bible and the Authority of Reason" which was subsequently published in *The Churchman* (75, no. 4, December 1961, 207–19). Here he demonstrated cogently the necessity for both those who advocate the authority of reason and those who acknowledge the authority of God and his Word to make a claim of universal right for their approach: they cannot compromise by dividing the field of knowledge and allowing each to keep sovereignty in his/her own sphere. He then proceeded to analyze the damage done to the Reformed faith by the progressive encroachments on the line Arminianism–deism–Kant. Only regeneration for the individual and revival for the church can overcome this deadly peril. After the reading of the paper there was a period of questions from the audience, and the poise, pertinence and adequacy of Packer's answers were so remarkable that I never attended a session equal or superior to this one.

In classical Protestant theology it is customary to recognize four perfections of Scripture: authority, necessity, sufficiency and perspicuity. Starting in 1961, J. I. Packer devoted a number of articles to the question of authority in addition to the contribution just mentioned. We note:

+ "The Authority of the Bible," 1961.
+ "The Holy Spirit and Authority," 1962.
+ "Hermeneutics and Biblical Authority," 1967.
+ "Biblical Authority, Hermeneutics and Inerrancy," 1971.
+ "Why Is Authority a Dirty Word?" 1977.
+ "The Reconstitution of Authority," 1982.
+ "Authority and Preaching," 1991.
+ "Authority" in *Concise Theology*, 1993.

The concept of biblical authority is inseparably connected with the truth of the divine authorship of Scripture, and this is emphasized in these articles and elsewhere.

+ The necessity of Scripture is emphasized in Packer's article in M. Tenney, ed., *The Bible: The Living Word of Revelation*, 1968.
+ The sufficiency of Scripture is the principal subject of "*Sola Scriptura* in History and Today," published in 1974.

The perspicuity of Scripture is tied up with the discussions of hermeneutics, the science of perceiving and expounding the true (and, as we strive, full) meaning of statements, specifically scriptured statements. It is obvious that if we are unable to discern the true meaning of Bible passages the value of its inspiration will be nullified, for Scripture does not affect us like a medical pill, which does its work irrespective of our understanding or ignorance of the nature of the chemical reactions it precipitates. The Scripture is a message in words, and our benefiting from it is tied with our understanding of this message and of its relevance to us.

Packer's first article of some length on hermeneutics was published in *The Churchman* in 1967 under the title "Hermeneutics and Biblical Authority." He begins by recounting seven elements that are constitutive of the evangelical acceptance of biblical authority, to wit, the recognition of divine inspiration, canonicity, self-authentication, sufficiency, clarity and mystery of Scripture, and our conscious and unreserved submission to it. The acceptance of this worldview of Scripture will lead us to a grammatico-historical method of exegesis and to observing of the principle of harmony, also known as "the analogy of Scripture." This will lead us to develop "a christo-centric, covenantal and kerygmatic exegesis of both Testaments" (p. 14) and enable us to escape the morass of some of the contemporary complicated discussions of hermeneutics.

Dr. Packer has often returned to this theme in a number of articles, such as

- "Biblical Authority, Hermeneutics and Inerrancy," 1971.
- "An Evangelical View of Progressive Revelation," 1978.
- "A Lamp in a Dark Place," 1979.
- "The Adequacy of Human Language," 1980.
- "Upholding the Unity of Scripture Today," 1982.
- "Infallible Scripture and the Role of Hermeneutics," 1983.
- "Response to Henry Krabbendam," 1984.
- "The Quest of Canonical Interpretation," 1985.
- "Bringing the Bible to Your Life," 1987.
- "The Challenge of Biblical Interpretation on Creation, Woman, Eschatology," 1988.
- "Interpretation," 1993.

In his preaching, understanding of Christian doctrine and ethics, and in the witness of his personal life and piety, Dr. Packer has surely provided an excellent application of the principles he advocated.

In 1964 we have the first of a series of articles dealing with John Calvin's doctrine of Scripture:

- "John Calvin: A Man of the Word," 1964.
- "Calvin the Theologian," 1966, especially pp. 162–67.

Two large articles, to some extent overlapping, constitute the mature and learned conclusions of this Calvin scholar: "Calvin's Doctrine of Scripture," 1974, and "John Calvin and the Inerrancy of Scripture," 1988. It is demonstrated that the dominant theme of John Calvin was the divine authority and truthfulness of Scripture, and this is in entire agreement with my own conclusions in "John Calvin and Inerrancy" in the *Journal of the Evangelical Theological Society* (25, no. 4, December 1982, pp. 425–42), in which a full survey is provided on the Calvin literature up to 1982. Dr. Packer has more affinities with Calvin than with any other Reformer. We should note here his own experience of the witness of the Holy Spirit to Scripture, which is like switching on an electric lamp: the filament is the same, but the electricity makes it incandescent. This is better than an analytical proof, and it is an important feature of the self-authentication of Scripture, as expressed also in the Westminster Confession (I.5), and in earlier Reformed Confessions such as the Gallican (Article 4) and the Belgic (Article 5).

In 1966 a significant conference took place in Wenham, Massachusetts, gathering many noted evangelical scholars from various parts of the United States and from a number of foreign countries (Great Britain, Australia, France, Netherlands, Norway). The purpose was to determine whether there was among evangelicals a consensus on the question of inspiration and inerrancy of Scripture. Some cracks in evangelical unity had surfaced, and this had given rise to accusations and suspicions of a very damaging nature. It was made clear at this meeting that there was a common desire to emphasize the authority of the Word, but that differences existed on the kind of biblical phenomena that could be alleged to be mistakes without impugning the concept of divine authorship. A concluding statement was made asserting "the entire truthfulness" of the Bible, but there was no consensus about the exact meaning of this term, and the language of "inerrancy" was avoided because a significant minority viewed it as misleading or just plainly false. Throughout this conference Dr. Packer was extremely active, representing ably and graciously the standpoint of strict inerrancy.

In 1977 the International Council on Biblical Inerrancy was established under the leadership of Dr. James Boice with the aim of defining, defending and implementing the doctrine of biblical inerrancy. Dr. Packer was a member of this council from the beginning, and he took a vigorous part in all three so-called Summit Meetings in Chicago in 1978, 1982 and 1987 and in the two Congress meetings in San Diego (1982) and Washington (1988). The Summits were intended for scholarly discussion and definition; the Congresses were intended to publicize our stance, and they were geared to large audiences. For each of these Dr. Packer had a major plenary paper. In each of the Summits he was a member of the Redaction committee, which was to prepare a draft of articles of affirmation and denial that we hoped would represent a large majority of the participants and thus be suitable for their individual endorsement. Dr. Packer wrote also the "Exposition" for the first two Summits. The Committee approved these but did not participate in their redaction. In addition to a chapter in each of the Summit Volumes, *Inerrancy* (1980), *Hermeneutics, Inerrancy and the Bible* (1984) and *Applying the Scripture* (1987), J. I. Packer wrote a chapter for some of the volumes produced under the auspices of the International Council on Biblical Inerrancy (ICBI): *Foundations of Biblical Authority* (1978), *Can We Trust The Bible?* (1979), *Scripture and Truth* (1983) and *Inerrancy and the Church* (1984). He also produced the brochure *Freedom and Authority*. Perhaps after Dr. Boice, the organizer, no one in the ICBI worked harder and more effectually than Dr. Packer.

The relation of the Bible to preaching has been a great concern for him, and he articulated it in the last chapter of *Inerrancy and Common Sense* (1980). The task of the preacher is to proclaim, expound and apply the Word of God. To do anything else is to abuse the pulpit and defraud the church. The same emphasis is found in the first chapter of *The Preacher and Preaching* (1986). In his preaching Dr. Packer has certainly practiced what he advocates. His articles "From the Scripture to the Sermon" (1990) and "Authority in Preaching" (1991) articulate the same principle.

In the 1980s a considerable controversy developed in the Southern Baptist Convention, the largest Protestant denomination in the United States, concerning biblical inerrancy and interpretation. Two large conferences were organized respectively in 1987 and 1988, and Prof. Packer was one of the very few non-Baptists invited to participate. He touched on a number of issues, as is apparent from the titles listed in my bibliography. He spoke with great conviction allied to a gracious spirit, so that he did not alienate those who differed from him. In fact one of his respondents grew so enthusiastic that he closed his address with the words: "My dear Doctor Packer, how desperately we need you in Southern Baptist life. . . . What prohibits you from being baptized?" (*Proceedings of the Conference on Biblical Inerrancy*, 1987, p. 150).

One of the latest contributions is found in the article "Thirty Years' War: The Doctrine of Holy Scripture" (1990). Here some of the developments mentioned in the present essay are reviewed by Dr. Packer himself. With characteristic humility he has understated rather than exaggerated his own participation in the debates. Here is a highly interesting account in twenty pages of the highlights of the discussions to which the Doctor has so liberally devoted his time and skills to the great benefit of those who love the Word.

Notes:

[1] J. I. Packer, "Revelation and Inspiration," in E. F. Kevan, A. M. Stibbs, and F. Davidson, eds., *The New Bible Commentary* (London: Inter-Varsity Press, 1954), p. 17.

Select Bibliography of J. I. Packer's Writings on Scripture

1954 "Revelation and Inspiration," in E. F. Kevan, A. M. Stibbs, F. Davidson, eds., *The New Bible Commentary*, 2nd ed. Also published as D. Guthrie, J. A. Motyer, A. M. Stibbs, D. J. Wiseman, eds., *The New Bible Commentary Revised*, pp. 24–30; and in *Eerdmans' Bible Commentary* (London: Inter-Varsity Press and Grand Rapids, Mich.: Eerdmans, 1954, 1970), pp. 12–18.

1955 Review of P. K. Jewett, *Brunner's Doctrine of Revelation*, *Churchman* 69, no. 2 (June 1955): 123-24; also *Theological Students Fellowship*, Summer 1955, pp. 5–7.

1956 "The Witness of the Spirit: The Puritan Teaching," in *The Wisdom of Our Fathers: Puritan and Reformed Studies Conference Reports, 1956* (privately printed, 1957), pp. 14–25 (reprint Clonmel, Ireland: Clonmel Evangelical Bookroom, 1993).

"Some Thoughts on General Revelation," *Christian Graduate* 9, no. 3 (September 1956): 114–21.

"The Inspiration and Infallibility of Holy Scripture," *Theological Students Fellowship Terminal Letter*, Spring 1956.

1957 Review of G. Hebert, *Fundamentalism and the Church of God*, *Christian Newsletter* 4, no. 3 (July 1957): 37–40.

1958 *"Fundamentalism" and the Word of God* (London: Inter-Varsity Fellowship and Grand Rapids, Mich.: Eerdmans, 1958).

"The Puritans as Interpreters of Scripture," in *A Goodly Heritage: Puritan and Reformed Studies Conference Reports, 1958* (London: Banner of Truth Trust, 1959), pp. 18–26.

"Foreword," in ibid., pp. 2–7. Also in *A Quest for Godliness* (Wheaton, Ill.: Crossway, 1990), pp. 97–106.

"The Fundamentalism Controversy: Retrospect and Prospect," *Faith and Thought* 90, no. 1 (Spring 1958): 35–45.

"Fundamentalism: The British Scene," *Christianity Today*, September 29, 1958, pp. 3–6.

"Contemporary Views of Revelation," in C. F. H. Henry, ed., *Revelation and the Bible* (Grand Rapids, Mich.: Eerdmans, 1958), pp. 89–104. Also in *Christianity Today*, November 24,

1958, pp. 3–6, and December 8, 1958, pp. 15–17.

Review of J. K. S. Reid, *The Authority of Scripture, Theological Students Fellowship,* Summer 1958, pp. 8–11.

1959   Review of E. Harris, *Revelation Through Reason, Churchman* 73, no. 3 (September 1959): 156–57.

"The Puritan View of Preaching the Gospel," in *How Shall They Hear? Puritan and Reformed Studies Conference Reports, 1959* (privately printed, 1960; reprint edition Clonmel, Ireland: Clonmel Evangelical Bookroom, 1993).

1960   Review of H. D. MacDonald, *Ideas of Revelation, Churchman* 74, no. 1 (March 1960): 42–43. Also *Bible League Quarterly* 17, no. 2 (June 1960): 81f.

"The Bible in Modern Theology," *Bible League Quarterly* no. 240 (January–March 1960): 129–32.

1961   "Origin and History of Fundamentalism," in T. Hewitt, ed., *The Word of God and Fundamentalism* (London: Church Book Room Press, 1961), pp. 100–27.

"Inspiration," in J. D. Douglas, ed., *New Bible Dictionary* (London: Inter-Varsity Press and Grand Rapids, Mich.: Eerdmans, 1961), pp. 564–66. Reprinted in later editions of this work.

"Revelation," in ibid., pp. 1090–93.

"The Bible and the Authority of Reason," *Churchman* 75, no. 4 (December 1961): 207–19.

"The Authority of the Bible," *HIS,* November 1961, pp. 24–37.

1962   *Our Lord's Understanding of the Law of God* (Glasgow: Pickering & Inglis, 1962).

"The Holy Spirit and Authority," *The Almond Branch,* 1962, pp. 9–12.

1963   "Our Lord and the Old Testament," *Bible League Quarterly* no. 252 (January–March 1963): 70–74.

Review of H. D. MacDonald, *Theories of Revelation, Churchman* 77, no. 3 (September 1963): 202–3.

1964   "Calvin: A Servant of the Word," in *Able Ministers of the New Testament: Puritan and Reformed Studies Conference Reports, 1964* (Battersea, England: Evangelical Magazine, 1965), pp. 36–55.

"John Calvin: A Man of the Word," *Evangelical Library Bulletin* no. 32 (1964): 2–7.

"The Bible, Yesterday, Today and Tomorrow," *The Gospel*

Magazine, March 1964, pp. 104–13.

1965   *God Has Spoken* (London: Hodder & Stoughton, 1965). The American edition is entitled *God Speaks to Man* (Philadelphia: Westminster Press, 1965).

"Ministry of the Word Today," *Presbyterian Guardian* 34, no. 6 (July–August 1965): 87–90. Also *Christian Heritage,* December 1965.

1966   "Calvin the Theologian," in G. Duffield, ed., *John Calvin* (Grand Rapids, Mich.: Eerdmans, 1966), pp. 149–75.

"John Owen on Communication from God," in *One Steadfast High Intent: Puritan and Reformed Studies Conference Reports, 1966* (London: Evangelical Magazine, 1967), pp. 17–30. Also in *A Quest for Godliness* (Wheaton, Ill.: Crossway, 1990), pp. 81–96.

1967   "Hermeneutics and Biblical Authority," *Churchman* 81, no. 1 (Spring 1967): 7–21.

1968   "The Necessity of the Revealed Word," in M. Tenney, ed., *The Bible: The Living Word of Revelation* (Grand Rapids, Mich.: Zondervan, 1968), pp. 31–53.

Review of J. Bright, *The Authority of the Old Testament, Churchman* 82, no. 2 (Summer 1968): 138f.

1971   "Biblical Authority, Hermeneutics and Inerrancy," in E. R. Geehan, ed., *Jerusalem and Athens* (Nutley, N.J.: Presbyterian and Reformed, 1971), pp. 141–53.

1973   "Revelation," in C. F. H. Henry, ed., *Baker's Dictionary of Christian Ethics* (Grand Rapids, Mich.: Baker, 1973), pp. 383–84.

1974   "*Sola Scriptura* in History and Today," in J. W. Montgomery, ed., *God's Inerrant Word* (Minneapolis, Minn.: Bethany, 1974), pp. 43–62.

"Calvin's Doctrine of Scripture," in ibid., pp. 95–114.

1975   Review of G. C. Berkouwer, *Holy Scripture, Eternity,* August 1975, pp. 45–46. Also in *Beyond the Battle for the Bible* (Westchester, Ill.: Crossway, 1980), pp. 140–42.

1977   "Why Is Authority a Dirty Word?" *Spectrum* 9, no. 3 (May 1977): 4–6.

Foreword, to R. C. Sproul, *Knowing Scripture* (Downers Grove, Ill.: InterVarsity Press, 1977), pp. 9–10.

1978   "Encountering Present-Day Views of Scripture," in J. Boice, ed., *Foundations of Biblical Authority* (Grand Rapids, Mich.: Zondervan, 1978), pp. 61–82.

"An Evangelical View of Progressive Revelation," in K. Kantzer, ed., *Evangelical Roots* (Nashville, Tenn.: Thomas Nelson, 1978), pp. 143–58.

1979 "Chicago Statement on Biblical Inerrancy" and "Exposition," in *God Has Spoken,* 3rd ed. of *God Speaks to Man* (Downers Grove, Ill.: InterVarsity Press, 1979), pp. 147–53.

"A Lamp in a Dark Place," in E. Radmacher, ed., *Can We Trust the Bible?* (Wheaton, Ill.: Tyndale, 1979), pp. 15–30.

"Battling for the Bible," *Regent College Bulletin* 9, no. 4 (Fall 1979).

Review of H. Lindsell, *The Bible in the Balance, Crux* 15, no. 4 (December 1979): 26–27. Also in *Beyond the Battle for the Bible* (Westchester, Ill.: Crossway, 1980), pp. 142–46.

1980 *Beyond the Battle for the Bible* (Westchester, Ill.: Crossway, 1980).

Review of J. B. Rogers and D. K. McKim, *The Authority and Inspiration of the Bible, Crux* 16, no. 1 (March 1980): 31–32. Also in *Beyond The Battle for the Bible* (Westchester, Ill.: Crossway, 1980), pp. 146–51.

"Preaching and Biblical Interpretation," in R. Nicole and J. Michaels, eds., *Inerrancy and Common Sense* (Grand Rapids, Mich.: Baker, 1980), pp. 187–203.

"The Adequacy of Human Language," in N. Geisler, ed., *Inerrancy* (Grand Rapids, Mich.: Zondervan, 1980), pp. 196–226. This work also includes the "Chicago Statement on Biblical Inerrancy" and "Exposition."

"Editor's Preface," in J. I. Packer et al., eds., *The Bible Almanac* (Nashville, Tenn.: Thomas Nelson, 1980), pp. 11–12.

1981 *God's Words* (Downers Grove, Ill.: InterVarsity Press, 1981).

Freedom and Authority (Oakland, Calif.: International Council on Biblical Inerrancy, 1981). Published in England as *Freedom, Authority and the Scripture* (Leicester, England: InterVarsity Press, 1982).

Review of L. R. Bush and T. J. Nettles, *Baptists and the Bible, Crux* 17, no. 3 (September 1981): 29–31.

1982 "Upholding the Unity of Scripture Today," *Journal of the Evangelical Theological Society* 25, no. 4 (December 1982): 409–14.

"The Reconstitution of Authority," *Crux* 18, no. 4 (December 1982): 2–12.

1983 "Infallible Scripture and the Role of Hermeneutics," in D.

Carson and J. Woodbridge, eds., *Scripture and Truth* (Grand Rapids, Mich.: Zondervan, 1983), pp. 321–56.

"God's Word and Changed Lives," *Canadian Report* 7 (September 1983).

1984 "Response to Henry Krabbendam, 'The New Hermeneutic,'" in N. Geisler and E. Radmacher, eds., *Hermeneutics, Inerrancy and the Bible* (Grand Rapids, Mich.: Zondervan, 1984), pp. 559–71.

"Exposition," in ibid., pp. 905–14.

"John Calvin and the Inerrancy of Holy Scripture," in J. Hannah, ed., *Inerrancy and the Church* (Chicago: Moody, 1984), pp. 143–88.

1985 "The Quest of Canonical Interpretation," in R. K. Johnston, ed., *The Use of the Bible in Theology: Evangelical Options* (Atlanta, Ga.: John Knox, 1985), pp. 32–55.

1986 "Why Preach?" in S. Logan Jr., ed., *The Preacher and Preaching* (Grand Rapids, Mich.: Baker, 1986), pp. 1–29.

1987 "The Holy Spirit and His Work," in K. Kantzer, ed., *Applying the Scripture* (Grand Rapids, Mich.: Zondervan, 1987), pp. 51–76.

"Inerrancy and the Divinity and Humanity of the Bible," in J. Gregory, ed., *Proceedings of the Conference on Biblical Inerrancy* (Nashville, Tenn.: Broadman, 1987), pp. 135–42.

"Problem Areas Related to Inerrancy," in ibid., pp. 205–13.

"Implications of Inerrancy for Christian Mission," in ibid., pp. 245–50.

"Bringing the Bible to Your Life," *Charisma* 12, no. 6 (January 1987): 43–44, 46.

1988 "Infallibility and Inerrancy," in D. Wright, S. Ferguson and J. I. Packer, eds., *New Dictionary of Theology* (Leicester, England and Downers Grove, Ill.: InterVarsity Press, 1988), pp. 337–39.

"Scripture," in ibid., pp. 627–31.

"The Challenge of Biblical Interpretation: Creation," in J. Gregory, ed., *Proceedings of the Conference on Biblical Interpretation* (Nashville, Tenn.: Broadman, 1988), pp. 21–33.

"The Challenge of Biblical Interpretation: Women," in ibid., pp. 103–15.

"The Challenge of Biblical Interpretation: Eschatology," in ibid., pp. 191–204.

1990 *A Quest for Godliness: The Puritan Vision of the Christian Life*

(Wheaton, Ill.: Crossway, 1990), chapters 3 "John Owen on Communication from God," pp. 81–96, and 4 "The Puritans as Interpreters of Scripture," pp. 97–105.

"From the Scriptures to the Sermon," *Ashland Theological Journal* 22 (1990): 42–64.

"Understanding the Bible," in M. Tinker, ed., *Restoring the Vision* (Eastbourne, England: MARC, 1990), pp. 39–58.

"Thirty Years' War: The Doctrine of Holy Scripture," in H. M. Conn, ed., *Practical Theology and the Ministry of the Church, 1952–1984* (Phillipsburg, N.J.: Presbyterian and Reformed, 1990), pp. 25–44.

"The Reformed Faith in the Modern World: I. Bible," *Evangelical Presbyterian* (New Zealand) no. 2 (December 1990).

1991 "Authority in Preaching," in M. Eden and D. Wells, eds., *The Gospel in the Modern World* (Downers Grove, Ill.: InterVarsity Press, 1991), pp. 198–212.

"Scripture, Inerrancy and the Church," *Touchstone* 4 (Fall 1991): 3–4.

1992 "Inspiration" (article from *New Bible Dictionary*, 1961), in P. Comfort, ed., *The Origin of the Bible* (Wheaton, Ill: Tyndale, 1992), pp. 29–36.

"The Word of Life," *The Evangelical Catholic* 4, no. 4 (July–August 1992): 1–8.

1993 "Revelation," in *Concise Theology* (Wheaton, Ill.: Tyndale, 1993), pp. 3–5.

"Interpretation," in ibid., pp. 6–8.

"Inward Witness," in ibid., pp. 13–15.

"Authority," in ibid., pp. 16–18.

These entries are also in *The New Geneva Study Bible* (Nashville, Tenn.: Thomas Nelson, 1995).

1995 *Knowing and Doing the Will of God* (Ann Arbor, Mich.: Servant, 1995), pp. 41–70.

"Revelation and Authority," in *Knowing Christianity* (Wheaton, Ill.: Harold Shaw, 1995), pp. 19–41.

12

J. I. Packer and the Shaping of American Evangelicalism

Mark A. Noll

EVEN TO BEGIN TO ASSESS THE IMPACT OF AN author and speaker like J. I. Packer in one country like the United States would require diligent research on a number of different levels. The task is made more difficult in Packer's case since, from the publication of *"Fundamentalism" and the Word of God* in 1958, he has been *in* the United States but never actually, or entirely, *of* it. While his books and essays have been widely read in the States, while he has traveled extensively to address evangelical, Episcopal and theologically conservative conferences and congregations, and while he has actively supported many American publishers, symposia, denominations and parachurch agencies, all of this activity has proceeded from bases outside the United States—first from a variety of posts in England and then since 1979 from his position as professor of theology at Regent College in Vancouver, British Columbia.

The special circumstances that shape Packer's influence are not limited to the fact that for nearly forty years he—a non-American— has traveled regularly, spoken frequently and been widely published in the United States. Those special circumstances also include the fact that Packer's wide-ranging labor has aimed directly at the shadowy intersection of popular and academic concerns—he is a scholar who yet found his vocation in popular communication, a popular communicator who never abandoned scholarship. That Packer's work has touched on substantial historical, exegetical and ecclesiastical concerns, as well as more narrowly theological (or spiritual-theological) matters, also adds complexity to the nature of his influence.

At this point it is also a temptation (which shall be resisted) to launch into tangents. One tangent—which it can be hoped that someone will someday study seriously—is the general question of influence on evangelicalism in the United States from the Church of England. The thinking of what might be called middle-brow American evangelicals, who are by habit and sometimes conviction systematically unecclesiastical, has been decisively influenced in the period since World War II by at least three English churchmen—C. S. Lewis and John R. W. Stott as well as Packer. How and why that influence came to be exerted—especially given the generally unevangelical drift of the American Episcopal Church—would make an interesting study in itself, especially if the differences between Lewis (who never recognized himself as an "evangelical" and who never visited North America) and Stott and Packer (who sought out links with self-confessed "evangelicals" in North America and who have both spent much time in the States) were given their due. This is a story that should be told, but cannot be attempted here.

Another tangent not to be pursued is the question of J. I. Packer's impact on his native England and his adopted Canada as compared to his influence in the United States. I attempt below a crude, preliminary explanation for one aspect of Packer's work that involves his English and Anglican provenance, but the subject is worth full-scale attention. Such a comparison deserves study and not only as a potentially significant question of first-order research in itself—e.g., are Packer's books that sell best in the United States also the ones that sell best in Canada and in England? It is also an intriguing question because of Packer's ecclesiastical identification in each of the three areas. In both England and Canada, Packer has labored on behalf of pan-evangelical causes, but in both nations he is also visibly identified with the Anglican communion. To be sure, Packer's identity has never been anything less than robustly *evangelical Anglican,* but from his teaching and research positions in British Anglican institutions to his special labors on behalf of the Anglican Church of Canada and in his honorary assistant rectorship at St. John's Shaughnessy Anglican Church on Granville Street in Vancouver, there has never been a doubt as to where Packer stands, ecclesiastically as well as theologically, in England and in Canada. The American situation is different.

Many of his American readers and auditors know that Packer is Anglican (sometimes mistranslated "Episcopalian" south of the 49th parallel), but Packer's position in America has depended much more on the content of his theology and the tenor of his spiritual encouragement than on any awareness of his position as an Anglican. The question—what has an Anglican evangelical (or evangelical Anglican?) done because he *is*, or *is not*, Anglican when examined comparatively in England, Canada and the United States—strikes me as a question that could yield much about the meaning of Christian experience in these nations. But here, alas, we are not able to pursue that question, or the even more far-ranging one of how Packer has been read and appropriated in Scotland, Wales, Northern Ireland, Australia, South Africa, Korea, Hong Kong and other areas where he would be uniformly prized as an evangelical, but variously received as an Anglican.

Tangents spurned, what this essay does attempt is an introductory sketch based on some of the questions concerning the nature of J. I. Packer's contribution to the postwar life of evangelicalism in the United States.[1] To make a start, it is possible to provide at least preliminary data or opinion to response to six relevant questions:

1. What has Packer published in America?
2. How widely have Packer's publications been distributed?
3. How has Packer participated in American institutions, denominations and parachurch agencies?
4. What has been Packer's spiritual influence in ecclesiastical, spiritual and personal dimensions?
5. What has been his intellectual influence among academics?
6. How should one interpret the nature of Packer's influence in relationship to the realities of American evangelical life?

1. What Has Packer Published in America?

Even the simple question of what J. I. Packer has published in America is not as straightforward as it sounds. When someone has been writing as persistently as he has on so many subjects, publishing history becomes a complex matter. As of early 1995 Packer (or an industrious secretary) was able to list 165 separate books, coauthored or coedited books, pamphlets and articles in books (plus nearly that many more journal or periodical articles) from his busy (manual!) typewriter. The complexity begins in asking which of these were published in the United States, which in Britain and which in both. Setting aside publications in periodicals, a rough count of the book and pamphlet publication shows that about 65 of these individual writings were published only in the U.K., slightly more than that only in the U.S., not quite 30 in both the U.K. and the U.S., and a handful elsewhere (e.g., Australia, Germany). Of course, following the Chestertonian principle to "never sell anything once," authors must be free to recycle, so it is probable that material published in one nation sometimes showed up in another form, or incorporated into another publication, on the other side of the Atlantic. Yet, once past the major books that are well known in both the U.K. and the U.S.—e.g., *"Fundamentalism" and the Word of God* (1958), *Evangelism and the Sovereignty of God* (1961), *Knowing God* (1973), *A Quest for Godliness* (U.S. title)/*Among God's Giants* (U.K. title) (1991)— something of a pattern does emerge. Certainly, Packer's historical, ecclesiastical, exegetical and theological interests have been given a wide hearing on both sides of the Atlantic. But there is a decided preponderance of historical and ecclesiastical writing published in Britain that has not been brought out in North America, and more writings that are "just" theological or exegetical published only in the United States.[2] This situation means that someone who wants to read Packer's entire *oeuvre* on the Puritans, or explore the length and breadth of his opinions on sacraments, church order or historical confessions, would best do so from a British library strong in contemporary Anglican writing. By contrast, someone who wished to explore the details of Packer's convictions on subjects like the gifts of the Spirit, the use of the Bible or the meaning of justification by faith would do well to pursue those inquiries in a North American library strong in materials from evangelical, interdenominational publishers. In one particularly interesting instance, I believe it is the case that Packer's introductory essay to John Owen's *Death of Death in the Death of Christ* was published separately in the United States as a pamphlet (and so intended to be taken as a defense of the doctrine of specific atonement), whereas in Britain the introduction has only appeared *with* Owen's text (and so has functioned primarily as a commendation of that work and only secondarily as a first-order contribution to contemporary theology).

To be sure, there is sufficient overlap in the pattern of Packer's publication so that North Americans who want to know Packer's views on the Puritans or on contemporary questions affecting the worldwide Anglican communion can do so from works published in North America, and the same can be said in Britain for Packer's views on a wide range of theological questions. Yet the differences in what has been published where are interesting, and perhaps of some significance.

2. How Widely Have Packer's Publications Been Distributed?

Sufficient evidence does not exist to speak definitively about the way Packer's writing has altered the direction of North American evangelicalism. In any case, North American scholars are not yet as adept as their Continental counterparts at linking the availability of books to the actual influence of books. Yet even with these limitations, it still is possible to say a few concrete things about the distribution of Packer's books in North America.

With the helpful assistance of several publishers—Crossway, Eerdmans, Harold Shaw, InterVarsity Press (IVP), Tyndale House—it is possible to gain some sense of the quantity of Packer's books and separately printed pamphlets that, as of mid-1995, had been distributed in the United States.[3] The total number of copies in print for eighteen different titles from these five publishers came to slightly more than one and three-quarters million. *Knowing God* from IVP accounts for over half that total; over 200,000 copies of *Evangelism and the Sovereignty of God* (IVP) have been distributed since that book was first released in 1961; two IVP pamphlets, *Meeting God* and *Finding God's Will*, had both topped the 100,000 figure; and *"Fundamentalism" and the Word of God* (Eerdmans) along with *I Want to Be a Christian* (Tyndale) had gone over the 50,000 mark.

That is a lot of books. Yet the figures are certainly not unprecedented for religious book sales in North America, where the numbers of volumes sold by some of Packer's publishing contemporaries like Hal Lindsey, Frank Peretti or Marjorie Holmes are many times higher. Perhaps the most remarkable thing about these figures is that they combine very solid sales for the volumes treating spiritual realities directly, but also include substantial distribution for books of sturdy theological casuistry like *"Fundamentalism" and the Word of God* and *Evangelism and the Sovereignty of God.*

3. How Has Packer Participated in American Institutions, Denominations and Parachurch Agencies?

The question of Packer's influence exerted through institutions is also difficult to research, but brief consideration of the range of his institutional connections reveals patterns that may suggest something about his impact on American evangelicalism.

I set aside here the question of how Packer's one-sermon or one-lecture speaking engagements have been influential, for that is a subject requiring unusual subtlety. In the United States, where the visiting lecturer (especially the visiting lecturer with a foreign accent) has always been a spectacle, it is not altogether clear how to assess the meaning of crowds gathered to listen. Certainly for those who have read Packer's books or articles, the chance to hear him in person is welcome for identifying a face behind the words. One can also assume that many of those who have heard Packer but not read his writings have carried away something important—whether historical, theological, exegetical or devotional—to ponder. But a certain degree of suspicion may still be appropriate about the effect of such one-off speaking engagements in light of the highly developed American taste for show.

Packer's involvement with North American evangelical institutions, however, has gone much deeper than his many single engagements. Despite his wide travels, he has taught full-time at Regent College (Vancouver, B.C.) since 1979. He has also served stints as a visiting lecturer (usually involving some kind of extended or repeated stay) at Reformed Theological Seminary (Jackson, Miss.), New College (Berkeley, Calif.), Westminster Seminary (Calif.), Conservative Baptist Seminary (Denver), Canadian Theological Seminary (Regina, Sask.), Gordon-Conwell Theological Seminary (Mass.), Trinity Evangelical Divinity School (Ill.) and Westminster Theological Seminary (Philadelphia). The collective identity of these institutions is strikingly different from the British institutions where Packer was employed before migrating to North America: Tyndale Hall (Bristol), Latimer House (Oxford) and Trinity College (Bristol). The British posts were Anglican; the North American posts have been Reformed, evangelical or evangelical and Reformed.

Packer has also actively supported several other enterprises in the American evangelical world. He has not only written frequently for but consulted regularly with *Christianity Today* and its sister publications. He has served several terms on the board of the Institute for Advanced Studies. And for many years he was a regular speaker for the "Philadelphia Lectures in Reformed Theology" and the Allies for Faith and Renewal conferences. He also has played an important part in many of the collaborative book projects that, at least for some academically inclined North American evangelicals, have functioned as denominations may have done for their predecessors in the nineteenth century. So it was that, among a wide variety of such offerings, Packer made special contributions to several of Carl Henry's memorable evangelical symposia in the 1950s and 1960s, to several of the books on biblical inerrancy from the 1970s and 1980s and to several more general symposia on theology and spirituality in the 1980s and 1990s.

Many of Packer's contributions to these institutional and collaborative projects feature his characteristic concentrations on churchly, historical and confessional matters. But, with the exception of a few of the specifically Reformed enterprises, very few of the forums themselves can be said to be overwhelmingly historical, confessional or churchly in their intents. In addition, Packer's identification as an Anglican on the other side of the water has not loomed large in his North American career, where assistance to the Anglican Church of Canadian and the American Episcopal Church has not been nearly as visible as his contributions to transdenominational evangelicalism.

4. What Has Been Packer's Spiritual Influence in Ecclesiastical, Spiritual and Personal Dimensions?

The question of spiritual influence is best left to the testimonies of those who have read, marked and inwardly digested Packer's "spiritual theology," and especially the luminous theocentricism of *Knowing God*. Packer writing on God may indeed resemble, as he said at the beginning of that book, "clowns" who "yearn to play Hamlet." But if so, he has played the role like a *jongleur de Dieu* and, like his Franciscan predecessors in at least this one way, has done more than a little to help theology perform "its basic task of holding the church to the realities of the gospel."[4] When G. K. Chesterton arrived in his study of Thomas Aquinas to the point where readers might expect a discussion of Thomas's theology, he begged off with a cryptic, but no less persuasive, explanation: "Anyone writing so small a book about so big a man, must leave out something. Those who know him best will best understand why, after some considerable consideration, I have left out the only important thing."[5] In a similar way, the profound spiritual impact of Packer's work is certainly the most important aspect of his influence in the Christian history of North America. But for that very reason, it is also the most difficult to discuss.

5. What Has Been His Intellectual Influence Among Academics?

Since academic influence is only relatively important in comparison with spiritual influence, it is possible to say something slightly more concrete about that subject. Again, a full search through the writings of Packer's contemporaries, and also in master's theses and doctoral dissertations, on the Puritans, twentieth-century evangelical Anglicanism and major doctrines of the Trinity, the Holy Spirit or the justifying work of Christ, would be necessary to assess academic influence. In the absence of such a thorough study, however, a preliminary substitute can be found in a research tool called the "Arts and Humanities Index."[6] This index catalogues the citations in several hundred academic journals in such a way that the use made by academics of works from other academics can be studied systematically. An exploration of this index in September 1995 turned up thirty references to Packer's works in eighteen different journals. Eleven of the journals were theological or biblical, four were historical and the rest were quite diverse, including *Christianity and Literature, Library Journal* and the *Journal of Psychology and Theology*.[7]

Even more revealing were Packer's twenty different works (ten books, ten articles) that were cited in these thirty articles. About ten of the citations were taken from his writings on Anglicanism, four were citations to *Knowing God* and *"Fundamentalism" and the Word of God,* three were to *Evangelism and the Sovereignty of God* and the rest came from a scattering of other works.

From this very preliminary search, it would seem that Packer's academic influence lies, again, in two areas—in theology *per se,* especially spiritual or lived theology, and also in historical-theological matters respecting the Church of England or (less prominently) the Puritans.

Ascertaining the exact dimensions of Packer's academic influence would require much fuller comparative study. At the least, however, even this preliminary measure indicates that he has been widely read, and read for more than one narrow purpose.

6. How Should One Interpret the Nature of Packer's Influence in Relationship to the Realities of American Evangelical Life?

A last question of influence is more interpretive. It is the question of how Packer's contribution fits into the particular landscape of American evangelical culture. Restated, it is the question of what Packer offered that American evangelicals have needed. Elsewhere I have tried to suggest what I think the particular strengths and weaknesses of American evangelicalism have been. To oversimplify an admittedly complex situation, my conclusion was that American evangelicalism is best defined as a traditional activistic pietism (or "experiential biblicism") which has featured mobilization for specific, tangible tasks like evangelism, institution building and political action (sometimes for ill, but often for good). As a consequence, American evangelicals have underemphasized (to their detriment) historical, contemplative, mediating and complex expressions of the faith.[8] If that analysis is correct, J. I. Packer's influence on American evangelicalism has been as critical as it is broad.

Packer has exerted that influence by combining characteristics that have rarely been joined together in America. In a word, he is an *educated, Reformed, Anglican evangelical,* with each of the four ascriptions vital as a counterweight to the other three. As the history of Christianity in America has shown so often, any of these commitments by itself can easily become a threat to clarity of Christian thought and integrity of Christian activity. Together, at least as they have been conjoined in Packer's writing and speaking, they have been water to a parched and weary land.

As a well-educated person grounded in both classical theology and the classics more generally, Packer readily perceives how complex many spiritual and intellectual problems really are. He has assumed that he has something to learn from authorities beyond his own inner circle. And he instinctively realizes that the canons of various disciplines and subdisciplines have intrinsic value, but also that perceptive canon-criticism is a requirement for any kind of self-critical wisdom. At the same time, he has displayed these scholarly virtues as a part of, rather than in revolt against, his Reformed, Anglican and evangelical identities. He has shown how learning not only can flourish with Reformed, Anglican and evangelical convictions, but can flourish to honor God and build up the church. In the history of American evangelicalism, such examples have been all too rare.

As a Calvinist, Packer has embodied the virtues of a weighty theological tradition. He has demonstrated the *gravitas* to be found in embracing one of the three or four truly consequential theological traditions in the Christian history of the last several centuries. His self-conscious Reformed theology has been displayed to best advantage in his explicitly biblical work—as careful exegete, resolute defender of the authority and inerrancy of Scripture, and self-conscious hermeneutical theorist. Against the widely prevailing, but intellectually suicidal, American tendency to act as if exegesis, hermeneutics and dogmatizing on the doctrine of Scripture take place in a vacuum, Packer has offered the principial thinking of a sturdy Calvinist. This means that, as with B. B. Warfield, the American theologian whom Packer resembles most closely, organic connections exist between his doctrine of the Bible, his methods of exegesis and his exegetical conclusions. And yet Packer the Calvinist has been simultaneously Packer the evangelical and Packer the Anglican, with each of the latter commitments taking the self-satisfied, triumphalist or demeaning edge off the spirit that so often has characterized the work of serious American Calvinists.[9]

As an Anglican, Packer is moderate, orthodox in the classical sense of the great Trinitarian creeds, open to theological insight from other points on the ecclesiastical compass (including the Roman Catholic and the Pentecostal), self-critical and historical. There are, in both the United States and Canada, Episcopalians or Anglicans who share these virtues, but none (to my knowledge) who do so along with such obvious commitments to Reformed and evangelical convictions. Packer is a churchman, but he has not been afraid to speak in chapels. He embodies the distilled wisdom of the ecclesiastical ages, but he has not scrupled to fellowship with those whose churches were founded yesterday.

Withal, Packer is an evangelical. He knows, teaches and lives the truth that knowledge of God must be personal, that the work of Christ was a ransom to be actively embraced and that the Holy Spirit is alive and active even today. At the end of *Knowing God,* Packer's evangelical convictions blended seamlessly with his recommendation of classical orthodoxy. Besides knowing what the Scriptures say about God, besides knowing that humans are sinners in need of divine grace, "we saw that knowing God involves a personal relationship whereby you give yourself to God on the basis of His promise to give Himself to you. Knowing God means asking His mercy, and resting on His undertaking to forgive sinners for Jesus's sake. Further, it means becoming a disciple of Jesus, the living Savior who is 'there' today, calling the needy to Himself as He did in Galilee in the days of His flesh. Knowing God, in other words, involves *faith*— assent, consent, commitment—and faith expresses itself in prayer and obedience."[10] The diction is British, the sentiment is evangelical. The unusual quality of Packer's evangelicalism, however, is precisely that it is so organically linked to his education, his Calvinism and his Anglicanism. This combination keeps it from the excesses that a largely unhistorical, mostly antitraditional and often anti-intellectual evangelicalism has suffered in the course of American history.

To illustrate the way that Packer sustains these commitments together, I close with a brief summary of three talks that Packer presented to an American audience only months after he had emigrated from England. In November 1979 Packer was asked to participate in a conference at Wheaton College on "The Bible in America." His role was to comment as a panelist at the end of the academic conference and also to bring two chapel addresses during the days of the conference to Wheaton College students and faculty. For those popular audiences, his messages were "Beyond the Battle for the Bible" and "How God's Word Is Heard."[11] Some of what Packer presented at these gatherings has appeared in print in other forms. But the combination of his concerns were also typical of his entire *oeuvre* and so particularly suited to provide what has often been lacking in the American setting.

In the course of these talks, Packer defended unequivocally an evangelical and orthodox view of Scripture. He reminded the chapel audience, for example, that it would be a grievous thing if evangelicals would "go the way of the world in continuing to doubt the Bible." And he told it that "the inerrancy of Scripture matters . . . because the authority of Scripture matters." He also sounded a characteristically evangelical note in driving home the point that an unapplied Bible is as good as an unread Bible. "Sometimes," he said, "God the Holy Spirit will . . . make a nuisance of himself by keeping applying Scripture to our consciences until we are willing to change our ways." And he made a decidedly evangelical conclusion to this chain of reasoning (though by using a quotation from W. H. Auden), that often "we would rather be ruined than changed."

Packer's defense of an orthodox and evangelical view of Scripture was, however, especially noteworthy by being buttressed with the weight of Christian tradition. Against flighty approaches to Scripture, Packer urged the Wheaton faculty and students to "study the Bible historically" (in the context of the day in which it was written), to study the Bible organically (as a whole) and to study it in connection with the whole history of Christianity. "If you get out of touch with . . . that heritage," he concluded, "you cannot find your own means and become a reliable interpreter of Scripture on your own."

To the academics at the conference he added Reformed and Anglican specificity to his historical recommendation of Scripture. Apropos the modern fascination with the vitality of "the word of God" set over against the relative passivity of the written Scripture, Packer reminded the academics that already in the Westminster Confession the church was using both containment language ("the Word of God contained in Scripture") and equation language ("the Word of God is Scripture") to speak about the Bible, well before this difference was posed as a dichotomy in modern theology. He also corrected a casual reference to Richard Hooker's use of reason in connection with Scripture by reminding his audience that Hooker's discriminations concerning Scripture had much more to do with the question of where the Bible spoke generally as opposed to where it spoke specifically to local situations, rather than with a contrast between the rights of Scripture, on the one hand, and the rights of reason, on the other.

To both the academics and the student body, Packer affirmed the need for evangelicals to sharpen their wits, even as they guarded their hearts. He forthrightly acknowledged that the new importance accorded to historical sensibility in western society over the last two centuries had created a situation where something more was needed to preserve an orthodox view of Scripture than merely updating the dogmas of the past. And he reminded his audiences repeatedly that sincere defense of Scripture could never replace the need for Christian humility. He warned specifically that "in the battle for the Bible, the . . . danger operates, that the folk engaged in the battle will just concentrate on the battle and never think of the issues for sake of which the battle is being fought."

Packer's major call for critical self-awareness, however, dealt at length with the need for critical discernment—of the world, of intellectual methods, but mostly of oneself. In this regard he used one of the chapel services to recommend the kind of searching self-criticism that activistic American evangelicalism has too rarely taken to heart. For their willingness to be self-critical as well as for their willingness to seek theological and spiritual help wherever it may be found, Packer's words are worth quoting at length:

> [Beware of] the blinkers that we wear. . . . We are victims because we are children of the Protestant tradition, of the evangelical tradition, of our own denominational tradition. . . . All of these traditions have brought us strengths and we ought to be grateful for them, but . . . all of them can serve as blinkers, narrowing our vision for things which folks from other traditions can see. Again, we are children and therefore victims of reactions, negative reactionary attitudes which are there in our own tradition. Reactions I mean against the sacramentalism of Rome, which has made us all distrust sacraments; against the liturgical formalism of Rome, which has made us all distrust set prayers; against the beauty and dignity of worship, which is characteristic of Rome and on which our traditions have tended to turn their back. We are victims of reaction against the heavy

theology of earlier generations, which has made us an unthe-
ological lot opposing head knowledge to heart knowledge and
treating the head knowledge as if it did not matter. We are victims of reaction against the love of the past. History, we say in
our hearts, is bunk. We are not the first to say it, but many
evangelical Christians in their hearts do say it these days and it is
a reaction. And we are victims too of a lot of reactions against
what is natural to man, what is human, but what in our traditions we are inclined to write off as being worldly. And what
does this produce? It produces something for which the sociologists have a name—they call it cultural prejudice and it keeps
us from seeing, brothers and sisters, a lot of what is there in the
Bible. The Psalmist prays, "Give me understanding that I may
keep thy law." One of the things that is needed for understanding is that we should find the way to freedom from cultural
prejudice.

As these words suggest, Packer's theological horizon is wide. Despite his own willingness to critique Catholic positions on several
important matters, for example, he also told the academics he felt
that it was "only in the Roman Catholic Church in the last generation, I would say, that the dimensions of this problem [of history and
tradition] have begun to be explored." And when Packer told the
chapel audience who they should be reading as partners in the past to
help understand the Scripture, the expected names headed the list:
Martin Luther, John Calvin, Augustine, Jonathan Edwards and the
Puritans. But then to these stalwarts of his own tradition he added
"John of the Cross and folk like that."

Above all, Packer's advocacy on behalf of Scripture was marked by
balance. He wanted first to accentuate the need for a vigorous doctrine of the Holy Spirit to accompany a vigorous doctrine of Scripture. "God gives understanding through the Holy Spirit." This in-
junction did not remove the need for careful study, but was part and
parcel of that need. "If you want to know what the Bible meant, you
must study. . . . But then, you haven't understood the Bible fully until
you are able to apply that and see what it means for yourself, for
your own folk, for your own situation, for your own church, for
your own time. And it is at this point that you and I can never make
any progress unless the Holy Spirit guides us to see the application."

If proper use of the Bible requires the Holy Spirit, so, Packer held,
it also requires the church. To make this point, Packer was once again
willing to critique his own tribe: "Here we are all at a disadvantage.

Our evangelical culture and heritage has wrong-footed us" with the evangelical stress on the individual appropriation of the Bible. But according to Packer, "that is not the Scripture pattern." Rather, "the understanding of God's revelation is given in the fellowship, first and foremost through preachers and teachers given by God in the fellowship for this very purpose." And it is given through reading the serious students of Scripture who have gone before. "We ought," said Packer, "to be taking very seriously the privilege of practicing fellowship with our Christian brothers across the ages by reading classic books from the past." Such an activity would liberate us "from the tyranny of being tied to our own thoughts . . . from the tyranny of being tied to our own time . . . from the tyranny of being tied to our own heritage. . . . The Christian ought to practice fellowship across those traditions. . . . The Holy Spirit has been with all God's people in all traditions in all centuries. You can expect to find wisdom and truth and vitamins in those traditions as well as finding mistakes."

So it was that a vigorous defense of the inerrancy and authority of the Bible became also a historically informed, realistic and anti-triumphalist lesson in pneumatology, ecclesiology, church history, ecumenical orthodoxy and humility. It was vintage Packer.

Although Packer's three talks on the Bible in the fall of 1979 were given only just after he had moved to North America, they displayed the historical acuity, the breadth of ecumenical orthodoxy, the balance and the winsome Christian savvy for which he was already well known. If the full extent of Packer's shaping influence cannot yet be adequately judged, the outlines of that influence are clear. The influence has been considerable, in part no doubt because of the gifts, wisdom and innate abilities Packer has brought to his tasks. More broadly and foundationally considered, however, James Packer has had a considerable influence because he has written and said what American evangelicals, under God, have needed to hear.

Notes:

[1] Influence remains a notoriously difficult historical subject to research and measure. The subject is even more difficult than its imposing contours initially suggest, since, to be treated properly, all questions of influence must be comparative questions—influential alongside what other influences? in comparison to whom else? as a force within which contexts? etc.

[2] An observation pertinent to U.S.-Canadian comparisons of Packer's influence is that none of Packer's books, book chapters or pamphlets seem to have been published in Canada, although some of his writing for periodicals originated there.

[3] For their assistance, I am grateful to Lane Dennis and Patricia Rodriguez (Crossway), Jon Pott (Eerdmans), Stephen Board (Harold Shaw), Andrew Le Peau (IVP) and Mark Norton

(Tyndale).

[4] J. I. Packer, *Knowing God* (Downers Grove, Ill.: InterVarsity Press, 1973), pp. 5, 7.

[5] G. K. Chesterton, *Saint Thomas Aquinas: "The Dumb Ox"* (New York: Doubleday/Image, 1933), p. 180.

[6] For providing this run through the index, I am grateful to John Fawcett of the Wheaton College Library.

[7] The full list of journals citing Packer's works included the following: *Catholic Biblical Quarterly, Christianity and Literature, Heythorp Journal, History, Interpretation, Journal of Ecclesiastical History, Journal of Ecumenical Studies, Journal of Psychology and Theology, Journal of Religion, Library Journal, New Testament Studies, Religious Studies, Scottish Journal of Theology, Sixteenth Century Journal, Sociological Analysis, Studies in Religion/Sciences Religieuses, Theology Today* and *Verbatim.* The greatest number of citations (7 of the 30) appeared in the *Journal of Psychology and Theology.*

[8] See Mark A. Noll, *The Scandal of the Evangelical Mind* (Grand Rapids, Mich.: Eerdmans, 1994); and "Revolution and the Rise of Evangelical Social Influence in North Atlantic Societies," in Mark A. Noll, David Bebbington and George Rawlyk, eds., *Evangelicalism: Comparative Studies of Popular Protestantism in North America, the British Isles, and Beyond, 1700–1990* (New York: Oxford University Press, 1994), pp. 128–31.

[9] I should write "us American Calvinists," for this is my identification too.

[10] Packer, *Knowing God*, p. 253.

[11] For careful transcriptions of the tapes of these addresses I am grateful to Carmin Ballou and Mary Noll.

13

A Vision for Preachers

Peter F. Jensen

THIS ARTICLE IS WRITTEN IN TRIBUTE TO JAMES I. Packer, who has done so much in our generation to impart a vision for biblical preaching.

❖ ❖ ❖

Introduction: The Absurdity of Preaching

I once had the privilege of seeing a most peculiar sight: a dog skateboarding. It was a famous animal, reported in the press, and its canine progress was followed by the public with rapt attention. The sight evoked a sort of wonder—but not the sort of wonder that you feel when an elephant or a dolphin performs its circus tricks. You could not help but sense that what you were seeing in this case was absurd.

So it seems to anyone who observes the preacher. Admittedly the sight of a preacher is a good deal more commonplace than the appearance of a dog skateboarding. Preachers are hardly given rapt and wondering attention. But preaching is absurd, and when we think about it we can see why. Here are four reasons. They are given by one who is himself a preacher, and whose business is to train preachers.

First, because of the contrast between the greatness of our subject matter and the frailty of our lives. Preachers are bolder by far than the most daring physicists. Physicists merely talk about the whole of space and time and the uncounted billions of stars; preachers talk about the God who made all these things, the high and lofty One who inhabits eternity. And yet who are we? "Frail children of dust, and feeble as frail," as the hymn writer so aptly remarks. Time is our enemy; our bodies are in constant decay; we are mere creatures. How dare we speak of the Creator-God? The contrast is painful and absurd.

Second, because of the contrast between the holiness of our subject matter and the sinfulness of our lives. The threefold "holy" of Isaiah's seraphim has forever impressed on us the knowledge that God is other than us, that he dwells in unapproachable light. When we think of him in all his glory, his sinlessness, his love, his work for us on the cross, and then compare him with ourselves, we find a sinfulness that brings us low. And yet we sinners have the temerity to stand up in the name of this holy God and to speak as his ambassadors! The contrast is painful and absurd.

Third, because of the comparison between the indifference of the world and our own weakness. The world, for its part, is mightily indifferent to preachers. Every Sunday preachers announce that the world has been redeemed and that a man has risen from the dead, but the world is not impressed enough to get out of bed. There may once have been a time and place where crowds would flock to hear a preacher, but that time is past, and most of us are not that preacher. If C. H. Spurgeon or George Whitefield or Billy Graham was the minister of my church, crowds might come; but even this is not sure, and what the locals have got in any case is seldom anything like Spurgeon, Whitefield or Graham. Compared with the job of preaching effectively to my contemporary world, I am insignificant, weak and foolish. Preaching is absurd.

Fourth, because of the insufficiency of our method. I have not paused to define "preaching" because I wanted to be quite straightforward and say that I have in mind exactly what most preachers do. I do not want to evade the point. For the purposes of this article, I mean by preaching what is done on Sunday mornings: a twenty- to thirty-minute monologue, attempting to expound a passage of Scripture and offering suggestions about its application. This is preaching as we experience it. As a method of educating anyone, it has its clear and obvious drawbacks. It is simply not the best way of imparting information and testing assimilation unless it is done very skillfully. And yet we preachers are filled more often with sloth than with skill. Confronted with the difficulties inherent in our method, we become lazy. We fall into routine. We prepare our passage, but we never think about how we are going to communicate. Alternatively we think that preaching consists of anecdotes with passing reference to Scripture. Our sloth creates dull preaching, lifeless congregations and superficial

Christianity. In these circumstances let's face it: preaching is absurd.

I am writing in the first place as a preacher to preachers. However, anyone concerned about preaching—and who in the church is not?—should find consideration of the subject of vital significance. Why, then, do we persist with the absurd? Why put the dog on the skateboard for all the world to laugh? We need answers which explain what preaching is about, and what God is doing through it. We need a vision of preaching which will inspire, sustain, rebuke, galvanize and refresh. We need to see that God cares about our preaching and has, therefore, commissioned us and resourced us for the task.

The Commissioning of Preaching

No one should preach by self-appointment. The absurdities would surely then be overwhelming. We preach only because we have been appointed by God himself, and we can do no other.

The Scriptures reveal a twofold way of talking about this appointment. It comes to us both from God and from man. In the first place, and most importantly, it forms an integral part of what God has done and is doing in the salvation of his people. By his own power he has created teachers of his Word—apostles, prophets, evangelists, pastors and teachers (to use one famous list)—who are his gifts to his church. They preach his Word and through his Word the church is gathered and established and built up. The way in which the apostles were chosen, gathered, trained and commissioned is a model for what God does in all ministry.

In one powerful metaphor, Paul speaks of ministers as ambassadors for Christ. It is the task of the ambassador to be the faithful servant and mouthpiece for his master. He does not invent the message or tamper with it; he transmits it faithfully as the appointed agent for the master. So it is with those who are preachers of Christ—they are his ambassadors, God "making his appeal through us" (2 Cor 5:20).[1]

The picture of the ambassador also gives us a clue as to why God may choose to bless preaching of the declarative type that we engage in. Such preaching reflects both his nature and the nature of what he has done and is doing. The gospel is a gracious act of God transmitted in good news; it draws us by its authority under Christ's lordship. Preaching reflects that. However much we rightly use different techniques in Christian education, including discussion and meditation on the Scriptures, we must give a central role to declaration. The ambassador, or the herald (to use another New Testament metaphor), is given the task of declaring the tidings. We are communicating about what God has done and what he wants of us; we are describing God's work, not ours. In all this, preaching reflects the reality of what has happened in a way that group discussion, for example, cannot do.

The picture of ourselves as ambassadors or heralds or watchmen gives us heart. So, too, do other New Testament images such as of undershepherds and guardians. In all this we see that it is God's work we are doing, in God's name at God's appointment. We are not responsible for creating the message or even for bringing about the results. With this commission we can preach anywhere; without it we should preach nowhere.

I referred earlier to a twofold way of talking about this appointment. We may, like Amos, be impelled to speak despite the reaction of the audience and despite our lack of human credentials. But God's ordinary means of appointment in this, as in so much else, is through his human servants. It is the work of others to recognize and to endorse our commission to preach both formally and informally. That the people of God are willing to receive the word of God from us is in itself a powerful encouragement. There is nothing wrong with the age-old method of the teachers of God's people being recognized, educated and ordained in a formal way, especially by those who are already acknowledged as having this role: "and the things you have heard me say in the presence of many witnesses entrust to reliable men who will also be qualified to teach others" (2 Tim 2:2). This is all the more so because there may come a moment when the people of God may not be willing to receive the word of God from us; like many of the Lord's servants we may suffer rejection and scorn. In the end we may be left with little encouragement save our sense of God's call mediated at a particular moment by the words and prayers of others, and from our side, responded to by solemn and memorable promises.

The Resources for Preaching

Just as commissioning has its divine and human sides, so too do the resources with which we absurd creatures go into battle. I am going to mention three sets of resources.

Before examining these resources, however, it is important to note that in each case they are twofold, having a human side and a divine side. Theologically, divine and human belong together, for it is fatal to divorce God from the means he ordinarily employs. Often this is done in the name of whatever is the latest version of super-spirituality, as though it were somehow especially honoring to God to emphasize the supernatural, the spectacular, the extraordinary, and hence by implication to denigrate or omit the human or the creaturely. Paradoxically we only succeed in making God tiny as we restrict him to the extraordinary, or we make him grotesque as we connect him to the bizarre.

There was once a preacher who was convinced of the need to let God speak through him. He therefore hit upon the following device: in the first part of each sermon he would follow his careful preparation; in the second part, he would say whatever came into his head on the assumption that he was thereby allowing the Holy Spirit free rein to communicate whatever the Lord wanted to the congregation. But one member of the congregation was a better theologian than he was. Having noticed the change in his preaching at about the halfway point each time, she challenged him to explain it. When she heard what he had to say, she summed up the situation like this: "Strange! You are a better preacher than the Holy Spirit!"

The preacher's fault was the common one of assuming that God operates best when the ordinary means are not in use: grace abolishes nature. On the contrary, grace renews, reinvigorates and uses nature. Having said that, however, it is necessary to emphasize the priority of grace. After all, our preaching is as we are sent by God; it is his message we bring; it is by his strength that we accomplish anything; any blessing comes from him alone. To use Paul's words as he confronts those who want to exalt the human messenger:

> What, after all, is Apollos? And what is Paul? Only servants through whom you came to believe—as the Lord has assigned to each his task. I planted the seed, Apollos watered it, but God made it grow. (1 Cor 3:5-6)

Grace may use nature, but it often does so in such a way as we can see a certain disjunction between grace and nature. Grace makes of nature what you would never expect:

> Where is the wise man? Where is the scholar? Where is the philosopher of this age? Has not God made foolish the wisdom of the world? For since in the wisdom of God the world through its wisdom did not know him, God was pleased through the foolishness of what was preached to save those who believe. (1 Cor 1:20-21)

Bearing in mind the priority given to grace, therefore, we now turn to the three sets of resources that enable absurd creatures to speak in the name of the everlasting God.

1. First, we speak by the power of the Holy Spirit;
second, we speak by the capacity of the human spirit.

First of all, we must turn to the role of the Holy Spirit in preaching. It is proper, when we preach, to ask that God's Holy Spirit will fill us. Our prayer is made conscious of the way that this phrase is used in Scripture to describe the enabling power of the Holy Spirit, and in particular his enabling to speak. Why is the Holy Spirit especially related to Christian utterance?

All salvation is the work of God, Father, Son and Holy Spirit. The unity of the Savior God is especially important, since it contrasts with the multiplicity of other saviors called upon by humanity ancient and modern. But it is also scriptural to distinguish the work of the Father who sends, of the Son who comes and of the Holy Spirit sent by Father and Son. It is the Son, not the Spirit, who is crucified. Although when the Spirit comes Father and Son are also present, there is nonetheless a unique office of the Spirit who comes to be *another* advocate, and to bear witness to the Son.

A study of Scripture makes clear that the Spirit's office is in the application of redemption. He takes and brings to us the saving benefit of the work of Christ on the cross, who died by the deliberate plan and foreknowledge of God. One of the most significant aspects of his office is in the area of knowing God. He is, of course, especially associated with the production of the Scriptures, since the inspiration of Scripture is attributed to him. This is the material or substantial part of his work in bringing knowledge—here is the content of what needs to be known. But as with the cross, so with Scripture: it is also part of God's saving work by the Spirit to make known, to enlighten the mind.

Our knowledge of God is relational, and it comes through words. But these words find a relating lodgment in our hearts only as our hearts are prepared and opened to receive them. The risen Lord "opened their minds so they could understand the Scriptures" (Lk 24:45); "the Lord opened [Lydia's] heart to respond to Paul's message" (Acts 16:14); God "made his light shine in our hearts to give us the light of the knowledge of the glory of God" (2 Cor 4:6); "what God has prepared for those who love him, [he] has revealed it to us by his Spirit" (1 Cor 2:9-10). These passages remind us of the intrusive impact of God's grace in bringing the knowledge of him, and the last one tells us that it is by the Spirit that his impact comes. In short, God brings people to himself through the gospel, which is "the sword of the Spirit" (Eph 6:17). Our part is the way of speaking the truth, of trusting him, of prayer. The finest oratory in the world will not make Christians. The power in preaching is spiritual not rhetorical.

That is why we connect both prayer and prophecy to preaching. Whatever the exact definition of prophecy and its distinction from teaching, God's preachers still exercise this gift. We may not be conscious of its operation; we may not allow for it as a category; but when the word strikes home to its listeners, elevating the Lord Jesus and bringing upbuilding, encouragement and consolation, I believe that it is present. It is a gift that we should earnestly desire (1 Cor 14:1), and it seems to me that the common complaint that preaching is dry and academic and unapplied may arise from our forgetfulness to pray that the Spirit will fill us and that we will speak that word of God which is

> sharper than any double-edged sword, it penetrates even to dividing soul and spirit, joints and marrow; it judges the thoughts and attitudes of the heart. (Heb 4:12)

We preach, therefore, by the power of the Holy Spirit. On the other hand, however, we speak by the capacity of the human spirit. God once chose an ass to speak for him; once he chose Caiaphas. But usually his choice falls on a Moses, a David, a Peter, a Paul or a Timothy. In choosing them he does not suppress their natural capacities. Even in the writing of Scripture, he uses human skills and dignifies them with responsibility. When the Israelites fought Amalek, Aaron and Hur steadied Moses' arms while Joshua engaged in the battle (Ex 17:8-13). The action of Moses was a reminder that it was by the Lord that the battle was won. Despite the Lord's work, however, Joshua and his men were by no means exempt from the task of fighting with all their might and at some risk to themselves.

In the same way, we need to realize that the Lord expects faithfulness from us:

> Watch your life and doctrine closely. (1 Tim 4:16)

> Preach the Word, be urgent in season and out of season, convince, rebuke, and exhort, be unfailing in patience and in teaching. (2 Tim 4:2 RSV)

There is no denigration of human effort here. On the contrary, it is an enormous stimulus to effort. First we must ensure that what we teach is the true foundation of the gospel; second we must bring our personal skills into play as we aim to persuade our hearers of the truth: the pastor must be "apt to teach."

Our human responsibility entails a careful study of the business of preaching. You recognize of course that doing God's work is useless without his enlivening power; but you recognize too that for stewards of God's gifts there is a place for reflection on the methods to be employed, that one can rightfully consider such matters as communication skills, the use of the voice and aids to delivery. It is here that God has given the modern preachers many resources, and we are failing our hearers if we do not give them careful thought and bring them into use as long as they serve the gospel message and do not conflict with it. Our aim must be simplicity and reality, not manipulation (2 Cor 4:2-3).

The initial set of resources, then, is the power of the Holy Spirit and the capacity of the human spirit. The second set is as follows.

2. First, the power of the Gospel;
second, the depth of human need.

From the very opening pages of the Bible we are informed about the creative energies of God's word. It is a word with enormous power, for the whole universe was created by the word. It is a word with relating power, since through his covenant God related himself to Noah, to Abraham, to Israel, to David and finally to his people in the new covenant. It is a word with ruling power, since the covenant is God's method of reestablishing his kingdom over the hearts of his people. It is a word with unfailing power, since it never returns to God empty, but always establishes the purpose for which he sent it forth.

In the New Testament it is revealed that "the Word" is a particularly apt title for Jesus Christ, the Son of God, and by the time that the New Testament is finished a linguistic usage is established by which the Word is a gospel which is also a person. To believe in the gospel and to trust in Jesus Christ are one and the same thing; to preach the kingdom, to preach the gospel and to preach Christ are not three activities but one. Nor is this gospel severed from the Old Testament word of God; it is the mightiest expression of the powerful, creative, relating, ruling, unfailing and personal word. This word causes controversy, opposition, hatred, even persecution. It has the power to stir people up, since part of the power of the gospel is its power to condemn as well as save. The gospel messenger retains the sins of some, just as we forgive the sins of others (Jn 20:23).

But more important than its power to provoke is its power to save. In two classic texts, Paul says:

[The gospel] is the power of God for the salvation of everyone

> who believes. (Rom 1:16)
> How can they believe in the one of whom they have not heard?
> And how can they hear without someone preaching to them?
> . . . Faith comes from hearing the message, and the message is
> heard through the word of Christ. (Rom 10:14, 17)

Here we must be very clear: there is no substitute for the gospel. It is God's appointed instrument for salvation.

There are many even within our churches who think otherwise. Some see no need for evangelism, since all are saved in any case; others regard the gospel as anything that liberates, and so have translated the original gospel out of existence. Others think that sacramental religion is the way to salvation. Others simply hope the best for the nominal Christians who make up their churches. Others, confronted by the numerically desperate plight of their denomination, are prepared to slough off the sloth of the ages and call for a decade of evangelism. Unfortunately, however, there is so little clear concept of the gospel that evangelism consists of trying to make more Christians by making religion more attractive. God's appointed gospel is omitted from the armory.

There may even be some success. Given a little planning and effort, almost anyone can grow a satisfactorily sized church. You can create a message which will attract and an ethos which will retain. The Mormons do this quite well. But without the gospel there is no saving power, and our work is offensive to God. If you are interested in the feeling of power, I would not suggest the gospel; its power is a power to salvation, and the gospel preacher may be completely unaware of the effects of his preaching whether for good or for ill.

God's word is powerful, and that gives us great heart. But there is the second side to this which is likewise a great encouragement—the gospel is explicitly directed to human need. I am not pretending, of course, that every audience will recognize its need. The gospel has to open the eyes of the blind to the reality of their own situation. But of these things we may be absolutely confident when we stand in the name of God as an ambassador of Christ: all those who listen are sinful; all need reconciliation; all are guilty; all are destined for death and judgment; all experience the effects of the wrath of God in their lives. In commending the gospel we are commending a message which is addressed to the very essence of the human experience. We are dealing with the biggest of issues, the largest in extent and the most profound.

All great literature raises the same issue. It is about sin and alienation, conflict, despair and spiritual sickness. Even comedy is premised on the idea of the disparity between what is and what should be. Of course preachers are perfectly capable of botching this advantage. We often seem to lack imagination and sensitivity; we often seem incapable of revealing the link between what the Bible is saying and how our people are living; we become engrossed with the small details and forget the large themes whether in Scripture or in life. In any learning situation people need to move from what they know to what they do not know. They do know from the inside all about sin, death, guilt and suffering; it is our job to identify what these experiences mean and to lead them to what they do not know—that the gospel of Jesus Christ addresses these needs.

I am not suggesting that people necessarily know all about sin, death, guilt and suffering under those names. These are abstractions, names for things, and our hearers may be inarticulate, unable to analyze or name their experiences. For them sin comes in the form of the swollen credit card, the taxation fiddle, the quarrel over behavior, a rebellious child, a pang of jealousy, a sexual betrayal. We need to be able to work from these knowns to the unknown of God and the gospel. Nor am I suggesting that we be driven in our preaching from human need to divine provision. We only know the significance of the need from the provision. The Bible's own agenda must direct the content of preaching.

The third set of resources continues the themes of the second.

3. First, the reality of the Bible;
second, the availability of our own experience.

I have remarked on great literature and how its themes, taken from human experience, are really the stuff of theology. But the greatest of all books is the book we are preaching from. "You are the man," says Nathan to a proud king, and instantly there is shame, depression and death, and the long entail of a family in dissolution begins. As preachers of the Bible we have the tremendous advantage that we are forced to address the things that really matter—God and the world, sin and death, atonement and forgiveness.

It must be said, of course, that the Bible is a strange book, an alien book. Every decade that passes distances it from us. These are the words of Helmut Thielicke after he had been preaching on the first chapters of Genesis:

> The Garden of Eden looked so completely different from our garden plot at home. . . . And never before had we met a ser-

pent like this, which was able to carry on a religious discussion, not even in a circus or zoo. The Flood was quite unlike any rainstorm we had ever experienced. . . . We citizens who live our lives between asphalt and concrete were somewhat at a loss as we contemplated the primitive rock of those strange, primeval, lunar peaks.[2]

Its very strangeness, however, is a powerful advantage. Most other communication comes from within the same postmodern world that we ourselves inhabit. But here is something quite evidently from the outside, something that gives us hope by being different. Here is Thielicke again:

Once we took hold of the words of these ancient texts and turned them over in our minds, these messages suddenly became relentless in the way they struck home to us. . . . The serpent suddenly became more aggressively present than the dog that barks at me in my neighbourhood. . . . And God's great "Let there be!" suddenly became so tremendously real that compared with it the screaming advertisements on the billboards, the human-fold ballyhooing of toothpastes, margarines, and tourist attractions became as unreal as soapbubbles.[3]

Thielicke's experience is true. Carefully and imaginatively expounded, the Bible creates its own audience. We can see it creating a taste, becoming more genuine than television and radio and novels to the Christian audience. We can see people bringing their Bibles and checking the message. We can hear people praying through their Bibles as it begins to take over and shape their minds, bringing them to maturity. But the Bible does not make them alien—it provides the key to contemporary experience and the exploration of contemporary culture. It is, after all, the word of the living God.

I deliberately wrote, "the Bible carefully and imaginatively expounded." It is the Bible that is the word of God, but it is human beings who are the preachers. Theological education ought to make us careful in the exposition of God's word, since truth matters. I do not think that education of this sort can make us imaginative; without imagination, however, our efforts of exposition are not gold but lead. By "imagination" I certainly do not mean a free-wheeling adaptation of the text to enliven an otherwise dull account. Such a method is close to the image-building which is idolatry. We do not need to improve the Bible. But we do need sympathy—the capacity to identify oneself imaginatively with others, to see things their way. In preaching we need both sympathy with the text as we "feel" (for want of a better word) what it is about in essence and sympathy with the audience as we understand what are their deepest concerns and how they would articulate them if they could.

It is not the business of the art critic to paint; it is not even his or her business to demolish. If the critic has a role, it is to stand beside us and help us see the truth of what we are observing. So, too, the preacher. The preacher is not to stand in the way, but to stand beside us and to help us by knowing us and knowing the text, with a sympathetic knowing that will let us see that the text is sharp and strong and true.

Our second resource remains our own personal experience, reflected on and used creatively. In the first place there is theological education, by which I do not mean merely time spent in seminary but also the study done since then. Some of us never read; others never read the big books; others will avoid theology and biblical studies at all costs. This is a tragic failure for preacher and for congregation. The preacher who is insulated from what challenges, who refused to wrestle with larger ideas, becomes flabby, mundane, routine, dull. He cannot be sympathetic to the text of the great book which it is his business to expound.

But theological education is not enough. The way to a sympathetic reading of an audience is through your own humanity, through being a member of the human race, through your pastoral work. Like the novelist who refracts life, the preacher must meditate on human experience. I do not by any means refer to using incidents as sermon illustrations. I am thinking of something more profound by far—the identification of the big issues in the community and the analysis of their meaning in the categories of Scripture. Have you preached on war? Have you addressed postmodernism? Does massive unemployment not impinge on you? What about the language we use these days? Have we nothing to say about environmental degradation? Where is justice to be found?

I do not refer here, of course, to those sermons which are simply issue-oriented attempts by the preacher to be relevant. Our task is far, far harder than that. It requires the bringing together of the Bible's themes with the concerns of the day; it requires that we address those themes with the gospel of God's grace. I believe that it can be done; I believe that it must be done; I do not think that it is easily done.

The Function of Preaching
The pastor who relies on preaching as the sole means of edifying the

flock is failing them. We must have a Christian education program that will touch our church members at a number of points and give them different ways of learning. Some of these ways of learning may well be more attractive educationally than the traditional sermon, and the question may well be asked whether we ought to persevere with the sermon or not.

The declarative form of the sermon reflects the nature of the message that God has given us in the gospel: news not views, as the old slogan used to say. This makes the sermon indispensable. At some point we need to sit quietly and listen to the word of God. But the sermon as we have it also reflects the nature of our gathering as the church of God. The purpose of our gathering is to meet the Lord Jesus Christ in the fellowship of our brothers and sisters. As two or three are gathered, he is in the midst, and our encounter with him is through his word. The branches of the vine remain in Christ's words; the sheep of Christ follow the voice of the shepherd; the people of Christ let the Word of Christ dwell in their midst. It is the chief function of the sermon to unleash the word of the Lord in the midst of his people. It is the chief means by which the Lord directs, rebukes, sustains and invigorates his people.

Preaching like this, of course, must be biblical. It is not our task to replace divine revelation with human inspiration. Having listened attentively to the text of Scripture ourselves, we must then share this knowledge of God with those who gather. A theologian once complained to me that in listening to many sermons, he never found the preachers talking about God. It was notable that in his tradition the expository sermon was virtually unknown. The sermon that expounds the Bible cannot help be about God, since he is the theme of the Bible. Even the weakest and dullest exponent of expository teaching will ensure that the faithful congregation has some awareness of the God in whose presence they meet. This is all the more the case if the preacher remembers his biblical theology and is able to shape his sermons by the wider context of Scripture until they truly become part of the story of what God has done in Christ, part of the gospel. Preaching like this has purpose and a sharp point; it is a call to repentance and faith.

We live in a time when considerable thought should be given to what constitutes "biblical" preaching. Despite protestations to the contrary, there is a manifest failure of confidence in the Bible amongst evangelicals. Their sermons have a biblical appearance, with references to texts and stories from the Bible, but the truth of the matter is that anecdotes and quotations take the place of exposition as the substance of what is said. Such preaching acts as a barrier between the listener and the Scripture, preventing the congregation from reading the Bible except in the most superficial way. Admittedly, expository preaching which actually puts the hearer in touch with the passage is difficult. Initially, it is not as interesting as anecdotal preaching. In the end, however, it both creates and satisfies a deep and serious hunger for God's word and a thoroughgoing impatience with human-centered, clever and entertaining pulpit oratory.[4] In the end, too, it is the only way to proclaim the transcendence and glory of God. Mere sermons on God will not achieve this important goal— we must allow Scripture to teach the truth in its own way.

There is a second function of preaching, less significant than the first, but with its own importance nonetheless. In preaching, the pastor confesses the creed to which he adheres. He says publicly week by week what it is he believes. He gives both God and the church an account of that deposit of the truth for which he remains responsible. The Sunday school teachers hear him; the youth leaders hear him; his assistant ministers and congregational leaders hear him; the leaders of the small group Bible studies hear him; the heads of families hear him. He is not able to evade his confession as he might be able to by deft handling of questions in a discussion group. This preaching sets the tone for the church; it feeds the flock and directs the leadership. It is essential to the care which he has promised to show his people. It is not accidental nor inappropriate that pastors still believe that when all their important tasks are done, the task of preaching remains as the first priority.

Conclusion: The Vision of Preaching

Isaiah the prophet was turned into a preacher by a vision. So too was Paul, who told Agrippa that he was not disobedient to the heavenly vision. In both cases of course the vision was a vision of God accompanied by the divine commissioning for service. In both cases the fulfillment of the mission involved hardship and opposition.

To keep on with the absurd task of preaching—and I do not mean saying a few words on Sunday because you are paid to do it—means that you need a vision. We certainly need to be clear about what preaching is all about, who we are and who God is and what he plans to achieve in this way. These are questions which I have been addressing in this paper. Finally, however, we need a vision of God, a vision that will inspire, sustain, rebuke, galvanize, refresh.

To very few is granted the visions that Isaiah and Paul saw. Even the "vision of angels" that set the women witnessing to the resurrection on Easter morning is not a common experience. But our hearts have been captured by the wonderful vision of God that is offered in the gospel itself, the vision that Israel was incapable of beholding, the vision of the glory of the Lord (2 Cor 3:14) which we see with unveiled face. And where is this glory to be found? It is "the light of the knowledge of the glory of God in the face of Christ" (4:6) which the gospel gives. It is this gospel which constitutes our vision. It is this vision which we preach, for we do not preach ourselves, but we preach Christ Jesus as Lord, with ourselves as your servants for Jesus' sake (4:5).

Notes:

[1] All scriptural quotations in this article are taken from the New International Version of the Bible, copyright the New York International Bible Society, unless otherwise noted.

[2] H. Thielicke, *How the World Began* (London: James Clark, ET, 1964), p. 7.

[3] Ibid., pp. 8, 9.

[4] See the many fine articles in C. Green and D. Jackman, eds., *When God's Voice Is Heard* (Leicester, England: Inter-Varsity Press, 1995), not least the one by Dr. J. I. Packer himself, entitled "The Preacher as Theologian."

14

Knowing God:
The Transmission of
Reformed Theology

James M. Houston

IT IS A GREAT PLEASURE TO CELEBRATE DR. PACKER'S threescore years and ten in this *Festschrift* volume, for we have been friends and colleagues since 1945. He was then already interested in the Puritans, especially John Owen and Richard Baxter, and he has been ever since. Through them and their great predecessor, John Calvin, he saw the central objective of theology to be pastoral. In his many books, Dr. Packer has communicated consistently the same pastoral concern for the theological education of all the people of God. So this Puritan transmission continues. That is why I thought it appropriate in this essay, and it is only an assay, to explore tentatively the efficacy of Reformed theology to Christianize sixteenth-century society by the transmission of this faith. Recent modern research, especially on Calvin, has intensified the search for the rootage of the Reformation, for its formative pre-Reformation ideas. But since Ernst Troeltsch's classic study at the beginning of the twentieth century, much less interest has been given to assess the efficacy of the transmission of the Reformed faith of Luther and Calvin.

In our own postmodern age of confusion, it is tempting to see the sixteenth century analogously, as being postmedieval, confused and full of contradiction and discord. Perhaps we can learn then from the process of reform and its consequences in that century in apposite ways for us now, as we enter the twenty-first century. For equally at stake for us today is the credibility and the relevance of the Christian gospel in our society. However, even our notion of "the decline of the church" is not inherited from the Reformation, but much earlier, from Augustine. For it is within late antiquity, with the transformation of the Roman Empire to the organized church, that notions such as "Christianization of society"[1] or "the shared culture" of Christian and pagan alike are traceable originally and still are persistent today. Perhaps it is also in Augustinian terms that we can see the failure of Christianization and the prospect of a new "dark ages" for the church in the future. Yet we now must make our own assessment in terms of the Calvinist reform, which has had profound influence upon the making of modern culture, in contradistinction to classical culture. Postmodernism is now in revolt against its Christian, and its Calvinist, foundations.

There is, however, another historical contrast between the assessment of "Christianization" and its failure in the fifth century and our own postmodern situation today. For Christianity was then tempted to fill the cultural void of the fall of Rome, whereas now it is the deliberate rejection of Christian values that is creating a new void in secular society. What will sustain the societal values that Reformed theology promoted in the constructs of modern life, such as the dignity of personal vocation, meaningful work, industry, empirical inquiry, stewardship of wealth, political commonweal, authority, social responsibility, etc.? Christian reformation in the next millennium will require not just the renewed correction of the church's errors, as the consequence of its past aberrations, but the challenge of the secular revolt against God himself. The nature of theology and of anthropology and therefore the questioning of ontological issues are now much more deeply at stake. It is not just the failure of Christianization within the world, but of its failure within the church also. "Who is a Christian?" becomes a haunting question indeed, for many more than Hans Küng.[2] At the beginning of this century, William James observed somewhere that "the average church-going civilizee realizes, one may say, absolutely nothing of the deeper currents of human nature." At the end of the century, the average nonchurched postmodernist has made himself his own god. Between them, theology has a great task ahead of it, to educate both parties.

Roman Catholic Reactions to the Reformation
Then and now, the challenge of Reformation has been, and is, a per-

sonal one. When Martin Luther (1483–1546) and John Calvin (1509–1564) shocked their contemporary churchmen in their public denunciation of the traditionalism of the church, the question was, how do you arrive at the truth? Even the gentle, spiritual-minded Francis de Sales (1567–1622), the Catholic bishop of Geneva, could ask in 1595:

> If then the Church can err, O Calvin, and O Luther, to whom will I have recourse in my difficulties? To Scripture, they say: but what will I do, poor man that I am? For it is with regard to Scripture itself that I have trouble. I do not doubt whether or not I could adjust faith to Scripture, for who does not know that it is the word of truth? What bothers me is the understanding of the Scripture.[3]

If the whole church is in error, why turn then to one individual rather than another to find the truth? Is it not being implied that not only is the collective mind unreliable, but all tradition also, all the history of the church? So to Francis de Sales this Protestant arrogance was "the absurdity of absurdities," to denounce the whole church for having erred for the past thousand years. "I am amazed," he concludes, "that you can live with so much assurance in the doctrine you follow, as if you could not err, and yet you hold it as certain that everyone has erred and can err."[4]

But Francis de Sales was protesting at the end of a century that had been full of skepticism. Michel de Montaigne (1533–1592) was the archetype of humanist skepticism, in the company of Rabelais and Bodin. In an age of fanaticism, such skeptics appeared as "moderates" in an ocean of doubt. The renewal of classical Pyrrhonism was interpreted as rescuing the mind to have recourse to common sense, as the Stoics and Epicureans had also sought.

Humanist Skepticism

Later in the seventeenth century, François Veron and others were to use skepticism as a war machine against French Protestants. Jesuits such as Marin Marsenne (1588–1668) and Petrus Gassendi, his friend, reasoned that this classical style of religious skepticism must be admitted, to distinguish religious uncertainty from the new rational certainty of a growing scientific knowledge; later, the Enlightenment and Kantianism brought this to a climax. René Descartes attempted to overcome skepticism with his famous formula *cogito ergo sum*, admitting the need to doubt everything other than "I am the thinker." But he only intensified the skepticism that was further induced by rationalism. For Montaigne, it is man who is in doubt. For Descartes, it is the universe that is the sphere of doubt. One must go on living, one must accommodate to doubts, argued Montaigne. For Descartes, the quest of certainty must be absolute, so that one must weigh probabilities against each other, as the Pyrrhonists did. However, the primary function of doubt for Descartes is to find assertions that are universally guaranteed as certain. Thus Descartes would remove all fiduciary foundations from knowledge, while Montaigne would not seek external authority but merely self-enhancement. So in different ways both men have profoundly infected the intellectual life of the modern world, to be faithless and empirical.[5] The Reformation opened Pandora's box in seeking for the foundations of certain knowledge. The reaction of Catholic intellectuals was to seek an increasingly impossible certitude within the church, while the Reformers sought it in God alone.

Ignatian Spirituality

A contrasting second Catholic reaction to the Reformation was the spirituality of Ignatius of Loyola (1491–1556), a contemporary of Montaigne and Calvin at Paris. He remained profoundly a layman, uneducated in theology, so when he was asked publicly in 1527 in Paris, was it by theological "science or by the Holy Spirit" that he wrote *The Spiritual Exercises,* he refused to reply. Later, in recounting his conversion privately, he spoke of "God instructing him as a child is at school."[6] Ignatius really believed that God had instructed him so he could teach others. His conversion had begun by reading the lives of the saints; they pointed him to the Gospels, to follow Christ himself. He was stimulated by biblical studies at the new university of Alcalá de Henares, but his desire to "help souls" rather than keep silent in academic life led him to leave and pursue studies in Paris, gather companions around himself and begin the organization which was to become the order of the Jesuits (1528–1535). The order was recognized by Pope Paul III in 1540, and *The Exercises* approved officially in 1548.

The clear design of *The Exercises* for lay Christian education aimed at a simple objective: "to conquer oneself and to order one's life without being influenced in one's decisions by any inordinate affection." In the hands of an experienced director this gave a strong psychological dynamism in an age of stoicism and rational concern. Activation of the affections and the deepening of the meditative life have made *The Exercises* appealing ever since. Intimacy with God has been the call for their lasting appeal. For those Catholics who wanted to remain within the church, *The Exercises* have provided an "election," an "ordering of life" and a deep "affectivity" for God. Ignatius's disciple Jerome Nadal (1507–1580) carried on this Ignatian tradition faithfully, with his call "to contemplation in action," linking the ideal of public service to the inner needs of the heart. It suited well the sentiment of Renaissance humanism that was "world-affirming" with seriousness of intent to do "religious works" in human freedom in an activist culture. Much of this was a reaction to Lutheranism by reinforcing its ongoing posture "what have I done for Christ, what am I doing, what ought I to do?"[7] By the seventeenth century, however, this approach had become methodical, certainly moralistic, and ascetical. It had also become expansive, syncretistic and undiscerning of doctrinal issues. Its authoritarian tone was reinforced by the prominence given to "spiritual direction," an emphasis renewed strongly today since Vatican II.

Like Calvin's *Institutes,* it is the key work of a reformer, and yet in contrast to Calvin's work, the *Exercises* are never intended to be a doctrinal treatise but simply a practical and personal guidebook. Like the Reformers, Ignatius recognizes the call of God, so vocation is of primary importance, as Ignatius experienced himself. But as a Catholic, Ignatius keeps the call within the church's teachings and practice. For he feared uncontrolled Spanish illuminism and unverified mysticism. Yet Ignatius emphasizes that it is a personal experience of God, not just a conceptual knowledge of God. The former he relates to the transcendent character of self-consolation, which has no apparent psychological cause, so he is open to attribute it to God, his Creator. It is the "awareness-become-consciousness" of one's complete openness to God, as a dynamic act of the will, in a free act of love. Ignatius often experiences such a "sense" of God that comes to him without words, which raises awareness within him, with deepest feeling. So it is "wordless." This complete "openness" to God also explains why Ignatius wishes to "find God in all things," so that election is carried out in everyday life. "Discernment of spirits" becomes the central theme of the *Exercises,* and the acceptance of both desolations and consolations develops a strong psychological bias for the human emotions to organize around, before God. However, as Catholic theologians now admit, the doctrinal implications of Ignatius's *Exercises* have never been worked out, even today.

Many issues then are left unexamined and therefore undefended in Ignatian spirituality, which the Counter-Reformation endorsed officially in 1549. Its preoccupation with the incarnation and redemption diverts attention from the verbal revelation of Christ to the activities of Jesus' earthly ministry. So the parables of Jesus are ignored, and Christ as the Word of God is also not treated. The seriousness with which sin is interpreted by Paul in his epistles is ignored, in contrast to the focal importance given this by the Reformers. Ignatius is an activist, and to him the golden age of activity is Jesus' earthly ministry, whereas the Reformers' emphasis upon the action of God is eternal and ever present. In tune with the Counter-Reformation that reacts to the Reformed doctrine of justification, *sola gratia*, Ignatius reverses love of God and love of neighbor, to become "the greater service of God" and "the service of souls."[8] The Ignatian preoccupation with the past earthly life and ministry of Jesus, unrelated to the resurrection, distracts the Christian devotee from the present reality that the Holy Spirit can be in his or her life. So the Reformers give much more scope and vitality to the Holy Spirit than to human psychology, in the proper exercise of one's imagination and in tune with the Augustinian tradition of "memory."

Yet as a spiritual underground movement, Ignatian contemplation spread a wide influence, even within the Protestant world. Spanish Catholic works were translated into English to become part of English "Recusant" devotional prose—that is, the underground Catholic publications. Such works were printed secretly in clandestine presses in the Netherlands and in England. While the translated works of Luis de Granada were popular, the influence of the Ignatian *Exercises* was basic in late Tudor popular meditation. Written and translated by men of letters, their appeal was both literary and psychological, as expressive of spiritual humanism. In an age of verbal controversy, personal sensibilities were found in them often more appealing to the inner life than the harsh presentation of external doctrines of controversy. Yet the line between controversial literature and devotional literature is very thin, for both need to be recognized as didactic in intent.

Moreover, the Recusants tend to think that when argumentation has failed, in an age of skepticism, a return to the life of prayer will bring about the effect of conversion more subtly. For Catholics of the time believed, probably more stubbornly than Protestants, that the age-long medieval practices of prayer and the ascetic disciplines deeply ingrained in the religious psyche would inevitably lead back to the Catholic faith. So Recusant literature was used subliminally as "dumb preachers," whereas the Protestants more overtly monopolized public preaching.[9] Moreover, insightful Catholics were well aware that the political policies of the Counter-Reformation would not win self-conscious converts so much as provide some renewal of the traditional spiritual life of the average Catholic. But to counteract the radical self-consciousness of Lutheranism, it was seen also as necessary to emphasize man's role in saving his own soul by making various practical, psychological suggestions. So these devotional manuals were the forebears of our religious "how-to" books today, Catholic and Protestant!

What some Puritans no doubt did not realize was how this Recusant literature influenced their own mindset. So behind Bishop Hall's art of meditation, and even that of his pupil, Richard Baxter, there was the Ignatian art of doing this. The *Christian Directory* of Richard Baxter is a compound of Ramus's secular system of education, as well as the whole Catholic tradition of spiritual directors and Protestant catechisms. All seek to blend doctrine with practical living in tune with educational theory. So historians of consciousness need to analyze such influences that doctrinally are assumed to have been separated, but in practice are not so. The recrudescence of spiritual direction since Vatican II is essentially the revival of Ignatius's *Exercises*. But now Protestants are adopting them more indiscriminately than before, because their own semi-Pelagian tendencies are well suited to accept them uncritically. This self-help approach is particularly evident in North American evangelicalism.

Valdesian Reform

In all the current Reformation scholarship, Juan de Valdes (c. 1509–1541) is scarcely mentioned and little appreciated. This is partly because he is a Spaniard, remote from the Reformation scene, and also because he left no Reformed church in Italy where he took refuge from the Inquisition after 1530. His roots of reform lie within the Franciscan revival of biblical scholarship at the Renaissance university of Alcalá de Henares, near Madrid (founded in 1509). Six years before Calvin first published his *Institutes,* Juan de Valdes was completing a doctoral thesis which was sufficiently "Lutheran" to attract the attention of the Inquisition, which had already condemned his colleague Pedro Ruy de Alcaraz. It was this biblical renaissance of scholarship at Alcalá that prompted the scholarship for a muted Spanish reform, so that Alcaraz's reform started as early as 1511, and only after 1517 did he come under Luther's influence. In turn, Alcaraz influenced Valdes, and during Valdes's residence in Italy (1530–

1541), he wrote many biblical commentaries. His discussions with influential friends (published as *The Considerations*[10]) help us to learn the doctrinal views he developed in their companionship.

In Lutheran fashion Valdes rejects natural theology, so he makes a clear break from Renaissance humanism, such as that expressed by Erasmus (1466–1536). Valdes's conclusion is that the whole penitential system of the Roman Catholic Church is grounded upon a false epistemology. Natural knowledge of God is void of true, soteriological knowledge. Knowing the Scriptures without the Spirit of God illuminating the Word is in vain, he argues.[11] For the only knowledge of God which is efficacious is the knowledge of God in Christ. So it is this "knowledge in Christ" that is focal to the theology of Valdes. This presupposes the twofold knowledge of man and God, identical with the consciousness of sin and of grace, given in man's confrontation with the Law and the Gospel, respectively.[12] This twofold knowledge of man and God, which comes through Law and Gospel, becomes manifest in the believer's consciousness of grace and forgiveness. Valdes bases this Christocentric knowledge on Matthew 11:27, where it is claimed that only Christ knows the Father. This knowledge, which is soteriological, is the regeneration of the image of God in man.[13] Further, this true knowledge is "illuminating," by which Valdes means it is always a personal encounter with God, clarifying the mind through the experience of justification and regeneration.

Valdes also appeals constantly to personal experience of the triune God, as a broad and inclusive understanding of the Christian life. Here Valdes appeals to no external authority of church or council, but only to his own experience of saving grace, in knowing God personally through his Word. So he cuts himself off from any ecclesial authority that would deny him his own experience of God. He locates this as the Christ-dependent and Christ-centered experience of the apostle Paul in the epistle to the Romans, of David in the Psalms, and also elsewhere in Scripture. For to have knowledge without experience is to misunderstand the true nature of the Christian life.[14] Freedom of conscience is evidence of the true experience. So it is not an experience one can create for oneself, but is God's gift to a justified and regenerated child of God. Moreover, he adds, "mortification and vivification are the most efficacious forms of experience by which our faith is confirmed, since only they who believe and know themselves righteous in Christ, have mortification and vivification."[15] These are truly to enter into "the benefits of Christ's death." In these benefits Christian knowledge, experience and ongoing faith are all interdependent. For the gift of God to man is Christ himself, who is our life.

Like Calvin, Valdes was checked from embracing the radical views of the Radical Reformers, because of his grasp of the seriousness of sin as affecting the mind as well as all other human faculties. Likewise, he distanced himself theologically from the *alumbrados,* devotees of pseudomystical, quietist tendencies. He is a reformer of doctrine, yet more perhaps than other reformers he believed in the practice of tolerance, love of one's neighbor and the exercise of Christian freedom. We can speculate that Valdes represents more of what young Luther might have remained, if he had not compromised in his political associations with the German princes. Possibly, Valdes's brother's association with Charles V as the king's secretary may have helped persuade the emperor to be conciliatory to the reformers in the early 1540s. Juan de Valdes influenced the minds of Italian humanists, even cardinals within the Vatican, without their becoming "Lutherans" or "Calvinists" publicly. Only after his death were they persecuted for their faith. If we measure the success of Valdesian reform doctrine by the effecting of institutional and cultural change, then it may not be judged to have been a reformation that had lasting power in Italy. However, to ignore the work of Juan de Valdes in Reformation studies is a serious mistake that persists today.

A Comparative Assessment of Luther and Calvin as Reformers

It is popular to generalize about Luther as "the evangelist" of the Reformation and Calvin as its "theologian." It is also easier to assess the personal experience of Luther as a man transformed by the gospel, but whose later life became engulfed in political and ecclesial distortions, in ways Calvin never allowed to happen to him. In this respect, Juan de Valdes stands closer to Calvin, while Zwingli, whom I will not assess, stands alongside Luther in perpetuating a more medieval view of "a Christian society."

Martin Luther

In strong reaction to the metaphysical speculations of the scholastics, Martin Luther (1483–1546) sees the centrality of the *theologia crucis.* "He deserves to be called a theologian," he observes, "who comprehends the visible and manifest things of God, seen through suffering and the Cross."[16] For in tune with Romans 1:22, the knowledge of God through his works of creation "does not make one worthy or wise," he says.[17] Such knowledge can only come from the way God has spoken in his Son, and this in the light of the cross. Hence Luther dismissed metaphysical speculation about God and his attributes. Rather it is in "the hidden God" of redemption, not the prevailing theological "school of the God of glory," and this not in speculation but in personal faith in God, that is revealed indirectly by salvation. For concealment is an essential characteristic of the exercise of faith. Nor is there then any contradiction between "the hidden God" and "the revealed God."

Interpreting faith in Pauline thought, Luther affirms that natural reason cannot know God. But the scholastics had established a doctrine of *synteresis* or conscience, as the meeting place between the finite man and the infinite God. For Jerome, this was "the spark" that had not been eliminated by the Fall. For Alexander of Hales, this was the retention of ethical consciousness, and for Thomas Aquinas, this was the "natural habit," indeed the practical intellect of man unimpaired by the Fall. Gabriel Biel went even further, to affirm that this gave man an infallible moral ability of knowledge. Luther wholly rejects this semi-Pelagian accumulative doctrine of *synteresis*.[18] Man does not possess the truth through natural aptitude but as one is turned *around* in conversion—not turned within in self-groundedness, but turned *to* the way of the cross, away from himself.

Faith then is hearing the Word of God, to be surrendered to God's self-revelation. "I live by faith, hope, and love alone, and I am weak, that is I suffer, for when I am weak, then I am strong."[19] So this delimitation of faith is over against every kind of empirically psychological and verifiable experience. For faith does not have its origin in any of the given abilities of the soul, nor can it be classified with the psychic functions of man. It is only the experience of God himself, of reaching out to him, with an orientation of selfhood that is Godward, not manward. In turn, all Christian works proceed from faith that is relational, not itself as human work, but expressive of divine grace.

For Luther, thought of God can never be seriously engaged in without Christ, any more than the content of faith can be explored without being determined by Christ. Where faith is, there Christ is present. Faith and Christ belong together as Word and Presence. Faith is expressed as humility, but humility is not a virtue, but the life as expressed by *sola gratia, sola scriptura*. Humility is the maturity of self-knowledge, gained by the cross of Christ.

Perhaps three dominant postures shape Luther's faith: *coram Deo;*

Christus pro me; and *Anfechtung.* Life is lived "before God" (*coram Deo*), or in "the presence of God." This is analogous to the Old Testament posture of "the fear of the LORD," for "to believe in such a God is to go down upon your knees," he says.[20] In the light of the cross, "Christ was given for me" (*Christus pro me*), so saving faith requires personal appropriation. This, however, is so comprehensive that no theory of atonement is adequate enough to describe what Christ has accomplished, other than appropriate it personally for the rest of one's life. So Luther urges: "read with great emphasis on these words 'for me,' 'me,' and accustom yourself to accept and apply this 'me' with certain faith. The words 'our,' 'us,' 'for us,' ought to be written in letters of gold—the man who does not believe them is not a Christian." But, adds Luther, "I did not learn my theology all at once, but I had to search deeper for it, where my trials/temptations [*anfechtungen*] took me . . . not standing, reading, or speculating, but living, nay, rather dying, and being damned makes a theologian."[21] Perhaps temperamentally too, Luther sees that his tendency to suffer from recurrent depressions forces him to live day-to-day under the cross.

To arrive then at the truth of justification and its experience in Luther's life is a long, painful journey. He has to go beyond the scholastics' doctrine of *synteresis* to recover Pauline epistemology from Augustinianism. Then in Romans 1:17 he sees three realities at once: the imputation of righteousness, its character by-faith-alone, then its experience both as a sinner and yet also as one made righteous. This transaction is indeed "the sweet exchange between Christ and the sinner." So Luther learns to pray: "Thou, Lord Jesus, art my righteousness and I am Thy sin; Thou hast taken on Thyself what Thou wast not, and hast given me what I am not."[22] It is the complete victory of the cross that has made this possible. Faith now remains as *fiducia,* an abiding personal trust, a grasping hold of Christ. But such faith in Christ is also nourished constantly by seeing Christ in all the Scriptures, the Lord and center of Scripture. So *sola fide* is held in balance by *sola scriptura,* while *sola gratia* remains the watchword to guard one's attitudes and gain one's assurance. It is receptivity, utter receptivity to the grace of God, through his Word, that engenders faith: faith as the revealed *fides,* and faith as the respondent *fiducia.*

How then is Luther's faith transmitted? As a conscientious Augustinian monk, he does not find a satisfactory answer to the question, How do I get right with God? So he overthrows the tradition, and ever after remains contemptuous of human traditions, *Menschensatzungen,* which he contrasts to the original message of the Word of God, unencumbered by the cultural accretions of the intervening centuries. The claims of the papacy are now untenable in the light of its institutional and doctrinal distortions. Thus, he leads the other Reformers in exploding the notion of "the consensus of centuries." What Luther is unable to see is that the denial of "traditionalism" is one thing, but wholehearted destruction of the past is much more serious, if it loses a historic sense of the continuity of God's sovereign grace throughout all the history of human waywardness. *Traditio* also refers to the *humanum* of human nature, of the cultivated sensibility that is bred and passed on to succeeding generations.[23] Here Luther is still rooted in mystics like Johannes Tauler, the unknown writer of the *Theologia Germanica,* and above all in Bernard of Clairvaux. But if Luther is the first "modern," then modernity has exacerbated the destruction of what is valid tradition, in the loss of the sense of the past that is needed to provide wisdom, human nurture and a much more holistic sense of the cultivation of *humanum.* Here Luther then is more radical, abstractive and unwise than Calvin, who makes a strong appeal to the legitimate authority of the patristic fathers, notably the Cappadocians, as a corrective to the Augustinian influence of Western traditionalism.

The priority of the gospel is transmitted effectively when the personal testimony of its transforming power is sustained as of basic importance. But the whole social fabric of Lutheranism buries this, or at least suffocates it, when "the late Luther" decides deliberately in favor of the territorial church system. Consequently, Lutheranism lost its dynamism and never spread very far from Germany, the Baltics and Scandinavia. Then it grew inwardly, as an *ecclesial* civilization, like a reversion to medieval Christendom, an ironic trend in view of Luther's own original aversion to tradition. Inherent within the developments of the Lutheran Church have been inbred contradictions. Luther the anti-Aristotelian embraces the classical educational system that Philipp Melanchthon (1497–1560) created, by which to build the church. The church spiritualized by Luther and the church rationalized by Melanchthon is an unholy enough alliance.[24] In addition, the furtherance of the doctrine of the two kingdoms leads eventually to the Kantian split between scientific rationalism and religious phenomenology. Should Luther never have associated himself with Melanchthon in the first place? For Luther is a redeemed sufferer who sees and knows that true theology comes through grace, and grace comes through the status of being a suffering beggar. This is an environment of the soul uncomfortable to the humanist Melanchthon. Luther had said it long before in the explanation he gave of the fourth of his Ninety-five Theses: "If a person's whole life is one of repentance and a Cross of Christ, . . . then it is evident that the Cross continues until death and thereby to entrance into the Kingdom."[25]

John Calvin

What then of John Calvin (1509–1564)? How effective is he in the transmission of reformed faith? Like Luther, he focuses upon the doctrine of justification which is so easy to understand theoretically and so difficult to accept in personal practice. It is easy because it is so utterly free, but it is so difficult because its absolute freeness devalues the moral and religious currency of our own self-understanding.[26] So the real test of Calvin is how effectively he transmits pastorally, as well as doctrinally. The aim of the *Institutes,* he tells us, is to "include in a brief compass, the summary of evangelical doctrine."[27] But while this need of doctrine is basic, the ultimate purpose is to give teaching to build up Christian life and character. "Make sure that you listen to doctrine," he writes to the faithful Christians in Angers. "This must not be with the purpose of acquitting yourselves before God, as though that were the aim of the whole of Christianity, but in order to grow and be confirmed in faith as well as in all holiness."[28] To another congregation he says the same thing: "The truth is that it is not enough to read and listen, for our aim is to live in all holiness and perfection in the eyes of our God." So all our life should reflect our faith. Thus Calvin fears intellectualism that studies Scripture in scholarly curiosity with an arrogant desire to penetrate divine mystery. Indeed, he expresses himself as a pastor at heart, who would guide his flock scripturally and practically so. Trained by some of the best French humanist scholars, with a keen legal mind and a very high intelligence, yet Calvin sees himself less as a professional theologian than as a biblical scholar with a pastor's heart.

As a spokesman of the Reformation he is both more acceptable and more formidable than Luther, for he is a Renaissance humanist, more sophisticated intellectually, yet more moderate in tone, and with an acute sense of social realities. Writing to Martin Bucer (1491–1551) in 1538, Calvin views Luther as a social embarrassment: a demanding priest, a violent rebel, "craving for victory," "haughty in manner," with "insolent fury" and using "abusive language."[29] In spite of these deficiencies Calvin does not doubt Luther's piety. Like Zwingli, Calvin does not see Luther as the *only* reformer, but as one of a group of associates, "not the only one in the church of God to be looked up to." However, it is perhaps easier for a second-generation reformer to have this more modest perspective. For originally Luther did feel temperamentally very much "on his own."

In terms of institutional assessments, Ernst Troeltsch has advanced the theory of the superiority of Calvinism over Lutheranism.[30] For the Lutheran ethic has an inbuilt dualism between private devotion and public life that accepts the secular norms of the culture without any serious attempt to integrate them doctrinally. Returning to the medieval scholasticism that Luther himself had rejected, his associate Melanchthon reintroduced the Stoicism of natural law, appealing to Roman law. Eventually, the school of Grotius in the next century severed both law and reason from theology, to intensify the massivity of the state church, against which even a genius like Søren Kierkegaard could not prevail later. In contrast, Calvinism maintained a far more consistent and critical intellectual acumen of reformed theology, that has contributed broadly and deeply to our Western modern culture. For Calvin's aim was always pastoral and socially practical, on an international level. So while Lutheranism handed over governance and control of social morals and education to the secular authorities, the Calvinist communities have always sought to exercise such control themselves, as "holy communities," whether in Geneva, Europe or indeed overseas.

But the primary distinction John Calvin was given by his colleagues, like Gregory Nazianzen in the late fourth century, was to be called "the theologian." Melanchthon himself discerned that the key to both Gregory and Calvin was their deep grasp of the doctrine of the Trinity.[31] In an illuminating essay, T. F. Torrance has traced this association of the two theologians. The Athanasian association of godliness with orthodoxy plays a significant role in both, while the deity of Christ provides the key to the divine Triunity. The consubstantiality of the three Persons is also upheld clearly by both theologians, so that the total Being and the total nature of the one God is in each Person. Yet both agree that the Essence of God is incomprehensible, so that later Calvinist speculations about what God might elect, outside the biblical narrative, is abhorrent as idle speculation. Yet for both theologians, the self-revelatory character of God in his triune Being has opened up for us a way of communion with himself that is the source of ceaseless worship and of meditation upon his

Word, through his Spirit. Indeed, we can say that the greatest impact made upon the Christianization of the world of the fourth century, as upon the sixteenth century, is the recovery of the doctrine of the Trinity.

For Calvin, the outcome is his reverential approach to the sheer Godness of God, as Lord and Father of humankind, which deepened his godly piety. This goes together with Calvin's profound sense of "God's unfathomable and Spiritual Being," which transcends all human thought. "Who is this God" is a far greater cause for wonder in Calvin's spirit than the mere "quiddity" about God that the schoolmen had argued about before him.[32]

Likewise, it is in trinitarian terms that Calvin teaches the Reformed doctrine of justification by grace alone. To counter medieval misuse of "scholastic causes," he asserts the eternal love of the Father to be the "efficient cause" of our salvation, while the obedience of the Son is "the material cause" and the power of the Holy Spirit is "the instrumental cause," in preaching and in faith.[33] Thus the inner structure of his *Institutes* takes on this trinitarian form, in the persons of the Father, the Son and the Holy Spirit, together with the fourth volume, which is on the life and worship of the church. Only at the end of book 3 does he treat the doctrine of election (unlike Beza, who puts it at the beginning of his work), to emphasize that only after the Christian has understood the vicarious humanity of Christ and his salvation, together with our union with him, is it permissible to explore election. Indeed, Calvin's doctrine of election, instead of being a speculative doctrine as it became in Federal Calvinism, sums up the reality that the triune God of grace is *both* the proximate and the ultimate cause of salvation. The permanence of our eternal salvation—unlike its insecurity in Lutheranism—can then be affirmed.

Calvin's consistent rejection of medieval scholasticism also challenges the sovereignty of natural reason. "If we wish to be his disciples," he declares, "we must unlearn everything we have learned apart from Christ. For example, our own pure teaching in the faith begins with forgetting and rejecting the whole instruction of the papacy."[34] Calvin turns to his advantage the culture of doubt and Pyrrhonism by his deep engagement with the nature of Christian knowledge. The first two books of the *Institutes* are thus entitled "The Knowledge of God the Creator" and "The Knowledge of God the Redeemer in Christ." This is the double knowledge he speaks of in the first sentence of his work, the natural knowledge of ourselves, and of the world around us, in contradiction to the knowledge of

God that only God can self-disclose to us. Since reason alone cannot grasp the gospel, natural theology is denied validity. Without divine revelation man is left in a state of agnosticism, as Calvin's sixteenth-century culture was experiencing. So idle speculation, detached observation, systems of thought that carry no ethical impact—Calvin scorns them all.

Instead, Calvin sees that all knowledge is ultimately theonomous, for no branch of knowledge can be interpreted as autonomous. Moreover, knowledge of God can never be theoretical, for it is personal experience that engages the whole person before God; mind, heart and conscience, and all spiritual faculties. So Calvin views scornfully as "Epicurean" any attempt to have a detached, abstract theology.[35] Instead, the first response of man to knowing God should be "the fear of the Lord" that leads to worship and adoration. Such knowledge of God becomes "persuasive of faith," for it is given by the Holy Spirit, sealing the heart by being "cordial knowing." This knowledge of God is not about divine existence but consists in actually "doing His will," so that divine knowledge can become more intimately personal.[36] Then such persuasive knowledge of God helps us to recognize that the principal underlying purpose of all authentic theological endeavors is to find Jesus Christ through the study of the Scriptures.[37] As Calvin puts it: "he alone has duly denied himself who has so totally resigned himself to the Lord that he permits every part of his life to be governed by God's will."[38] Thus obedience, humility and self-mortification are all expressive of "knowing God," for John Calvin.

One of the finest biographical studies of the twentieth century has been William Bouwsma's portrait of John Calvin.[39] In an unusual event, a whole international congress on Calvin studies was recently devoted to the review of the book. Why? Perhaps it is because of the growing recognition that this great Reformer most effectively transmits Reformed doctrine by a transformed personal portrait. What modern scholarship is appreciating is the authentic humanity of Calvin, his devout spirituality, as well as doctrinal intellect, so that Catholics and Protestants alike are now exploring appreciatively his quality of godly personhood. Bouwsma himself has admitted that if there is any fault in his portrait, it is that Calvin's own spirituality has not been more critically explored by him.[40] Perhaps what he means by this—and what is certainly needed today—is the profoundly personal nature of theology. For knowledge of God does not deal merely with a concept of God, but with God himself. God is not an object outside us, an object of science, but the experience of the Subject who knows us and encounters us so intimately. Hence knowledge of God challenges and enhances our moral sensibility and our own self-understanding. Through it, a profound sense of commitment develops which will penetrate every aspect of our behavioral and conceptual existence. Yet this does not mean that theology is subjective and relative. With his doctrine of Word and Spirit, Calvin correlates the objective and subjective factors of knowledge, to break the antithesis of objectivism and subjectivism. Calvin understands theology to be vital and experiential, demanding constant daily openness to the Word of God and to the guidance of the Holy Spirit. Generationally, this can only be transmitted personally, not institutionally. Not even associates, as Melanchthon was to Luther or as Beza was to Calvin, succeeded in transmitting the Reformed faith of their leaders. How much less did the later institutionalized forms of Lutheranism and Federal Calvinism really reflect their founders' convictions.

The Christian Spirit of Transmission
The more deeply we probe the issues of transmission of faith, the more readily we may admit the failure of "Christianization." This is being admitted by recent scholarship, both for late antiquity and for the Reformation period.[41] As Gerald Strauss affirms, "official Christianity" throughout the centuries has been able to capture a narrow, elite layer of the population, not "the underground," constituted by popular culture. So the notion of the "Christian West," then and now, should be seen as an illusion. If "the deep currents of popular life nourishing the subterranean religion were beyond the theologian's proof, the preacher's appeal or the writer's power to compel" then "its central purpose to make all people think, feel and act as Christians, to imbue them with a Christian mind-set, motivational drive and way of life . . . failed."[42] Yes, if Christian faith can ever be conceived of as a mass movement, then it did fail. But Strauss's assumption may itself be wrong. For is the faith not personal in a primary sense of the word? Moreover, the assumption that it is man and not God who brings reform may also be challenged.

Steven Ozment couches his judgment of the Reformation more wisely: "the great shortcoming of the Reformation was its naive expectations that the majority of people were capable of radical religious enlightenment and moral transformation whether by persuasion or coercion."[43] Luther was fully aware that irrational apocalyptic expectations, such as advocated by Joachim de Fiore and his millennial successors, were false. Sober realism about the sinfulness of man marked the spiritual reforms of the great leaders. Freedom of the will before God suggests a personalist approach to reform, not mass hysteria, then and now.

A fundamental issue raised by the Reformation is the determination of the interdependence of the kingdom of Christ and the structures of profane society. It was contextualized very differently in Wittenberg, Zurich and Geneva.[44] The challenge of the transmission of reform is how to avoid immediate "political triumphs" that ultimately seduce us into "spiritual tragedies," such as the Lutheran Church's compromise with Hitler's regime in the 1930s, which the Barmen Declaration sought to resist. Again, the linkage between Federal Calvinism and its logical premises for apartheid policies within the Dutch Reformed Church in South Africa reveals how the nature of God can be so distorted. And again, we think of all the travesty of religion in Northern Ireland. If we trace back to when such distortions in the transmission of reform actually began, we have to start with the immediate collegiality of Luther with Melanchthon, and of Calvin with Beza. Then within the second and third generation of the Reformation, there was already a self-confident elite of theologians, jurists, politically active preachers and learned city councilors, making negation of the doctrinal reforms personally exemplified by Luther and Calvin, by the institutionalizing processes that tended to generate "Constantinian churches," politicized within the prevailing culture. Discernible is the admixture of classicism and biblical thought, stoicism and grace, reason and faith, conditional contract and covenant.[45] Such institutional "success" is spiritual "tragedy."[46]

Perhaps then we should interpret "massivity" as the enemy of reform. It is appealing to see grow a popular ecclesial culture, as we are naturally fascinated by quantity. Growth in size gives the appearance of progress, as North American Christianity still believes it to be. But what size does is to exaggerate the inconsistent flaws already inherent, as Luther's dualism had, in the kingdom of reason before one's fellows and the kingdom of Christ before God. The educational utilization of "Ramism" in the sixteenth century and later was a rhetorical and diagrammatic rationalization that created dialectical flaws in Calvinism, to generate a double election—to salvation or damnation.[47] It kept several generations of simple believers on a neurotic edge of personal uncertainty and even despair, as John Bunyan expresses poignantly in *Grace Abounding to the Chief of Sinners*.

The juridical spheres of sovereignty, of family, work, church and state also left many Lutherans wholly encapsulated in "Prussian" legalisms, which are far removed from Luther's own early personal testament, "On the Freedom of the Christian Person." Neither Kierkegaard's protest to the state church in Denmark in the nineteenth century nor Bonhoeffer's protest of "cheap grace" in Germany in the twentieth century has freed their kinsmen, other than in the massive secular rejection of the church itself, today.

But complete break with tradition does not serve the purpose of reform, either. Severance from error, yes, is essential. But is there a living *traditio,* reflecting the tacit dimension—to use Michael Polanyi's language—that intuits communal and personal sensibilities that are the heritage of *humanum?* As Andrew Louth has expressed very well: "to be a Christian is not simply to believe something, to learn something, but to *be* something, and experience something." So "joining a fellowship, commitment to a community, involves more than assent to its beliefs, but rather a sharing in its way of life, in its ceremonies, and its customs and practices."[48] Thus, renewal movements today that remain wholly oblivious to previous reforms and their traditions of practice do not generate lasting reform but dissipate quickly into disillusionment later.

Calvin especially lives conscious of the theological contributions made by Bernard of Clairvaux, Augustine and above all the Cappadocians headed by Gregory Nazianzen. He knew, as they had taught him, that *theologia* means not just the *doctrine* of the Trinity but the *contemplation* of the Trinity. As a friend of the Cappadocians, Evagrius Ponticus, put it: "if you are a theologian, you pray, and if you pray truly, you are a theologian."[49] This is not taught nor understood by modernist theology, too saturated by Enlightenment thought. Likewise, no one can study a great Reformer like Calvin without realizing the great traditional values he reflects, of a life of godliness as the prerequisite to becoming a theologian. Then neither academic ambition nor the quest for favor is the real passion of reform. Rather it is the glory of God alone.

True reform always rejects appearances for the pursuit of the reality in one's own life. That is why personal brokenness, conversion and personal conviction are the drive behind all such reform movements. Idolatries of the mind, of the spirit, of the will, all tend to create shadows of illusion as expressive of our fallen condition. So the idolatry of feeling can be a substitute for the transforming encounter with God himself. The idolatry of ideas can eclipse the self-disclosure of God's revelation in his Word. The idolatry of organization in "churchism" can be a substitute for the community of Christian fellowship. The idolatry of "ethicism" can replace Christian obedience, in the shadows of human "goodness" and "goodwill."[50] The mark then of reform is the return to what is determined solely by God's own character.

There can be no human substitute for "knowing God." Yet the natural desires for clarification, rationalization, organization, moralization are all confronted there, by mystery—the central mystery of God in Christ—realized in us by the Holy Spirit. Transmission of reform requires us to live trustingly, to live in, through and by the Mystery of God. So as Pieper puts it, Christian theology "should hinder and resist the natural craving of the human spirit for a clear, transparent, definite system."[51] They have their place, but they must be transcended by "the fear of the Lord, which is the beginning of wisdom." We need constant vigilance in reexamining the educational model we adopt, whether it be "Ramism" in the sixteenth century or "inductive study" in the twentieth century. These are but "earthen vessels" for the transmission of "knowing God."

Notes:

[1] See Peter Brown, *Authority and the Sacred: Aspects of the Christianization of the Roman World* (Cambridge: Cambridge University Press, 1995), pp. 1–26.

[2] Hans Küng, *Who Is a Christian?* (London: William Collins, 1976).

[3] François de Sales, *Les Controverses,* in *Oeuvres* (Annecy, France: 1892), 1:73.

[4] Ibid., p. 335.

[5] See the excellent study of the two philosophers in Richard H. Popkin, *The History of Skepticism, from Erasmus to Descartes* (New York: Harper & Row, 1964), pp. 175–217.

[6] Gilles Cusson, *Pédagogie de l'experience spirituelle personelle* (Paris: Descle de Brouwer, 1976), p. 19.

[7] Quoted by John O'Malley, "Early Jesuit Spirituality: Spain and Italy," in *Christian Spirituality: Post-Reformation and Modern,* eds. Louis Dupré and Don E. Saliers (New York: Crossroad, 1991), p. 12.

[8] Friedrich Wulf, ed., *Ignatius of Loyola: History, Personality and Spiritual Heritage, 1556–1956* (St. Louis, Mo.: Institute of Jesuit Sources, 1977), p. 7.

[9] John R. Roberts, *A Critical Anthology of English Recusant Devotional Prose, 1558–1603* (Pittsburgh, Penn.: Duquesne University Press, 1966), p. 3.

[10] James M. Houston, ed., *The Benefit of Christ* (Portland, Ore.: Multnomah Press, 1984).

[11] José C. Nieto, *Juan de Valdes and the Origins of the Spanish and Italian Reformation* (Geneva: Librarie Dioz, 1970), p. 209.

[12] Ibid., p. 214.

[13] Ibid., p. 221.

[14] Ibid., p. 266.

[15] Ibid., p. 269.

[16] Quoted by Rowan Williams, *The Wound of Knowledge* (London: Darton, Longman & Todd, 1979), p. 146.

[17] G. Ruff and B. Drewery, *Martin Luther, Documents of Modern History* (London: Edward Arnold, 1970), p. 29.

[18] Walther von Loewenich, *Luther's Theology of the Cross,* trans. Herbert J. A. Bouman (Minneapolis, Minn.: Augsburg, 1976), pp. 52–58.

[19] Ibid., p. 57.

[20] Timothy George, *Theology of the Reformers* (Nashville, Tenn.: Broadman, 1988), p. 59.

[21] Ibid., p. 60.

[22] Ibid., p. 70.

[23] See Andrew Louth, *Discerning the Mystery: An Essay on the Nature of Theology* (Oxford: Clarendon, 1989), pp. 73–95.

[24] See Sachiko Kusukawa, *The Transformation of Natural Philosophy: The Case of Melanchthon* (Cambridge: Cambridge University Press, 1995). This helpful study shows how Melanchthon used a philosophy based on Aristotle, Galen and Plato, as well as Stoicism, to promote university education in aid of "Lutheranism"!

[25] *Heidelberg Disputation;* see Ruff and Drewery, *Martin Luther,* p. 27.

[26] T. F. Torrance, "Cheap and Costly Grace," in *God and Rationality* (Oxford: Oxford University Press, 1971), p. 70.

[27] John Calvin, *The Institutes of the Christian Religion,* 3.19.1.

[28] Quoted by Jean-Daniel Benoit, *Calvin in His Letters* (Oxford: Appleford, 1991), p. 17.

[29] William Bouwsma, *John Calvin* (Oxford: Oxford University Press, 1988), p. 18.

[30] Ernst Troeltsch, *The Social Teaching of the Christian Churches,* trans. Olive Wyon (Chicago: University of Chicago Press, 1981), 2:576–78.

[31] T. F. Torrance, "The Doctrine of the Holy Trinity in Gregory Nazianzen and John Calvin," in *Trinitarian Perspectives* (Edinburgh: T. & T. Clark, 1994), pp. 21–40.

[32] Ibid.

[33] James B. Torrance, "The Concept of Federal Theology: Was Calvin a Federal Theologian?" in *Calvinus Sacrae Scripturae Professor,* ed. Wilhelm Neuser (Grand Rapids, Mich.: Eerdmans, 1994), p. 17.

[34] *Commentary,* 2 Tim 3:14.

[35] Edward A. Dowey, *The Knowledge of God in Calvin's Theology* (Grand Rapids, Mich.: Eerdmans, 1994), p. 27.

[36] Iain Paul, *Knowledge of God in Calvin, Einstein and Polanyi* (Edinburgh: Academic Press, 1987), p. 7.

[37] Ibid., p. 11.

[38] Ibid., p. 15.

[39] Bouwsma, *John Calvin.*

[40] Quoted by John Hesselink, "Reactions to Bouwsma's Portrait of John Calvin," in *Calvinus Sacrae Scripturae Professor,* ed. Wilhelm Neuser, p. 211.

[41] See Brown, *Authority and the Sacred,* pp. 1–26.

[42] Gerald Strauss, *Luther's House of Learning: Indoctrination of the Young in the German Reformation* (Baltimore, Md.: Johns Hopkins University Press, 1978), pp. 303, 307.

[43] Steven Ozment, *The Age of Reform, 1250–1550* (New Haven, Conn.: Yale University Press, 1980), p. 437.

[44] Heiko A. Oberman, *The Reformation: Roots and Ramifications,* trans. Andrew Colin Gow

(Grand Rapids, Mich.: Eerdmans, 1994), pp. 23–52.

[45] James B. Torrance, "The Concept of Federal Theology," pp. 15–40; see also David A. Weir, *The Origins of the Federal Theology in Sixteenth Century Reformation Thought* (Oxford: Clarendon, 1990).

[46] Heiko A. Oberman, *Masters of the Reformation*, trans. Dennis Martin (Cambridge: Cambridge University Press, 1981), pp. 260–95.

[47] Walter Ong, *Ramus, Method and the Decay of Dialogue: From the Art of Discourse to the Art of Reason* (Cambridge, Mass.: Harvard University Press, 1958). This is an excellent description and critique of the influence of the sixteenth-century educationalist, adopted widely by Puritan and continental reformers.

[48] Louth, *Discerning the Mystery*, pp. 73–74. See also Jaroslav Pelikan, *The Vindication of Tradition* (New Haven, Conn.: Yale University Press, 1984).

[49] Evagrius Ponticus, *Treatise on Prayer*; quoted by St. Nilus of Sinai, *Early Fathers from the Philokalia*, trans. E. Kadlonbovsky and G. E. H. Palmer (London: Faber & Faber, 1954), p. 134.

[50] John A. Mackay, *Christian Reality and Appearance* (Richmond, Va.: John Knox, 1969). This is an excellent survey of the ecclesial temptations.

[51] Quoted by Louth, *Discerning the Mystery*, p. 146.

15

Immanuel and the Purpose of Creation

Loren E. Wilkinson

*There is but one God, the Father, from whom all things came and
for whom we live; and there is but one Lord, Jesus Christ, through
whom all things came, and through whom we live. But not everyone knows this. (1 Cor 8:6-7)*[1]

I MET JIM PACKER IN THE SPRING OF 1981, SHORTLY
before I joined the faculty at Regent College, where he had come
two years earlier as professor of systematic theology. I had heard his
name and read his works for twenty years (since reading *"Fundamentalism" and the Word of God* as an undergraduate), and so was aware,
when I knocked on his office door, that this was an Important Man. I
was expecting to be impressed (or intimidated); I was not prepared
to be befriended. But I was met then (as countless times since) not
only by a daunting British accent and flawless syntax (here is a man
who seems to think, if not dream, in alliterated parallel clauses) but
also, surprisingly, by warmth, attention and a great readiness to turn
intelligence and learning to the purposes of friendship.

So I remember well the main outlines of that conversation. It
moved quickly from literature in general onto two writers whom we
both admired: Gerard Manley Hopkins and Charles Williams. And
from there we turned to a theological theme which those writers
shared, along with the fourteenth-century Franciscan scholastic Duns
Scotus. That theme is the idea—some would say the *speculation*—that
the incarnation of Christ was only secondarily for our redemption:

primarily, it was God's intention from the beginning to unite himself in self-giving love to the creation.

Jim's response to this idea was immediate and forthright: it is fruitless speculation, he said. For the fact is, humanity *did* sin. And in the purposes of God, the Incarnation, leading to the death and resurrection, took place *for our salvation*. What *would have happened,* on this subject, as on all other conditions contrary to fact, is a door which must remain closed to us.

I must have been crestfallen at this apparently unanswerable refutation of the idea—for Jim Packer's last words on the subject graciously kept it alive, at least in my own mind, as a matter for future thought and discussion. "Well," he said, with that magisterial Packerian twinkle, "at least it's not *heretical.*"

So in the spirit of that first conversation with an old friend I would like to reopen that particular discussion. Immanuel, "God with us," the Word made flesh in Jesus, is more than a kind of divine mission, to be understood only within "the order of redemption." Rather, the incarnation is basic to God's action in creation, quite apart from human sin. For it shows us the *purpose* of creation, and hence, our own purpose and direction as creatures.

There are two good reasons for maintaining this belief. The first is that it seems most consistent with the abundant biblical witness which links Christ and creation. The second is that this generation desperately needs to rediscover the depth of God's love for the whole creation. And this need is as desperate within the church as it is outside it.

There is no question, however, that, at least in Western Christendom, the creational centrality of the Incarnation is a minority view. In dismissing the belief, Packer stands in a long theological tradition. Consider, for example, the words from the two preeminent theologians in Western Christendom. Aquinas and Calvin, though separated by three centuries and enormous differences in other areas, are united on this matter.

In the *Summa Theologica,* in the midst of a leisurely reflection on the Incarnation, Thomas considers, "Whether, if Man had not sinned, God would have been Incarnate?" His answer has a Packerian ring to it, for while admitting the validity of the question, he firmly closes the door on any answer outside those affirmations of Scripture which directly link Incarnation with atonement from sin. Thomas cites, in evidence, Luke 19:10: "For the son of man came to seek and to save what was lost." On this text Aquinas quotes Augustine as saying: "Therefore if man had not sinned, the Son of Man would not have come."[2] Likewise, Thomas cites First Timothy 1:15, "Christ Jesus came into the world to save sinners," and responds by quoting an unattributed gloss on that text: "There was no cause of Christ's coming into the world except to save sinners. Take away diseases, take away wounds, and there is no need of medicine."[3]

In summing up his conclusion, Thomas observes (as does Packer) that we have no insight into this matter beyond what is revealed in Scripture, and that "hence, since everywhere in the Sacred Scripture the sin of the first man is assigned as the reason of the Incarnation, it is more in accordance with this to say that the work of the Incarnation was ordained by God as a remedy for sin."[4]

But significantly (as in Jim's comment—"at least it's not heretical"), Aquinas leaves the door on the question slightly ajar. He concludes his statement with the words, "And yet the power of God is not limited to this—even had sin not existed, God could have become incarnate."

So much for that most magisterial of theological voices from the Middle Ages. When we turn to the Reformation, and to one of Packer's own great models for theology, we find the question considered, but dismissed even more quickly. In the *Institutes* John Calvin writes, in a comparable reflection on the Incarnation:

> He who considers these things with due attention, will easily disregard vague speculations, which attract giddy minds and lovers of novelty. One speculation of this class is that Christ, even though there had been no need of his interposition to redeem the human race, would still have become man.[5]

Calvin grants, barely, that there is reason for the speculation on the place of Christ in "the first ordering of creation," and mentions Colossians 1:15 (in which Christ is designated "the firstborn over all creation"). But, like Aquinas, Calvin closes the door on the subject because of the firm linking of Christ with redemption: "Since the whole Scripture proclaims that he was clothed with flesh in order to become a Redeemer, it is presumptuous to imagine any other cause or end." Calvin goes on to point out the biblical connection of Christ with sacrifice and blood:

> Since from the earliest age, even before the Law was promulgated, there was never any promise of a Mediator without blood, we justly infer that he was destined in the eternal counsel of God to purge the pollution of man, the shedding of blood being the symbol of expiation.[6]

Calvin sums up his comments on the subject with a decisive and dismissive declaration:

> After hearing that Christ was divinely appointed to bring relief to miserable sinners, whoso overleaps these limits gives too much indulgence to a foolish curiosity.[7]

In the face of these decisive voices from both Catholic and Protestant theology, it would seem foolish to pursue the matter further: a matter only, in Calvin's phrase, for "giddy minds and lovers of novelty."

Yet not even for these masters is the matter quite closed. As we have seen, Aquinas admits that the possibility of the Incarnation apart from sin is consistent with the power of God; Calvin considers the elusive significance of at least one of the "cosmic Christology" texts linking Christ and creation. And Jim Packer says of the idea, "At least it's not heretical."

Far from being heretical, I would like to argue, tentatively, that a Christ-centered creation is the best way to understand the many New Testament texts which link Christ and the created order. Further, to affirm that God intended the Incarnation from the beginning (whether or not it would entail suffering and death) puts love (with its necessary risk and self-emptying) at the center of the Godhead and provides a deep answer to the problem of pain and suffering in creation.

Such an understanding of the Incarnation is a necessary corrective to two current (and persistent) errors in our thinking about God. The first exaggerates God's transcendence, picturing him as a distant, detached lawgiver and judge. The second stresses only God's immanence, eliminating distinctions between Creator and creation—and between God and humanity. Such a view, which collapses all things—humanity and the cosmos—into the divine, is particularly evident in a great deal of contemporary "creation spirituality" and "ecofeminism."

When we understand Christ, the "new Adam," as the exemplar and end of creation, we gain a deep insight—as created image bearers of God, fallen and redeemed—into our own purpose in creation.

A Biblical "Cosmic Christology" and the Incarnation

The New Testament writers are insistent in their fundamental linking of Christ and creation. The central texts are well-known. Here are the main ones.

> In the beginning was the Word, and the Word was with God, and the Word was God. He was with God in the beginning. Through him all things were made; without him nothing was

made that has been made. In him was life, and that life was the light of men. (Jn 1:1-4)

Yet for us there is but one God, the Father, from whom all things came and for whom we live; and there is but one Lord, Jesus Christ, through whom all things came and through whom we live. (1 Cor 8:6)

And he made known to us the mystery of his will according to his good pleasure, which he purposed in Christ, to be put into effect when the times will have reached their fulfillment— to bring all things in heaven and earth together under one head, even Christ. (Eph 1:9-10)

He is the image of the invisible God, the firstborn over all creation. For by him all things were created: things in heaven and on earth, visible and invisible . . . all things were created by him and for him. He is before all things, and in him all things hold together. . . . For God was pleased to have all his fullness dwell in him, and through him to reconcile to himself all things, whether things on earth or things in heaven, by making peace through his blood, shed on the cross. (Col 1:15-20)

In the past God spoke to our forefathers through the prophets at many times and in various ways, but in these last days he has spoken to us by his Son, whom he appointed heir of all things, and through whom he made the universe. The Son is the radiance of God's glory, and the exact representation of his being, sustaining all things by his powerful word. (Heb 1:1-3)

Each of these texts has its place in the theology of the author, and the development of that author's argument. But some things can be learned from grouping them together like this.

The most obvious thing which these texts share is that they express a close link between Christ and creation. The nature of that link we will consider shortly. But for now it is enough to note that they together express the significance of Christ in terms of the whole creation—past, present and future.

Another important point about the texts is the diversity of their authorship, both in origin and in time. Three are Pauline, but one comes from the earliest of Paul's books, and two from late in the corpus. Of the remaining two, one is Johannine, and the other comes from the unknown author of the letter to the Hebrews. Taken together, they obviously reflect a very widespread understanding in the early church that Jesus, "God with us," was of importance for the whole cosmos. In the mystery of the Spirit's leading of the church into truth, this particular truth—that Jesus' concern was with the whole cosmos—was clearly fundamental to the early church.

It is worth noting that of these five texts, four occur very early in the books in which they occur, and stand as a kind of foundational premise for what will follow. John's prologue (as has often been noted) is written in deliberate echo to Genesis 1's description of creation: the linking of Christ and creation "in the beginning" is thus a foundational theme of John's Gospel.

The writer to the Hebrews likewise stresses the link between Christ ("through whom he [God] made the universe") and creation, stressing that Christ is the completion of all God's revelation in the past. In Ephesians, Paul's declaration that all creation will be summed up in Christ stands as the climax of the extraordinary outpouring of praise and adoration which begins this general letter. And in Colossians, that letter in which Paul is most concerned to persuade his readers of the uniqueness of Christ, Paul founds his argument on the repeated truth that "all things" hold together in him.

The remaining "cosmic Christology" passage (1 Cor 8:6) is in the context of a specific ethical question—the matter of eating food offered to idols. But the fact that Paul deals with this very particular question by appeal to such a cosmic principle—that "there is but one Lord, Jesus Christ, through whom all things came and through whom we live"—indicates the importance of the immense premise of the linking of Christ and creation. This premise is clearly foundational for his thought.

Thus far we have established only the centrality of the connection between Christ and creation. What does that connection, as it is expressed in these passages, say about the issue at hand: whether the Incarnation was in God's purpose from the beginning?

On the one hand, nothing: in none of these cases is it in the intention of the author to speculate on the "what if?" of human sinlessness. As both Aquinas and Calvin point out, these descriptions of the Incarnation are all in the overall context of the realities of our condition: we are alienated from God, in desperate need of reconciliation. Clearly the Incarnation of the One "in whom all things hold together" *has been* our redemption: literally our salvation, our only hope.

But let us ask a further question in the light of these texts. At least three of them—John, Colossians, Hebrews—have a clear focus backwards to "the beginning." In all of them Christ is spoken of in terms of the purpose and intention of God in the very origin of creation. Christ is presented as the *means* of creation. But what can this mean? What did it mean to the first-century writers (and hearers) of these texts? What can it mean to us?

One of the things it must mean is that Christ (the Anointed One whom we can only know as the man Jesus) is prior to creation, prior to the universe. The cosmos must be "made by" or "held together in" one who precedes it. The only thing that can predate creation is the Creator. Thus these passages point inescapably to the deity of Christ, and ultimately to the doctrine of the Trinity.

But they point also to the fact that the love which led God to enter his creation—and the *cost* of that love—is central to the very being of God. He did not create out of need. Nevertheless, creation and the incarnation shows the character of God—which is to pour out love. James Torrance and Roland Walls make this point very clearly in a little book on Duns Scotus:

> In terms of this trinitarian understanding of the love of God, Duns sees the inner purpose and destiny of creation and re- demption as that of sharing in the inner life of the Trinity. Man's chief end is to glorify God by enjoying communion with God forever. In the eternal Trinity, God loves himself and enjoys communion in himself. But he freely wills to share this life of love and communion. And so freely decides to create "co- lovers" of his infinitely lovable nature.[8]

It is this will to love in the very character of God, rather than the fact of human sin, which is the purpose of the incarnation. As Torrance and Walls put it:

> This purpose of sharing his love and his glory is the basis of the incarnation—the predestination from all eternity of Christ's human nature, in which we see the perfect example . . . of man as God's co-lover, and in which we see the ultimate purpose and destiny of our humanity. The incarnation was God's purpose for us from all eternity *even if sin had not come*. This is the inner meaning of grace in creation.[9]

We cannot overlook the *costliness* of creation, and the fact that creation by an all-good God makes evil possible. Here we must avoid the gnostic tendency to equate creation with the fall: there is no trace of such an idea in Scripture. But we must avoid also a tendency to drive a wedge between creation and redemption by implying that God was not prepared, from the beginning, for the suffering which Creation might entail.

Colin Gunton reflects on this tendency to distance redemption from creation in his work *Christ and Creation*. He asks:

> What . . . are we to say of the relation of creation and redemption? Much has been made already of their close relation. The divine self-emptying is the actualizing in time and space of the very love which gives being and form to the world. What, however, is the first of the works of God?[10]

Gunton then considers—and dismisses—the Thomistic (and implicitly the Calvinist) answer to the question, which he describes as "the view that redemption is second in the intention of God, because it represents an attempt to make the best of the first, failed, enterprise . . . of creation." Such an attitude, says Gunton, "fail[s] to articulate the initial christological and eschatological thrust of creation."[11]

It is precisely that "christological and eschatological thrust" which is expressed in those New Testament "cosmic Christology passages" we have been considering. If redemption is God's way of "making the best" out of a failed situation, then there is no reason to affirm (as these texts do) the involvement of Christ in creation at the beginning. They suggest creation would seem to have a purpose which is to be fulfilled in Christ quite apart from human sin: God's purpose from the beginning is to bring "all things into completion" in Christ. So Gunton draws his conclusion:

> If creation is to an end, namely that all that is should within the structures of time and space come to be perfected in praise of the creator, what we call redemption is not a new end, but the achievement of the original purpose of creation. It only takes the form of redemption—of a "buying *back*"—because of sin and evil. . . . What is realized in the incarnate involvement of the Son in time and space is the redirection of the creation to its original destiny, a destiny that was from the beginning *in Christ,* for all creation is through and to the Son.[12]

A little later in his argument Gunton touches on the question of the place of the Incarnation in God's purposes, and takes a position which is clearly different from the one which we saw expressed at the beginning of this essay by Aquinas, Calvin—and Packer:

> We can therefore agree with those who have argued that, had there been no fall, it would still have been the Father's good pleasure to come into personal relation with us through the incarnation of his Son.[13]

The Incarnation of a Loving Creator and the Pain of Creation
The texts we have considered clearly suggest that it was God's pur-

pose for creation to join it in his Son. The human story, however, has from the first been one of rebellion and alienation. And so, though the Incarnation was intended for communion, it has become, through God's gift and our need, first of all our salvation. Nevertheless we can see that hidden in redemption is the restoration of God's intention in creation, which is to unite all things in Christ.

There is another sense, however, in which we must understand redemption to be *implicit in creation*. For with creation there enters the possibility of pain, death and sin. And because the God who holds creation in being is a loving God, willing to give himself for the preservation of that which he has made, creation, from the beginning, has implied the willingness of the Creator to suffer.

This divine suffering implied by creation is hinted at in another passage of Scripture which links Christ and creation. It occurs in Revelation 13:8—where the book of life is described as belonging to the Lamb "slain from the creation of the world."

The Greek phrase here translated "the creation of the world" occurs several times in the New Testament to indicate "the beginning." Sometimes it clearly refers to God's foreknowledge: in Ephesians 1:4, for example (cited above), the same phrase describes Paul's certainty of being "chosen in him." But it also can indicate a state of affairs existing from the beginning—as, for example, in John 17:24, where Jesus says of the Father, "You loved me before the creation of the world." Here Jesus seems to be referring not simply to God's intention to love him, but to a state existing from the beginning: the sort of time referred to earlier in the prayer as "the glory I had with you before the world began."

"The Lamb . . . slain from the creation of the world" seems to refer, therefore, to God's willingness, from the beginning, to suffer out of love for his creatures. Kallistos Ware, in his work on the Creation, lays the basis for this uniting of love with suffering:

> God's motive in creation is his love. Rather than say that he created the universe out of nothing, we should say that he created it out of his own self, which is love. We should think, not of God the Manufacturer or God the Craftsman, but of God the Lover.[14]

And later, continues Ware:

> Even before the Incarnation God is directly involved in the sufferings of his creation. . . . It has been truly said that there was a cross in the heart of God before there was one planted outside Jerusalem.[15]

Jürgen Moltmann, in his recent Gifford Lectures published as *God in Creation,* explores further these Christological—and sacrificial—implications of creation itself. If, he speculates, creation is indeed "from nothing," then before creation there was no cosmos: only God. To create at all, God must allow for there to be a space which is not God: a kind of wound or emptiness in the very being of God. Creation is founded on God's willingness to let something besides God exist. The potential for suffering in God is thus implicit from the beginning, for creation rests at every moment on a kind of self-emptying:

> God "withdraws himself from himself to himself" in order to make creation possible. His creative activity outwards is preceded by this humble divine self-restriction. In this sense God's self-humiliation does not begin merely with creation, inasmuch as God commits himself to this world: it begins beforehand, and is the presupposition that makes creation possible. God's creative love is grounded in his humble, self-humiliating, love. This self-restricting love is the beginning of that self-emptying of God which Philippians 2 sees as the divine mystery of the Messiah. Even in order to create heaven and earth, God emptied himself of his all-plenishing omnipotence, and as Creator took upon himself the form of a servant.[16]

Something like this "self-emptying of God" must lie at the source of creation (whether or not that was the understanding of the author of the book of Revelation when he wrote "The lamb that was slain from the creation of the world"). If this is so, then creation itself is informed by the Incarnation, for its origin is the very love of God: God's willingness to give himself for his creatures. Thus there is a kind of symmetry between creation and redemption. Redemption is a restoration of creation: but creation is, at the very beginning, a demonstration of the self-giving love which will stop at nothing for the good of the beloved.

James Cotter, in a profound study on the theology of Gerard Manley Hopkins, describes Duns Scotus's understanding of the Incarnation in a way which casts light on this closeness of creation and redemption:

> The Lamb is slain from the beginning. The act by which the Father sums up all the *pleroma* in his crucified Son, this is the one creative act of love from and to which all being flows. Creation and atonement, two decrees from man's temporal points of view, are actually simultaneous in God. . . . Nature ex-

ists from the start in a supernatural order, creation in Christ, and waits patiently for the deliverance of man and his passing over into completion in his Lord.[17]

This harmony between the creation and redemption is an ancient theme in Christian thought, which has, at least in the West, been obscured by exclusive emphasis on legal understandings of the atonement. In the second century Irenaeus sounds the note clearly, in his insistence (following Ephesians 1:10) that in Christ we see the summing up, the "recapitulation of all things."

> For the Creator of the world is truly the Word of God: and this is our Lord, who in the last times was made man, existing in the world, and who in an invisible manner contains all things created, and is inherent in the entire creation, since the Word of God governs and arranges all things; and therefore He came to his own in a visible manner, and was made flesh, and hung upon the tree that He might sum up all things in himself.[18]

We see it again in Athanasius's repeated affirmation that there is no inconsistency between creation and redemption, for in his words, "the renewal of creation has been wrought by the Self-same Word Who made it in the beginning."[19] Hans Urs von Balthasar, in his introduction to the anthology of Irenaeus's writings on the Incarnation, observes that

> the thought of Irenaeus forms a great axis. Its first movement is steep and Godward . . . it flies straight to the saving heights of the ever greater God, whom no finite mind can grasp. The other movement is broad, slow, heavy, a line drawn across the face of the earth. . . . If there is to be real redemption, this earth and no other, this body and no other, must have the capacity to take God's grace into itself.
>
> At the centre of this axis is the image of the Son of Man, who unites heaven and earth. . . . This uniting of God and world takes place in the Passion of Christ, when He is stretched out between height and depth, breadth and length. The cross-beams are the world's centre, and since it is in this sign that all creation is redeemed, they become the "watermark" of any kind of existence in the world.[20]

Charles Williams, in a similar meditation on the cross, describes vividly this identity of Christ the Creator and Christ the Redeemer:

> He was stretched, He was bled, He was nailed, He was thrust into, but not a bone of Him was broken. The dead wood drenched with the blood, and the dead body shedding blood,

have an awful likeness; the frame is doubly saved. It was the
Cross which sustained Him, but He also sustained the Cross.
He had, through the years exactly preserved the growth of the
thorn and the wood, and has indued with energy the making of
the nails and the sharpening of the spear; say, through the centuries He had maintained vegetable and mineral in the earth for
this. His providence overwatched it to no other end, as it over-
watches so many instruments and intentions of cruelty then and
now. The Cross therefore is the express image of His will; it depends in its visible shape and strength wholly on Him.[21]

It is no longer possible (if it ever was) to assume that biological
death is simply the consequence of sin. On the most obvious level,
death is one of the things which we share with all other living creatures, which (geologically speaking) predate human beings by vast
periods of time. There is abundant evidence that living creatures were
dying long before God's image-bearers, male and female, exercised
their will to sin. Though we are given hope that "the last enemy
which shall be destroyed is death," the creation which God recognized as "good" is woven on a loom of pain, which cannot in any
way be attributed to sin. To see the Incarnation as central to God's
very purpose in creation is to recognize that God, the great lover, has
chosen to follow his risky experiment to its painful conclusion. He
has, for the sake of creation, submitted himself to the very conditions
of the creation which he sustains.

The more we understand about the way the world works—the
destruction of stars being necessary for the birth of planets, the
burning of the sun being necessary for the maintenance of life, biological creation itself being a painful process of death and extinction,
day-to-day nourishment being a matter of metabolism, one body
burning calories stored by another—the more our hearts cry for an
answer to the pain that is woven into creation. So the more we know
about creation, the more welcome is this possibility: that at the very
beginning of creation, God the Creator determined to become flesh,
and dwell among us.

God's Otherness and His Nearness to Creation

Our era is characterized by a growing number of voices engaged in
an agonizing reassessment of the consequences of that ambitious
modern experiment which sees humanity as transcendent, with
a godlike power over nature. One of the most common features of
that reassessment has been an angry criticism of the very notion of a

transcendent God. Such a view of God is rejected as the legacy of a repressive patriarchalism which has tyrannized both women and nature.

The argument proceeds as follows. Because in Judeo-Christianity God (unlike the divine in various monisms, animisms and pantheisms) is perceived to be wholly, radically other than creation, and because we humans are made in his image, we have come to think of ourselves as likewise "other" than nature, and have acted accordingly. The accelerating decline of the planet's health can thus be directly linked to the spreading of a technological worldview which has its source in a Christian culture. It is a secularized Christian culture which has fostered a worldwide attitude of superiority to the rest of creation. It has encouraged viewing the whole earth as a stockpile of resources to be used for the human good. Unless we change radically, such an attitude can only end disastrously for the planet and all its life, including us.

The changes proposed by many feminists and environmentalists today are primarily religious changes. And the religious attitude which is emerging—patched together from various bits of native spirituality, Eastern monism and "human potentials" therapy—is one of radical immanence. If the problem is caused by the belief that "the Sacred" is transcendent, wholly other than ourselves and the earth, the solution must be to come to believe in the immanent divinity of everything, including ourselves. Most commonly the divine is spoken of in feminine terms as "the goddess." The attitude is well expressed in the words of the self-declared white witch Starhawk, who has worked in close conjunction with the founder of the Creation Spirituality Institute, former Catholic (now Episcopal) Matthew Fox. Declares Starhawk, in a widely viewed Canadian film on eco-feminism:

> For me the goddess is immanent, she is the world, she is us, she is nature, she is the changing of the seasons, she is the earth herself. It is as if the whole universe were one living being that we are a part of.[22]

Others, like Matthew Fox, speak of "Cosmic Christology" (indeed one of Fox's books is titled *The Cosmic Christ*) but mean by that term nothing more than a kind of impersonal principle of cosmic interconnectedness, for which the historical Jesus was simply a sort of avatar.

Another "ecofeminist," Susan Griffin, writes in *Reweaving the World* that the divine as immanent is "a concept foreign to those raised in Judeo-Christianity. . . . The view that we've grown up with is that the divine and matter are separate and that matter is really dangerous."[23]

We must acknowledge that there is some reason for these extreme reactions: many Christians *have* communicated an idea of God which is little more than deistic, stressing only the distance and otherness of the Creator, showing little understanding that "all things hold together" in Christ.

A prose poem by Stanley Wiersma (writing as "Sietze Buning") illustrates very well the tendency to distance God from creation and to use that transcendence as a basis for asserting a destructive human distance. In "Calvinist Farming" Wiersma describes how, in the Calvinist farming community he grew up in, in northwest Iowa, the farmers were suspicious of contour planting, for it confused the transcendent grid of equal spacing by the infinitely varied contours of the earth beneath the field.

> Our Calvinist fathers . . . rode
> their horse-drawn corn planters like chariots, planting the corn
> in straight rows, each hill of three stalks three feet from each hill
> around it, up and over the rises. A field-length wire with a metal knot
> every three feet ran through the planter and clicked off three kernels
> at each knot. Planted in rows east-west, the rows also ran north-
> south for cross-cultivating. Each field was a checkerboard even to
> the diagonals. No Calvinist followed the land's contours.[24]

And they had theological reasons for their suspicion of contour planting: they had to do with the analogy between God and the farmer:

> Calvinists knew
> the distance between God and people was
> even greater than the distance between people
> and corn kernels. If we were corn kernels in God's
> corn planter, would we want him to plant us at random?

But, Wiersma continues:

> We youngsters pointed out that the tops
> of our rises were turning clay-brown, that bushels of black dirt
> washed into creeks and ditches every time it rained, and that in
> the non-Calvinist counties the tops of the rises were
> black.

Wiersma's purpose in the whole poem is to defend, not criticize, the reality of God's transcendence. But he is sensitive to the way that the concept of transcendence needs to be softened by an understanding of the God who suffers, even in the erosion of hills and the loss of soil.

Not all who affirm a belief in the otherness of the transcendent God are aware of the deep immanence of God. They continue to overlook God's purpose, in Christ, to restore the creation which is made "through" the incarnate Word, and thus they drive many to reject the God of Scripture.

Paul, in Acts 17, speaks to the pagans of his own day (similar in many ways to the pagans of today) by reaffirming that immanence of God: "He is not far from each one of us. 'For in him we live and move and have our being'" (vv. 27-28).

One of the ways by which we can begin to understand the closeness of God is to recognize that the Incarnation is not simply a rescue operation to take us out of creation. It is rather the transcendent God's fulfillment of his intention from the beginning: to lead his image-bearing creatures to be, with the incarnate Word of God "filled with delight day after day, rejoicing always in his presence, rejoicing in his whole world and delighting in mankind." These are the words of Proverbs 8:30-31 and refer immediately to God's wisdom, but they have long been understood by the church to speak of the preincarnate Christ.

There is, of course, no proof for such a view. But clearly it provides a deep answer to those who feel that God is distant, unconcerned about nonhuman creation. There are strong biblical and apologetic reasons for reopening this way of viewing the Incarnation. We can affirm (with the Franciscan thinker Duns Scotus) that

> God loves himself.
> God loves himself in things other than himself,
> and this love is unclouded and pure.
> God wills to be loved
> by each human being,
> who is able to love him to the highest degree
> and here I speak of the love given to him from
> outside himself.
> *God sees the union between himself and that*
> *eternal existence which owes him the highest love*
> *even if there were nothing created that had betrayed his love.*
> God sees the mediator who comes as the one who

suffers and redeems his people.[25]

Believing that the incarnation was God's intention, even had we not sinned does not in any way detract from our understanding of the atonement. But it deepens our understanding of God's love.

Earlier I quoted the words of an ecofeminist who felt, bitterly, that the separation of God from matter implied that "matter is really dangerous." This understanding that God chose to unite himself in love to the matter which he had made, in the words of Charles Williams (speaking of Scotus), "subtly modified" our view of matter.[26]

Such an understanding was certainly one of the insights behind Gerard Manley Hopkins's powerful poetry. Hopkins declared, with a clear understanding of God's immanence, that

> Christ plays in ten thousand places,
> Lovely in limbs, and lovely in eyes not his,
> To the Father, through the features of men's faces,[27]

and that "the world is charged with the grandeur of God,"[28] that God is "ground of being, and granite of it."

Not only does such an understanding seem to make the most sense out of those texts which speak of Christ as the source, means and end of creation; they give us, adopted into sonship with the "second Adam," the privilege of working in the task of bringing all things together under Christ: Immanuel, "God with us," who shows us the purpose of creation.

Notes:

[1] All scriptural quotations in this article are taken from the New International Version of the Bible, copyright the New York International Bible Society, unless otherwise indicated.

[2] Thomas Aquinas, *Summa Theologica*, 3.1.3, *contra.*, trans. by the Fathers of the English Dominican Province, 5 vols. (Westminster, Md.: Christian Classics, 1981), 4:2022.

[3] Ibid.

[4] Acquinas quoting Augustine, *De Verb. Apost.* VIII, 2. in ibid.

[5] John Calvin, *Institutes of the Christian Religion,* trans. Henry Beveridge (Grand Rapids, Mich.: Eerdmans 1962), p. 402 (2.12.4).

[6] Ibid., p. 403.

[7] Ibid.

[8] James B. Torrance and Roland C. Walls, *John Duns Scotus in a Nutshell* (Edinburgh: Handsel Press, 1992), pp. 8–9.

[9] Ibid., p. 9.

[10] Colin Gunton, *Christ and Creation* (Grand Rapids, Mich.: Eerdmans, 1992), p. 93.

[11] Ibid., pp. 93–94.

[12] Ibid., p. 94.

[13] Ibid., p. 96.

[14] Bishop Kallistos Ware, *The Orthodox Way* (Oxford: Mowbray, 1979), p. 83.

[15] Ibid., pp. 82–83.

[16] Jürgen Moltmann, *God in Creation* (San Francisco: Harper, 1985), p. 88.

[17] James Finn Cotter, *Inscape: The Christology and Poetry of Gerard Manley Hopkins* (Pittsburgh, Penn.: University of Pittsburgh Press, 1972), pp. 122–23.

[18] Irenaeus, *Against the Heresies,* in *Early Christian Fathers,* ed. and trans. Edward Rocie Hardy (Philadelphia: Westminster Press, 1955), 1:385.

[19] Athanasius, *On the Incarnation,* trans. a Religious of C.S.M.V. (Crestwood, N.Y.: St. Vladimir's Press, 1954), p. 26.

[20] Iranaeus, *The Scandal of the Incarnation,* from *Against the Heresies,* selected and with an introduction by Hans Urs von Balthasar (San Francisco: Ignatius Press, 1990), p. 13.

[21] Charles Williams, "The Cross," in *The Image of the City and Other Essays,* ed. Ann Ridler (Oxford: Oxford University Press, 1958), p. 136.

[22] *Full Circle,* a film directed by Donna Read, the Great-Atlantic and Pacific Film Company in cooperation with the National Film Board of Canada, 1992.

[23] Susan Griffin, "Curves Along the Road," in *Reweaving the World: The Emergence of Ecofeminism,* ed. Irene Diamond and Gloria Feman Orenstein (San Francisco: Sierra Club Books, 1990), p. 87.

[24] Sietze Buning [pseudonym of Stanley Wiersma], "Calvinist Farming," in *Purpaleanie and Other Permutations* (Orange City, Iowa: Middleburg Press, 1978), p. 61.

[25] *Reportata Parisiensis* 3.7.4, cited in Torrance and Walls, p. 16. Italics added.

[26] Charles Williams, *Descent of the Dove* (Grand Rapids, Mich.: Eerdmans, 1968), p. 122.

[27] G. M. Hopkins, untitled poem in *Poems and Prose* (New York: Penguin Books, 1953 [1985]), p. 51.

[28] "God's Grandeur," in ibid., p. 27.

Appendix

A Select Bibliography of J. I. Packer's Works

I. **Books (sole author; including pamphlets [P])**
1. *"Fundamentalism" and the Word of God* (London: Inter-Varsity Fellowship and Grand Rapids, Mich.: Eerdmans, 1958).
2. *Evangelism and the Sovereignty of God* (London: Inter-Varsity Press, 1961).
3. *The Thirty-nine Articles* (London: Falcon, 1961). (P)
4. *The Plan of God* (London: Evangelical Press, 1962). (P)
5. *Our Lord's Understanding of the Law of God* (Glasgow: Pickering & Inglis, 1962). (P)
6. *Keep Yourselves from Idols* (London: Church Book Room and Grand Rapids, Mich.: Eerdmans, 1963). (P)
7. *God Has Spoken* (London: Hodder & Stoughton, 1964). Also published as *God Speaks to Man* (Philadelphia: Westminster, 1964); new enlarged edition (London: Hodder & Stoughton and Downers Grove, Ill.: InterVarsity Press, 1979).
8. *Tomorrow's Worship* (London: Church Book Room, 1966). (P)
9. *The Gospel in the Prayer Book* (Abingdon, England: Marcham, 1966). (P)
10. *The Thirty-nine Articles Today* (London: Church Book Room, 1968). (P)
11. *We Believe* (London: Nurses Christian Fellowship, 1972). (P)
12. *Knowing God* (London: Hodder & Stoughton and Chicago: InterVarsity Press, 1973).
13. *I Want to Be a Christian* (Wheaton, Ill.: Tyndale House and London: Kingsway, 1977); reissued as *Growing in Christ* (Wheaton, Ill.: Crossway, 1994).
14. *For Man's Sake* (London: Paternoster, 1977).
15. *The Evangelical Anglican Identity Problem* (Oxford: Latimer

House, 1978). (P)

16. *Knowing Man* (Westchester, Ill.: Cornerstone, 1979).
17. *Beyond the Battle For the Bible* (Westchester, Ill.: Cornerstone, 1980). Also published as *Under God's Word* (London: Marshall, Morgan, and Scott, 1980).
18. *God's Words* (London: Inter-Varsity Press and Downers Grove, Ill.: InterVarsity Press, 1981).
19. *A Kind of Noah's Ark? The Anglican Commitment to Comprehensiveness* (Oxford: Latimer House, 1981). (P)
20. *Freedom and Authority* (Oakland, Calif.: International Council on Biblical Inerrancy, 1981). Also published as *Freedom, Authority and Scripture* (Leicester, England: Inter-Varsity Press, 1982).
21. *Keep in Step with the Spirit* (Old Tappan, N.J.: Revell, 1984).
22. *The Thirty-nine Articles: Their Place and Use Today,* with additions by R. T. Beckwith (Oxford: Latimer House, 1984).
23. *Your Father Loves You* (Wheaton, Ill.: Harold Shaw, 1986).
24. *Meeting God* (LifeGuide Bible Study) (Downers Grove, Ill.: InterVarsity Press, 1986).
25. *God in Our Midst* (Ann Arbor, Mich.: Servant, 1987). (P)
26. *Hot Tub Religion* (Wheaton, Ill.: Tyndale House, 1987).
27. *A Quest for Godliness* (Westchester Ill.: Crossway, 1991). Also published as *Among God's Giants* (Eastbourne, England: Kingsway, 1991).
28. *A Man for All Ministries* (Richard Baxter), St. Antholins Charity Lectureship (London: Needham's, 1991). (P)
29. *Rediscovering Holiness* (Ann Arbor, Mich.: Servant, 1992). Also published as *A Passion for Holiness* (Cambridge: Crossway, 1992).
30. *Concise Theology* (Wheaton, Ill.: Tyndale House, and Leicester, England: Inter-Varsity Press, 1993).
31. *A Passion For Faithfulness* (Wheaton, Ill.: Crossway, 1995).
32. *Knowing and Doing the Will of God* (Ann Arbor, Mich.: Servant, 1995).
33. *Knowing Christianity* (Wheaton, Ill.: Harold Shaw, 1995).

II. Books (joint author)
34. ed. and trans. with O. R. Johnston, *Luther's Bondage of the Will* (London: James Clarke and Old Tappan, N.J.: Revell, 1957).
35. with J. A. Motyer, *Reservation* (London: Church Book Room Press, 1960). (P)

36. with A. M. Stibbs, *The Spirit Within You* (London: Hodder & Stoughton, 1966); reissued (Glasgow: Pickering and Inglis and Grand Rapids, Mich.: Baker, 1980).

37. with C. O. Buchanan, E. L. Mascall, G. Leonard, *Growing into Union: Proposals for Forming a United Church in England* (London: S.P.C.K., 1970).

38. with Thomas Howard, *Christianity the True Humanism* (Waco, Tex.: Word, 1985).

III. Books (contributor)

39. "Revelation and Inspiration," in E. F. Kevan, A. M. Stibbs, F. Davidson, eds., *The New Bible Commentary*, 2nd ed. Also published as D. Guthrie, J. A. Motyer, A. M. Stibbs, D. J. Wiseman, eds., *The New Bible Commentary Revised*, pp. 24–30; and in *Eerdmans' Bible Commentary* (London: Inter-Varsity Press and Grand Rapids, Mich.: Eerdmans, 1954, 1970), pp. 12–18.

40. "Modern Theories of Revelation," in C. F. H. Henry, ed., *Revelation and the Bible* (Grand Rapids, Mich.: Baker, 1959 and London: Inter-Varsity Press, 1960), pp. 87–104.

41. "Call," "Faith," "Freedom," "Ignorance," "Justification," "Orthodoxy," "Puritan," "Regeneration," in C. F. H. Henry, ed., *Baker's Dictionary of Theology* (Grand Rapids, Mich.: Baker, 1959).

42. "Introductory Essay," in John Owen, *The Death of Death in the Death of Christ* (London: Banner of Truth, 1959), pp. 1–25; also published separately (P).

43. "The Origin and History of Fundamentalism," in T. Hewitt, ed., *The Word of God and Fundamentalism* (London: Church Book Room Press, 1960), pp. 100–127.

44. "Assurance," "Authority," "Conversion," "Earnest," "Election," "Good," "Inner Man," "Incarnation," "Inspiration," "Justification," "Liberty," "Perfection," "Piety," "Predestination," "Providence," "Obedience," "Revelation," "Temptation," in J. D. Douglas, ed., *The New Bible Dictionary* (London: Inter-Varsity Press and Grand Rapids, Mich.: Eerdmans, 1961). Also published as N. Hillyer et al., eds., *The New Bible Dictionary*, 2nd ed. (Leicester, England: Inter-Varsity Press and Wheaton, Ill.: Tyndale House, 1982); and published in *The Illustrated Bible Dictionary* (same publishers).

45. "Introductory Essay," in J. Buchanan, *The Doctrine of Justification* (London: Banner of Truth, 1961), pp. 1–9.

46. "Lambeth 1958," in J. I. Packer, ed., *Eucharistic Sacrifice* (London: Church Book Room Press, 1962), pp. 1–21.

47. "The Nature of the Church," in C. F. H. Henry, ed., *Basic Christian Doctrines* (New York: Holt, Rinehart & Winston, 1962), pp. 241–47.

48. "Episcopacy," and two other essays, in J. I. Packer, ed., *The Church of England and the Methodist Church* (Abingdon, England: Marcham, 1963).

49. "Thomas Cranmer's Catholic Theology," in G. E. Duffield, ed., *Thomas Cranmer* (Abingdon, England: Sutton Courtenay Press, 1963), pp. 10–37.

50. "What Is Revival?" in D. Winter, ed., *The Best of Crusade* (London: Victory Press, 1963), pp. 89–93.

51. "British Theology in the Twentieth Century," in C. F. H. Henry, ed., *Christian Faith and Modern Theology* (New York: Channel Press, 1964), pp. 23–41.

52. "The Status of the Articles," in H. E. W. Turner, ed., *The Thirty-nine Articles of the Church of England* (London: Mowbrays, 1964), pp. 25–57.

53. "The Wretched Man in Romans 7," in F. L. Cross, ed., *Studia Evangelica* (Berlin: Akademie-Verlag, 1964); reprinted as an appendix to *Keep in Step with the Spirit* (21), pp. 621–27.

54. "Wanted: A Pattern for Union," and (with C. O. Buchanan) "Unification and Ordination," in J. I. Packer, ed., *All in Each Place* (Abingdon, England: Marcham, 1965), pp. 17–40.

55. "Calvin the Theologian," in G. E. Duffield, ed., *John Calvin* (Abingdon, England: Sutton Courtenay Press, 1966), pp. 149–75.

56. "Expository Preaching: Charles Simeon and Ourselves" and "The Revised Catechism," in *Churchmen Speak,* selected essays from *Churchman* (Abingdon, England: Marcham, 1966), pp. 64–70, 88–99.

57. "Gain and Loss," in R. T. Beckwith, ed., *Towards a Modern Prayer Book* (Abingdon, England: Marcham, 1966).

58. "Isn't One Religion as Good as Another?" in F. Colquhoun, ed., *Hard Questions* (London: Falcon, 1967), pp. 16–19.

59. "The Good Confession," in J. I. Packer, ed., *Guidelines* (London: Falcon, 1967), pp. 11–38.

60. "The Necessity of the Revealed Word," in M. C. Tenney, ed., *The Bible: The Living Word of Revelation* (Grand Rapids, Mich.: Zondervan, 1968), pp. 31–52.

61. "Anglican-Methodist Unity: Which Way Now?" in J. I. Packer, ed., *Fellowship in the Gospel* (Abingdon, England: Marcham, 1968).
62. "Training for the Ministry," in C. Porthouse, ed., *Ministry in the Seventies* (London: Falcon, 1970).
63. "Biblical Authority, Hermeneutics and Inerrancy," in E. R. Geehan, ed., *Jerusalem and Athens* (Philadelphia: Presbyterian and Reformed, 1971), pp. 141–53.
64. "Towards a Corporate Presbyterate," in R. P. P. Johnson, ed., *Ministry in the Local Church: Problems and Pathways* (Bramcote, England: Grove Books, 1972). (P)
65. "Reservation: Theological Issues," in C. O. Buchanan, ed., *Reservation and Communion of the Sick* (Bramcote, England: Grove Books, 1972). (P)
66. "Representative Priesthood?" and "Postscript: I Believe in Women's Ministry," in G. E. Duffield and M. Bruce, eds., *Why Not?* (Abingdon, England: Marcham, 1972; 2nd ed. 1976), pp. 78–80, 164–74.
67. "Taking Stock in Theology," in J. C. King, ed., *Evangelicals Today* (London: Lutterworth Press, 1973), pp. 15–30.
68. "Thoughts on the Role and Function of Women in the Church," in R. C. Craston, ed., *Evangelicals and the Ordination of Women* (Bramcote, England: Grove Books, 1973). (P)
69. "Revelation," "Myth," "Puritan Ethics," in C. F. H. Henry, ed., *Baker's Dictionary of Christian Ethics* (Grand Rapids, Mich.: Baker, 1973).
70. "Introductory Essay," in Richard Baxter, *The Reformed Pastor* (London: Banner of Truth, 1974), pp. 9–19.
71. "'*Sola Scriptura*' in History and Today," and "Calvin's Doctrine of Scripture," in J. W. Montgomery, ed., *God's Inerrant Word* (Minneapolis: Bethany, 1974), pp. 43–63, 95–114.
72. "Life in Christ" (95 Bible studies), in *Bible Characters and Doctrines*, vol. 11 (London: Scripture Union, 1974).
73. "Abolish," "Accuse," "Carpenter," "Defile," "Despise," "Ruin," "Present," "Dirt," "Firm," in C. Brown, ed., *New International Dictionary of New Testament Theology*, vol. 1 (Exeter, England: Paternoster Press and Grand Rapids, Mich.: Zondervan, 1975).
74. "Introductory Essay," in E. Hindson, *Introduction to Puritan Theology* (Grand Rapids, Mich.: Baker, 1976), pp. 9–12.
75. "What Is Evangelism?" in H. Conn, ed., *Theological Perspectives on Church Growth* (Nutley, N.J.: Presbyterian and Reformed,

1976), pp. 91–105.

76. "The Reformed Doctrine of Justification," in R. C. Sproul, ed., *Soli Deo Gloria, Festschrift* for John Gerstner (Philadelphia: Presbyterian and Reformed, 1976), pp. 11–25.

77. "Jesus Christ the Lord: The New Testament Doctrine of the Incarnation," in J. R. W. Stott, ed., *Obeying Christ in a Changing World, Vol. I: The Lord Christ* (London: Collins, 1977), pp. 32–60.

78. "Theology of the Reformation" and "Ignatius Loyola," in T. Dowley, ed., *Lion Handbook of Church History* (Berkhamsted, England: Lion, 1977).

79. "Are Pain and Suffering Direct Results of Evil?" in F. Colquhoun, ed., *Moral Questions* (London: Falcon, 1977), pp. 26–29.

80. "On Knowing God," in J. M. Boice, ed., *Our Sovereign God* (Grand Rapids, Mich.: Baker, 1977), pp. 61–76.

81. Foreword to R. C. Sproul, *Knowing Scripture* (Downers Grove, Ill.: InterVarsity Press, 1977), pp. 9–10.

82. "Oxford Evangelicals in Theology," in John Reynolds, *The Evangelicals at Oxford,* 2nd ed. (Abingdon, England: Marcham, 1977), pp. 82–94.

83. Preface to 1977 reprint of W. H. Griffith Thomas, *The Principles of Theology* (London: Vine Books and Grand Rapids, Mich.: Baker, 1978), pp. 5–14.

84. "An Evangelical View of Progressive Revelation," in K. Kantzer, ed., *Evangelical Roots* (Nashville: Nelson, 1978), pp. 143–58.

85. "Situations and Principles" and "Conscience, Character and Choice," in G. J. Wenham and B. Kaye, eds., *Law, Morality and the Bible* (Downers Grove, Ill., InterVarsity Press, 1978), pp. 151–92.

86. "Encountering Present-Day Views of Scripture," in J. M. Boice, ed., *Foundation of Biblical Authority* (Grand Rapids, Mich.: Zondervan, 1978), pp. 61–84.

87. "A Lamp in a Dark Place: II Peter 1:19-21," in E. Radmacher, ed., *Can We Trust the Bible?* (Wheaton, Ill.: Tyndale House, 1979), pp. 15–32.

88. Preface to centenary edition of J. C. Ryle, *Holiness* (Welwyn, England: Evangelical Press, 1979).

89. "The Gospel: Its Content and Communication," in J. R. W. Stott and R. Coote, eds., *Gospel and Culture* (Pasadena, Calif.: William Carey Press, 1979); shorter version, *Down to Earth,* same eds. (Grand Rapids, Mich.: Eerdmans, 1980), pp. 97–114.

90. "Preaching as Biblical Interpretation," in J. R. Michaels and R. Nicole, eds., *Inerrancy and Common Sense* (Grand Rapids, Mich.: Baker, 1980), pp. 187–203.

91. "The Adequacy of Language," in N. Geisler, ed., *Inerrancy* (Grand Rapids, Mich.: Zondervan, 1980), pp. 197–228.

92. "Editor's Preface," in J. I. Packer, M. E. Tenney and W. White Jr., eds., *The Bible Almanac* (Nashville, Tenn.: Nelson, 1980), pp. 11–12.

93. "My Path to Prayer," in D. Hanes, ed., *My Path of Prayer* (Brighton, England: Henry E. Walter, 1981), pp. 55–66.

94. "Sacrifice and Satisfaction" and "To All Who Will Come," in J. M. Boice, ed., *Our Saviour God* (Grand Rapids, Mich.: Baker, 1981).

95. "Is Christianity Credible?" in D. Stacey, ed., *Is Christianity Credible?* (London: Epworth, 1981), pp. 64–72.

96. "Response to Stephen Clark," in P. Williamson and K. Perrotta, eds., *Christianity Confronts Modernity* (Ann Arbor, Mich.: Servant, 1981), pp. 187–93.

97. Preface to Elisabeth Elliot, *No Graven Image*, new ed. (London: Hodder & Stoughton, 1981).

98. Preface to Sinclair B. Ferguson, *The Christian Life* (London: Hodder & Stoughton, 1981), pp. ix–x.

99. Preface to Michael Baughen, *Breaking the Prayer Barrier* (Wheaton, Ill.: Harold Shaw, 1981).

100. "God: From the Fathers to the Moderns" and "The Puritans," in R. Keeley, ed., *Lion Handbook to Christian Belief* (Berkhamsted, England: Lion, 1982). Also published as *Eerdmans' Handbook to Christian Belief* (Grand Rapids, Mich.: Eerdmans, 1982).

101. Preface to A. Wetherell Johnson, *Created for Commitment* (Wheaton, Ill.: Tyndale House, 1982).

102. Foreword to Bruce Milne, *Know the Truth* (Leicester, England: Inter-Varsity Press, 1982), pp. 5–6.

103. "Infallible Scripture and the Role of Hermeneutics," in D. A. Carson and J. B. Woodbridge, eds., *Scripture and Truth* (Grand Rapids, Mich.: Zondervan and Leicester, England: Inter-Varsity Press, 1983), pp. 325–56.

104. "Introductory Essay," in John Owen, *Sin and Temptation*, ed. and rewritten by James M. Houston (Portland, Ore.: Multnomah, 1983), pp. xvii–xix.

105. "Steps to the Renewal of the Christian People" and "Agenda for

Theology," in P. Williamson and K. Perrotta, eds., *Summons to Faith and Renewal* (Ann Arbor, Mich.: Servant, 1983), pp. 107–27.

106. "Response to Henry Krabbendam: The New Hermeneutic," in N. Geisler and E. Radmacher, eds., *Hermeneutics, Inerrancy and the Bible* (Grand Rapids, Mich.: Zondervan, 1984), pp. 559–71.

107. "A Christian View of Man," in C. F. H. Henry, ed., *The Christian Vision: Man in Society* (Hillsdale, Mich.: Hillsdale College Press, 1984), pp. 101–19.

108. "John Calvin and the Inerrancy of Holy Scripture," in J. Hannah, ed., *Inerrancy and the Church* (Chicago: Moody Press, 1984), pp. 143–68.

109. "How to Recognize a Christian Citizen," in *The Christian as Citizen* (Wheaton, Ill.: Christianity Today Institute; bound into *Christianity Today* April 19, 1985), pp. 4–8.

110. "Divisions in the Church" and "Reformation in the Church," in *The Church: God's New Society* (Philadelphia: Philadelphia Conference on Reformed Theology, 1985).

111. "Arminianisms," in R. Godfrey and T. Boyd, eds., *Through Christ's Word* (Phillipsburg, N.J.: Presbyterian and Reformed, 1985), pp. 121–48.

112. "In Quest of Canonical Interpretation," in R. K. Johnston, ed., *The Use of the Bible in Theology: Evangelical Options* (Atlanta, Ga.: John Knox Press, 1985), pp. 35–55.

113. "David Martyn Lloyd-Jones," in C. Turner, ed., *Chosen Vessels* (Ann Arbor, Mich.: Servant, 1985). Also published as *Heroes* (Servant, 1991), pp. 109–23.

114. "Justification in Protestant Theology," in J. I. Packer and others, *Here We Stand: Justification by Faith Today* (London: Hodder & Stoughton, 1986), pp. 84–102.

115. "A Kind of Puritan," in C. Catherwood, ed., *Martyn Lloyd-Jones: Chosen by God* (Crowborough, England: Highland Books, 1986), pp. 33–57.

116. "Why Preach?" in S. Logan, ed., *The Preacher and Preaching* (Phillipsburg, N.J.: Presbyterian & Reformed, 1986), pp. 1–29.

117. "Theism for Our Time," in P. T. O'Brien and D. G. Peterson, eds., *God Who Is Rich in Mercy* (Homebush West, N.S.W.: Lancer Books, 1986), pp. 1–23.

118. "Foreword: No Little Person," in R. W. Ruegsegger, *Reflections on Francis Schaeffer* (Grand Rapids, Mich.: Zondervan, 1986), pp. 7–17.

119. "The Holy Spirit and His Work," in K. Kantzer, ed., *Applying the Scriptures* (Grand Rapids, Mich.: Zondervan, 1987), pp. 51–76. Also published in *Crux* 23, no. 2 (June 1987): 2–17.

120. "Foreword: Why We Need the Puritans," in Leland Ryken, *Worldly Saints* (Grand Rapids, Mich.: Zondervan, 1987), pp. ix–xvi.

121. Introduction to P. Fromer and J. I. Packer, eds., *The Best in Theology* (Carol Stream, Ill.: Christianity Today, 1987), 1:13–23.

122. "Introduction: On Being Serious About the Holy Spirit," in David Wells, *God the Evangelist: How the Holy Spirit Works to Bring Men and Women to Faith* (Grand Rapids, Mich.: Eerdmans, 1987), pp. xi–xvi.

123. "The Trinity and the Gospel," in R. A. Bodey, *Good News for All Seasons* (Grand Rapids, Mich.: Baker, 1987), pp. 91–98.

124. "Inerrancy and the Divinity and Humanity of the Bible," "Problem Areas Related to Biblical Inerrancy," "Implications of Biblical Inerrancy for the Christian Mission," in *Proceedings of the Conference of Biblical Inerrancy 1987* (Nashville, Tenn.: Broadman, 1987), pp. 135–42, 205–13, and 245–50.

125. Introduction to P. Fromer and J. I. Packer, eds., *The Best in Theology* (Carol Stream, Ill.: Christianity Today, 1988), 2:13–22.

126. "The Christian and God's World," in J. M. Boice, ed., *Transforming Our World* (Portland, Ore.: Multnomah, 1988), pp. 81–97.

127. "God the Image-Maker," in M. Noll and D. Wells, eds., *Christian Faith and Practice in the Modern World* (Grand Rapids, Mich.: Eerdmans, 1988), pp. 27–50.

128. "John Calvin and Reformed Europe," in J. Woodbridge, ed., *Great Leaders of the Christian Church* (Chicago: Moody Press, 1988), pp. 208–15.

129. "Baptism in the Spirit," "Baxter," "Farrer," "Glory of God," "Holiness Movement," "Holy Spirit," "God," "Infallibility and Inerrancy," "Method," "Paradox," "Revival," "Scripture," in D. Wright, S. Ferguson and J. I. Packer, eds., *New Dictionary of Theology* (Leicester, England: Inter-Varsity Press and Downers Grove, Ill.: InterVarsity Press, 1988).

130. "The Challenge of Biblical Interpretation: Creation," "The Challenge of Biblical Interpretation: Women," "The Challenge of Biblical Interpretation: Eschatology," in *The Proceedings of the Conference on Biblical Interpretation* (Nashville, Tenn.: Broadman, 1988), pp. 21–33, 103–15, and 191–204.

131. Introduction to H. Smith and J. I. Packer, eds., *The Best in Theology* (Carol Stream, Ill.: Christianity Today, 1988), 3:vii–xiv.

132. "Is the Charismatic Movement . . . from God?" in *Tough Questions Christian Ask* and *Pentecostals* (both Carol Stream, Ill.: Christianity Today Inc./Wheaton, Ill.: Victor, 1989), pp. 49–60. Also published as "Piety on Fire," *Christianity Today*, May 12, 1989, pp. 18–23, and *Renewal*, July 1990, pp. 28–32.

133. "Christian Morality Adrift," in K. Perrotta and J. Blattner, eds., *A Society in Peril* (Ann Arbor, Mich.: Servant, 1989), pp. 57–76.

134. Introduction to J. I. Yamamoto and J. I. Packer, eds., *The Best in Theology* (Carol Stream, Ill.: Christianity Today, 1989), 4:vii–xiv.

135. Introduction to Jeremiah Burroughs, *Hosea,* reprint (Beaver Falls, Penn.: Soli Deo Gloria, 1989).

136. Introduction to Richard Baxter, *Christian Directory,* reprint (Beaver Falls, Penn.: Soli Deo Gloria, 1990).

137. Introduction to H. Witsius, *On the Covenants,* reprint (Phillipsburg, N.J.: Presbyterian and Reformed, 1990).

138. Introduction (biographical) to John Gwyn-Thomas, *Rejoice Always* (Edinburgh: Banner of Truth, 1990), pp. ix–xv.

139. Introduction to J. Tolhurst, ed., *Men, Women and Priesthood* (Leominster: Gracewing, 1990), pp. vii–xvi.

140. "The Christian's Purpose in Business," in R. C. Chewning, ed., *Biblical Principles and Business: The Practice* (Colorado Springs: NavPress, 1990).

141. "Evangelicals and the Way of Salvation: New Challenges to the Gospel—Universalism and Justification by Faith," in C. F. H. Henry and K. Kantzer, eds., *Evangelical Affirmations* (Grand Rapids, Mich.: Zondervan, 1990), pp. 107–36.

142. "Understanding the Bible: Evangelical Hermeneutics," in M. Tinker, ed., *Restoring the Vision* (Eastbourne, England: MARC, 1990), pp. 39–58.

143. Foreword, "The Means of Conversion" and "Godliness in Ephesians," in D. M. Lewis, ed., *With Heart, Mind and Strength: The Best of Crux, 1979–1989* (Langley, B.C.: Credo, 1990), pp. 7–8, 63–79, and 129–43. "The Means of Conversion" originally published in *Crux,* 25, no. 4 (Dec. 1989): 14–22; "Godliness in Ephesians" originally published in *Crux,* 25, no. 1 (March 1989): 8–16.

144. "Babel," in R. A. Bodey, ed., *Inside the Sermon* (Grand Rapids, Mich.: Baker, 1990), pp. 185–200.

145. "Thirty Years' War: The Doctrine of Holy Scripture," in H.

Conn, ed., *Practical Theology and the Ministry of the Church, Festschrift* for E. P. Clowney (Phillipsburg, N.J.: Presbyterian and Reformed, 1990), pp. 25–44.

146. *Aspects of Authority* (Disley, U.K.: Orthos, 1990).

147. *The Problem of Eternal Punishment,* Leon Morris Lecture, 1990 (Victoria, Australia: Evangelical Alliance Publishing, 1990). Also published in *Crux,* 26, no. 3 (Sept. 1990): 18–25.

148. Introduction to Richard Baxter, *Practical Works IV,* reprint (Ligonier, Penn.: Soli Deo Gloria, 1991).

149. "Evangelical Foundations for Spirituality," in M. Bockmuehl and K. Burkhardt, eds., *Gott Lieben und Seine Gebote Halten* (Giessen, Germany/Basel, Switzerland: Brunnen Verlag, 1991), pp. 149–62.

150. "Authority in Preaching," in M. Eden and D. Wells, eds., *The Gospel in the Modern World* (Leicester, England: Inter-Varsity Press, 1991), pp. 198–212.

151. "Richard Baxter on Heaven, Hope, and Holiness," in J. I. Packer and L. Wilkinson, eds., *Alive to God, Festschrift* for James M. Houston (Downers Grove, Ill.: InterVarsity Press, 1992), pp. 161–75.

152. "The Comfort of Conservatism," in M. Horton, ed., *Power Religion* (Chicago: Moody Press, 1992), pp. 283–99.

153. "The Holy Spirit in the Book of Common Prayer," in S. Harris, ed., *The Holy Spirit* (Charlottesville, Va.: St. Peter Publications, 1993).

154. "Election," "Predestination," in D. Jeffrey, ed., *Dictionary of Biblical Tradition in English Literature* (Grand Rapids, Mich.: Eerdmans, 1993).

155. "The Empowered Christian Life," in G. Grieg and K. Springer, eds., *The Kingdom and the Power* (Ventura, Calif.: Regal, 1994), pp. 207–15.

156. with A. McGrath, G. LeMarquand and J. P. Westin, "Anglicanism Today: The Path to Renewal" and "Jesus Christ the Only Saviour," in G. Egerton, ed., *Anglican Essentials* (Toronto: Anglican Book Centre, 1995), pp. 53–63, 98–110.

157. "The Spirit with the Word: The Reformational Revivalism of George Whitefield," in W. P. Stephens, ed., *The Bible, the Reformation and the Church, Festschrift* for James Atkinson (Sheffield, England: Sheffield Academic Press, 1995), pp. 166–89.

158. "Atonement," "Richard Baxter," "Godliness," "Holy Spirit," "D. M. Lloyd-Jones," in David Atkinson and David Field, eds.,

New Dictionary of Christian Ethics and Pastoral Theology (Leicester, England and Downers Grove, Ill.: Inter-Varsity Press, 1995).

159. "The Preacher as Theologian," in C. Green, ed., *When God's Voice Is Heard, Festschrift* for Dick Lucas (Leicester, England: Inter-Varsity Press, 1995), pp. 79–95.

160. "Crosscurrents Among Evangelicals," in C. Colson and R. J. Neuhaus, eds., *Evangelicals and Catholics Together: Toward a Common Mission* (Dallas, Tex.: Word, 1995), pp. 147-74.

161. "Robert Aitken," in D. M. Lewis, ed., *The Blackwell Dictionary of Evangelical Biography: 1730–1860* (Oxford: Basil Blackwell, 1995).

IV. Articles in *Puritan and Reformed Studies Conference Reports*

162. "The Witness of the Spirit: The Puritan Teaching," in *The Wisdom of Our Fathers: Puritan and Reformed Studies Conference Reports, 1956* (privately printed, 1957), pp. 14–25 (reprint ed. Clonmel, Ireland: Clonmel Evangelical Bookroom, 1993).

163. "The Puritans and the Lord's Day," in *Servants of the Word: Puritan and Reformed Studies Conference Reports, 1957* (London: Banner of Truth Trust, 1958), pp. 1–24.

164. Foreword and "The Puritans as Interpreters of Scripture," in *A Goodly Heritage: Puritan and Reformed Studies Conference Reports, 1958* (London: Banner of Truth Trust, 1959), pp. 2–7, 18–26.

165. "The Puritan View of Preaching the Gospel," in *How Shall They Hear? Puritan and Reformed Studies Conference Reports, 1959* (privately printed, 1960; reprint ed. Clonmel, Ireland: Clonmel Evangelical Bookroom, 1993).

166. "Jonathan Edwards and the Theology of Revival," in *Increasing in the Knowledge of God: Puritan and Reformed Studies Conference Reports, 1960* (privately printed, 1961; reprint ed. Clonmel, Ireland: Clonmel Evangelical Bookroom, 1992).

167. "The Puritan Idea of Communion with God," in *Press Toward the Mark: Puritan and Reformed Studies Conference Reports, 1961* (privately printed, 1962; reprint ed. Clonmel, Ireland: Clonmel Evangelical Bookroom, 1992).

168. "The Puritan Conscience," in *Faith and a Good Conscience: Puritan and Reformed Studies Conference Reports, 1962* (privately printed, 1963; reprint ed. Clonmel, Ireland: Clonmel Evangelical Bookroom, 1992).

169. "The Puritans and Worship," in *Diversity in Unity: Puritan and Reformed Studies Conference Reports, 1963* (Battersea, England: Evangelical Magazine, 1964), pp. 3–14.

170. "Calvin: A Servant of the Word,"in *Able Ministers of the New Testament: Puritan and Reformed Studies Conference Reports, 1964* (Battersea, England: Evangelical Magazine, 1965), pp. 36–55.

171. "Luther," in *Approaches to the Reformation of the Church: Puritan and Reformed Studies Conference Reports, 1965* (Battersea, England: Evangelical Magazine, 1966), pp. 25–33.

172. "John Owen on Communication from God," in *One Steadfast High Intent: Puritan and Reformed Studies Conference Reports, 1966* (Battersea, England: Evangelical Magazine, 1967), pp. 17–30.

173. "The Puritans and Spiritual Gifts," in *Profitable for Doctrine and Reproof: Puritan and Reformed Studies Conference Reports, 1967* (privately printed, 1968; reprint ed. Clonmel, Ireland: Clonmel Evangelical Bookroom, 1992), pp. 15–27.

174. "Arminianisms," in *The Manifold Grace of God: Puritan and Reformed Studies Conference Reports, 1968* (London: Evangelical Magazine, 1969), pp. 22–34.

175. "The Doctrine of Justification in Development and Decline Among the Puritans," in *By Schisms Rent Asunder: Puritan and Reformed Studies Conference Reports, 1969* (London: Evangelical Magazine, 1970), pp. 18–30.

V.   Other articles (a selection of the more significant)

176. "The Puritan Treatment of Justification by Faith," *Evangelical Quarterly* 24, no. 3 (July 1952): 131–43.

177. "Sanctification—Puritan Teaching," *The Christian Graduate* 5, no. 4 (Dec. 1952): 125–28.

178. "Richard Baxter," *Theology* 55 (May 1953): 174–78.

179. "Blind Spots," *Discipulus*, Advent 1954, pp. 5–8.

180. "'Keswick' and the Reformed Doctrine of Sanctification," *Evangelical Quarterly* 27, no. 3 (July 1955): 153–67.

181. "Baptism: Sacrament of the Covenant of Grace," *Churchman* 69, no. 2 (June 1955).

182. "Some Thoughts on General Revelation," *Christian Graduate* 9, no. 3 (Sept. 1956): 114–21.

183. "Puritan Evangelism," *Banner of Truth* 4 (1957).

184. "With All Thy Mind," *Inter-Varsity*, Autumn 1957, pp. 4–8.

185. "Seventeenth Century Teaching on the Christian Life,"

Churchman 71, no. 4 (Dec. 1957); 72, no. 1 (March 1958).

186. "The Fundamentalism Controversy: Retrospect and Prospect," *Faith and Thought* 90, no. 1 (Spring 1958): 35–45.

187. "Fundamentalism: The British Scene," *Christianity Today,* Sept. 29, 1958, pp. 3–6.

188. "The Inspiration and Infallibility of Holy Scripture," *Symposium of Articles from Theological Students Fellowship Bulletin* (no date), pp. 16–18.

189. "Calvinism in Britain," *Torch and Trumpet* (1959).

190. "Christianity and Non-Christian Religions," *Christianity Today,* Dec. 21, 1959, pp. 3–5.

191. "The Bible in Modern Theology," *Bible League Quarterly* no. 240 (Jan.–March 1960): 129–32.

192. "Puritan Preaching," *The Evangelical Christian,* Oct. 1960, pp. 18–21.

193. *The Theological Challenge to Evangelicalism Today,* F. E. C. (1961).

194. "Training for Christian Service," *The Evangelical Christian,* Sept. 1961, pp. 10–15.

195. "The Bible and the Authority of Reason," *Churchman* 75, no. 4 (Dec. 1961): 207–19.

196. "The Holy Spirit—and Authority," *The Almond Branch,* 1962, pp. 9–12.

197. "Questions About Inter-Varsity Fellowship," *Break Through* no. 11 (May 1962): 13–19.

198. "Our Lord and the Old Testament," *Bible League Quarterly* no. 252 (Jan.–March 1963): 70–74.

199. "Fellowship: The Theological Basis," *Christian Graduate* 16, no. 3 (Sept. 1963): 7–11.

200. "Episcopal Idol—A Consideration of *Honest to God,*" *The Evangelical Christian,* Oct. 1963, pp. 4–5, 32–35.

201. "The Bible Yesterday, Today and Tomorrow," *The Gospel Magazine,* March 1964, pp. 104–13.

202. "Atheism," *Inter-Varsity,* special introductory issue (1964), pp. 4–6.

203. "The Holy Spirit and the Local Congregation," *Churchman* 78, no. 2 (June 1964): 98–108.

204. "A Broad Church Reformation?" *London Quarterly and Holborn Review* 189 (Oct. 1964): 270–75.

205. "All Men Won't Be Saved," *Banner of Truth* 41 (March 1965).

206. "Death: Life's One and Only Certainty," *Eternity* 16, no. 3 (March 1965): 22–26.

207. "Ministry of the Word Today," *The Presbyterian Guardian* 34, no. 6 (July–Aug. 1965): 87–90.

208. "One Body in Christ: The Doctrine and Expression of Christian Unity," *Churchman* 80, no. 1 (March 1966): 16–26.

209. "Luther Against Erasmus," *Concordia Theological Monthly* 37, no. 4 (April 1966): 207–21.

210. "Led by the Spirit of God," *The Life of Faith*, May 26, 1966, pp. 499–500.

211. "A Calvinist—and an Evangelist!" *The Hour International* no. 31 (Aug. 1966): 25–27.

212. "Must We Demythologize?" *Theological Students Fellowship Bulletin* no. 50 (Spring 1968): 1–5.

213. "Letter to a Leader," *CFYA Leaders' Newspaper* 1, no. 3.

214. "Retooling the Clergy Factories," *Churchman* 82, no. 2 (Summer 1968): 120–24.

215. "The Church of South India and Reunion in England," *Churchman* 82, no. 4 (Winter 1968): 249–61.

216. "Revival," *Christian Graduate* 14, no.4 (Dec. 1971): 97–100.

217. "The Way of Salvation: I. What Is Salvation? II. What Is Faith? III. The Problems of Universalism. IV. Are Non-Christian Faiths Ways of Salvation?" *Bibliotheca Sacra* 129, no. 515 (1972): 105–25; 129, no. 516 (1972): 291–306; 130, no. 517 (1973): 3–10; 130, no. 518 (1973): 110–16.

218. "Acquitted!" *Span* no. 1 (1973): 10–11.

219. "What Did the Cross Achieve?" (Tyndale Lecture) *Tyndale Bulletin* 25 (1974): 3–45.

220. "Revival and Renewal," *Renewal* 62 (April 1976): 14–17.

221. "A Secular Way to Go," *Third Way* 1, no. 7 (April 7, 1977): 3–5.

222. "Why Is Authority a Dirty Word?" *Spectrum* 9, no. 3 (May 1977): 4–6.

223. "Who Is God?" in *Simple Faith?* (Berkhamsted: Lion, 1978).

224. "People Matter More Than Structures," *Crusade* 23, no. 11 (April 1978): 24–25.

225. "The Uniqueness of Jesus Christ," *Churchman* 92, no. 2 (1978): 101–11.

226. "Battling for the Bible," *Regent College Bulletin* 9, no. 4 (Fall 1979).

227. "Puritanism as a Movement of Revival," *Evangelical Quarterly* 52 (Jan. 1980): 2–16.

228. "Theological Reflections on the Charismatic Movement,"

Churchman **94**, nos. 1–2 (1980): 7–25, 108–25.

229. "George Whitefield: Man Alive," *Crux* 16, no. 4 (Dec. 1980): 23–26.

230. "The Means of Growth" and "Body Life," *Tenth,* July 1981, pp. 2–11.

231. "Walking to Emmaus with the Great Physician," *Christianity Today,* April 10, 1981, pp. 20–23.

232. "A View from a Jacuzzi," *Regent College Bulletin* 11, no. 4 (Fall 1981).

233. "Poor Health May Be the Best Remedy," *Christianity Today,* May 21, 1982, pp. 14–16.

234. "Knowing Notions or Knowing God?" *Pastoral Renewal* 6, no. 9 (March 1982): 65–68.

235. "The Message Is Unchanged," *Alliance Witness,* June 23, 1982, pp. 11–14.

236. "The Reconstitution of Authority," *Crux* 18, no. 4 (Dec. 1982): 2–12.

237. "Upholding the Unity of Scripture Today," *Journal of the Evangelical Theological Society* 25, no. 4 (Dec. 1982): 409–14.

238. "Predestination in Christian History" and "Predestination and Sanctification," *Tenth,* July 1983, pp. 2–16.

239. "Lord, Send Revival," *The Bulletin,* Winter 1983, pp. 4–5.

240. "Feet in the Clouds," *Regent College Bulletin* 14, no. 1 (Spring 1984).

241. "Renewal and Revival," *Channels,* Spring 1984, pp. 7–9.

242. "Meeting God," *Spiritual Counterfeits Project: Special Collections Journal* 6, no. 1 (Winter 1984).

243. "'Good Pagans' and God's Kingdom," *Christianity Today,* Jan. 17, 1986, pp. 27–31.

244. Three articles on guidance, *Eternity,* April–May–June 1986, pp. 19–23, 32–37, and 36–39.

245. "What Do You Mean When You Say 'God'?" *Christianity Today,* Sept. 19, 1986, pp. 22–25.

246. "Does It Really Matter?" *Eternity,* Jan. 1987, p. 30.

247. "Dying Well Is Final Test," *Eternity,* Jan. 1987.

248. "How Christians Should Understand Themselves," *Eternity,* July 1987, p. 36.

249. "The Way of the Weak Is the Only Healthy Way," *Eternity,* Nov. 1987, p. 28.

250. "Keeping Your Balance: A Christian's Challenge," *Eternity,* Jan. 1988, p. 18.

251. "Soldier, Son, Pilgrim: Christian Know Thyself," *Eternity*, April 1988, p. 33.

252. "Christian *Gravitas* in a Narcissistic Age," *Eternity*, July 1988, p. 46.

253. "Bringing the Double Mind to Singleness of Faith," *Eternity*, Nov. 1988, p. 59.

254. "Bringing the Bible to Your Life," *Charisma*, January 1987.

255. "A Modern View of Jesus," *Faith Today*, January 1987, pp. 28–30, 32–33.

256. "Packer on Preaching," *New Horizons*, January 1987.

257. "Shy Sovereign," *Tabletalk*, June 1988.

258. "Jewish Evangelism and the Word of God," *Christian Witness to Israel Herald*, June 1988.

259. "Is Hell out of Vogue in This Modern Era?" *United Evangelical Action*, Sept. 1989.

260. "Westminster and the Roller-Coaster Ride," *Tabletalk* 14, no. 3 (March 1990): 6–10.

261. "An Introduction to Systematic Spirituality," *Crux* 26, no. 1 (March 1990): 2–8.

262. "The Gospel and the Lord's Supper," *Mission and Ministry* 8 (Summer 1990): 18–24.

263. "Shepherds After God's Own Heart," *Pastoral Renewal*, Nov. 1990.

264. "From the Scriptures to the Sermon: I. Some Perspectives on Preaching; II. The Problem of Paradigms," *Ashland Theological Journal* 22 (1990): 42–64.

265. "Let's Stop Making Women Presbyters," *Christianity Today*, Feb. 11, 1991, pp. 18–21.

266. "Understanding the Lordship Controversy," *Tabletalk*, May 1991.

267. "The Reformed Faith in the Modern World: I. Bible; II. Gospel; III. Church," *Evangelical Presbyterian* (N.Z.), Dec. 1990/ March 1991/June 1991.

268. with T. Beougher, "Go Fetch Baxter," *Christianity Today*, Dec. 16, 1991, pp. 26–28.

269. "Scripture, Inerrancy, and the Church," *Touchstone* 4 (Fall 1991): 3–4.

270. "The Empowered Christian Life," *Faith and Renewal* 16, no. 4 (Jan. 1992): 3–9.

271. "The Word of Life," *The Evangelical Catholic* 4, no. 4 (July–Aug. 1992): 1–8.

272. "Holiness," *Faith and Renewal* 17, no. 5 (March 1993): 3–11.
273. "George Whitefield: The Startling Puritan," *Christian History* 12, no. 2 (May 1993): 38–40.
274. "A Reasonable Faith," *Decision*, Dec. 1993.
275. "Why I Signed It," *Christianity Today*, Dec. 12, 1994, pp. 34–37.
276. Forewords to books in Crossway Classic Commentary Series, Calvin (*Acts, John*), J. C. Ryle (*Matthew, Mark*), C. H. Spurgeon (*Psalms*), C. Hodge (*Romans, 1 Corinthians, 2 Corinthians, Ephesians*), T. Manton (*James*) (Wheaton, Ill.: Crossway, 1993–1995).
277. "Higher Criticism" in *New Geneva Study Bible* (Nashville, Tenn.: Nelson, 1995), pp. 2044f.